MEGHAN

MISUNDERSTOOD

Also by Sean Smith

Spice Girls
Ed Sheeran
George
Adele
Kim
Tom Jones: The Life
Kylie
Gary
Alesha
Tulisa
Kate
Robbie
Cheryl
Victoria
Justin: The Biography
Britney: The Biography
J.K. Rowling: A Biography
Jennifer: The Unauthorized Biography
Royal Racing
The Union Game
Sophie's Kiss (with Garth Gibbs)
Stone Me! (with Dale Lawrence)

MEGHAN
MISUNDERSTOOD

BY SEAN SMITH
SUNDAY TIMES BESTSELLING AUTHOR

HarperCollins*Publishers*

HarperCollins*Publishers*
1 London Bridge Street
London SE1 9GF

www.harpercollins.co.uk

First published by HarperCollins*Publishers* 2020

3 5 7 9 10 8 6 4 2

A catalogue record of this book is
available from the British Library

ISBN 978-0-00-835957-7
TPB 978-0-00-835959-1
EB ISBN 978-0-00-835957-7

Printed and bound in Great Britain by
CPI Group (UK) Ltd, Croydon

To the Queen of Boop

CONTENTS

INTRODUCTION

Meghan Markle looked up, wide-eyed, lips quivering and said her now-famous words: 'It's not enough to survive something, right; that's not the point of life. You've got to thrive; you've got to feel happy ...'

Like thousands of others I probably only watched *Harry and Meghan: An African Journey* because of all the advance publicity the programme had received, the headlines written and the opinions voiced about Meghan's decision to sue the *Mail on Sunday*.

The documentary by broadcaster Tom Bradby, a long-time friend of Prince Harry, was riveting as it lurched between triumph and despair – the jubilation of Meghan dancing with young African girls being given the chance of a better life thanks to wonderful local charities, and the darker, private moments of introspection, admitting that while she never thought her new life would be easy, she had thought it would at least be fair.

I decided then and there to write a book about Meghan, chronicling her journey up to this point in her life – little realising that within three months she, Harry and their baby, Archie, would leave the UK, perhaps never to return.

Up until the moment the couple announced that Meghan was taking legal action against the newspaper for publishing part

1

of a private letter to her father, the trip to Africa had been described as a 'textbook royal tour', full of waving and cheering as a posse of royal reporters and photographers enjoyed an expenses-paid escape from a dull British autumn.

There was plenty to fill the pages of the newspapers and dominate the news channels back home. Meghan gave an empowering speech to the women of the Nyanga township in Cape Town, which ended in stirring fashion: 'I am here with you as a mother, as a wife, as a woman, as a woman of colour and as your sister. I am here with you and I am here for you ...'

For the first time the world was introduced properly to Archie; not in the dull, traditional way of posed pictures of tired mum and baby leaving hospital, but in a gloriously uplifting meeting between the new parents and Archbishop Desmond Tutu, one of the legendary figures of South African history alongside Nelson Mandela and Steve Biko, the anti-apartheid activist assassinated in 1977.

Meghan and Harry chatted with the Archbishop for half an hour at the headquarters of the Desmond and Leah Tutu Legacy Foundation in Cape Town. They met at the Old Granary, a beautifully restored building in Buitenkant Street that was originally built by slaves in the early nineteenth century. It used to be a symbol of colonial expansion but now houses a collection chronicling the acclaimed cleric's life.

Meghan explained, 'It's not lost on us what a huge and significant moment this is.'

Archbishop Tutu, approaching his eighty-eighth birthday, could not conceal his delight at meeting five-month-old Archie and planted a kiss on his forehead. Meghan said proudly, 'I think Archie will look back in so many years and understand that right at the beginning of his life, he was fortunate enough to have this moment with one of the best and most impactful leaders of our time.'

An African Journey tellingly contrasted the affluent present-day, largely white suburbs of Cape Town with the black township of Nyanga, where women face a daily threat of violence and rape and more than three hundred murders a year, making it one of the most dangerous places to live in the world. Meghan and Harry visited an initiative run by The Justice Desk, a human rights charity in southern Africa, where they saw for themselves young women being trained to defend themselves.

Harry, perhaps understandably, was a little overshadowed on the tour by the megawatt star quality of his wife (and son!), but he has charm and charisma in his own right. He is also undeniably sensitive and endures private inner struggles, which he movingly admitted to Tom on a solo trip to Botswana and Angola, countries that brought back sad memories of his mother. Harry strolled purposefully through a minefield in Angola, retracing Diana's steps for a photographic opportunity, although the actual field through which she famously walked is now a paved street in the middle of a new development.

Behind those poignant pictures was the painful story of Harry's reality, as he revealed to Tom how he really felt about photographers: 'Every single time I see a camera, every single time I hear a click, every single time I see a flash, it takes me straight back.' His mother's death is a wound that will not heal. The photographers are still the 'worst reminders of her life' and, presumably, her death. He openly discussed his mental health issues with Tom, who has also been candid about his own need to take five months off work in 2018 because of severe insomnia.

Meghan had stayed behind in Cape Town with Archie. While Tom and his camera crew and most of the press corps were following Harry, his wife paid a visit that would have been high on Diana's list of things to do. She took a bag of baby clothes that Archie had already outgrown to a mothers2mothers centre, a charity that offers counsel and mentoring to young mums living with HIV.

On another occasion, Meghan quietly visited the memorial for the murdered 19-year-old South African student Uyinene Mrwetyana. She had been raped, tortured and killed at Cape Town's Clareinch Post Office in August 2019. Her brutal death sparked demonstrations throughout the country against gender-based crimes of violence in South Africa. Meghan tied a yellow ribbon there that bore the message 'we stand together in this moment', written in the local language of Xhosa as a further mark of respect.

Meghan expressed her concerns for women and her desire to encourage change and progress: she said, 'In a world that can seem so aggressive, confrontational and dangerous, you should know that you have the power to change it.' In particular, she made a connection with people of colour in a way that nobody else in the Royal Family could. She had a natural ease with everyone, whether giving a warm hug to a young African boy in the crowd or having a laugh with Graça Machel, the widow of Nelson Mandela. Only Harry came close to demonstrating such rapport.

So much positivity turned to dust, however, when she was reunited with Harry in Johannesburg. His return coincided with their announcement about her legal suit and the unequivocal statement from Harry released on their website in which he said his wife had become 'one of the latest victims of a British tabloid press that wages campaigns against individuals with no thought to the consequences.'

The legal action, he explained, involved the 'contents of a private letter' being 'published unlawfully in an intentionally destructive manner'. He also referenced Princess Diana: 'I've seen what happens when someone I love is commoditised to the point that they are no longer treated or seen as a real person. I lost my mother and now I watch my wife falling victim to the same powerful forces.'

It was strong stuff but it did not seem to be met with anything resembling contrition or apology from those 'powerful forces' – far from it. The general consensus was that Harry's outburst, for that was how it was viewed, had ruined the tour. The couple had made it all about them. The wish-you-were-here postcards home, designed to depict a wholly varnished scene of local life and typify the self-congratulatory royal tours around the old Empire had been replaced with a giant slice of bitter reality.

Meghan, it seemed, was not playing the game as the media wanted her to do. But who are the so-called royal experts and columnists shouting the odds about how she should behave at every opportunity? And what exactly is this media invention of a 'royal expert' – someone who knows the correct way to bow or curtsy when you meet the Queen? It strikes me as a truly meaningless label, especially since Harry and Meghan were shining a light on such important global issues.

What, I wondered, had Meghan done to deserve all the negativity – the 'bullying', as Harry called it – that surrounds her? Was she really a victim of rampant racism, sexism and xenophobia because she's American, or was it just old-fashioned British snobbery at her being an actress?

When I had watched Harry and Meghan's wedding in May 2019 – less than eighteen months earlier – the most memorable elements for me were her mother Doria's quiet grace, the exquisite playing of cellist Sheku Kanneh-Mason, the Kingdom Choir singing 'Stand By Me' acapella and the long, passionate sermon by the Most Rev Michael Curry on the power of love. As he spoke, the reactions from the Royal Family that we were allowed to see were priceless: Prince Charles read and re-read the order of service as if it was the latest fascinating issue of *Country Life* magazine; his wife Camilla and Kate Middleton were desperately trying not to make eye contact with each other; Prince Andrew looked as pompous as ever. Prince William adopted a superior smile, Princess Beatrice seemed to be on the verge of laughing out loud, while, best of all, Zara Tindall appeared gobsmacked. The Queen had the familiar look of grim determination that was never going to waver. Harry, meanwhile, held Meghan's hand.

Meghan, it seemed, had been determined to recognise her heritage as a woman of colour on the most important day of her life so far. So, was the Royal Family itself fundamentally racist or just bogged down with stuffy traditions and protocol? And as a society, are we, the UK, really as tolerant as we like to proclaim?

There seemed so many questions for me to answer on my Meghan adventure. In particular, I wanted to find out more about her quest for female empowerment. Was feminism of fundamental importance to her or something she had adopted as a fashionable cause? And what about racism? How badly has she been affected by prejudice in her life? Watching Tom's documentary a second time, I was struck by the words of a biracial woman in Cape Town: 'It is quite a struggle when you grow up as a mixed-race child – either you are not white enough or you are not black enough, so you are in the middle; and you have to find your identity based on the middle – and with Meghan creating awareness about this, it makes people feel that it's ok to be me.'

For me, that begged the question: did Meghan have that same struggle with identity growing up in Los Angeles? I wanted to follow her journey from Hollywood to the balcony of Buckingham Palace and back again and answer the questions, is she misunderstood? And if she is, why?

PART ONE

THE SEARCH FOR IDENTITY

1

MOMENTS OF HISTORY

The eyes of the entire world were on Meghan Markle as she walked serenely and gracefully down the aisle of St George's Chapel in Windsor. They have remained on her ever since.

Her wedding to Prince Harry was an occasion of great joy, representing happiness at last for the Queen's grandson, who had captured the hearts of the nation when he disconsolately but bravely followed his mother Diana's coffin on that eternally sad day twenty years earlier. Now he was marrying a breathtakingly beautiful woman in a story that the screenwriters of Hollywood, where Meghan had made her name, could scarcely have imagined.

At least her mother Doria was there, the only member of her family to take a place at the ceremony. She had sat beside her daughter in the Rolls-Royce as she set out on the nine-mile drive that would take her from the luxurious Cliveden House Hotel to the steps of the chapel. They were two strong women strangely unsupported in a foreign land on this grandest of May days. As always, they had each other, sharing an unshakeable bond.

A crowd estimated to be in excess of 100,000 had poured into the Berkshire town to celebrate the day with flags, bunting, laughter and cheers. Doria could have been forgiven for punching the air with exuberant joy as if her beloved daughter had just won an Olympic gold medal.

Instead of drawing attention to herself, though, Doria sat quietly in a pew across from the Queen and the Duke of Edinburgh. Her eyes glistened with pride and excitement but she stayed composed, watching a woman of colour, her 'Flower' as she still called her, hammer loudly on the door of stuffy tradition and protocol.

There is nothing traditionally royal about Doria Loyce Ragland, memorably described by her daughter as a free spirit with dreadlocks and a nose ring. Her yoga class back in Los Angeles would scarcely have recognised the demure, stylish lady in a pale green Oscar de la Renta dress and coat. Her long hair was styled and partly hidden beneath a matching hat.

What a journey it has been for a family that historians and genealogists have eagerly traced back to the shameful days of slavery in America's Deep South, where the persecution of the black population did not stop with the Emancipation Proclamation of 1865 that officially freed all slaves. Meghan herself has admitted that trying to unravel her family tree is a bewildering task but she is intensely proud of her biracial heritage, describing herself as a 'strong, confident, mixed-race woman'.

Her maternal ancestors continued to face poverty and persecution for generation after generation, battling against the oppression of the Jim Crow laws, the legislation that enforced racial segregation in the southern states until 1965, two years after Dr Martin Luther King Jr's iconic 'I Have a Dream' speech at the Lincoln Memorial in Washington. Then, he implored, 'My four little children will one day live in a nation where they will not be judged by the colour of their skin but by the content of their character.'

The first known records of Doria's family show that they were slaves working on the plantations of Georgia around the town of Jonesboro, the setting for the epic novel *Gone with the Wind* and the famous film of that name. Fittingly, perhaps, Hattie McDaniel won Best Supporting Actress at the 1940 Academy Awards for her role as the maid 'Mammy', the first black winner of an Oscar.

While that was a win to be celebrated, the ceremony itself was, in retrospect, an appalling indictment of racism and segregation at the time. Hattie would not normally have been let into the Ambassador Hotel in Los Angeles where the ceremony was held, in its Coconut Grove nightclub; it had a whites-only policy. The film's famous producer, David O. Selznick, called in a favour to ensure that they let the great actress in, but, even then, she had to sit at a small segregated table at the back and well out of sight.

The role of Mammy represented a dreadful white stereotype of black servants, but Hattie's emotional acceptance speech would have inspired both Doria and Meghan. Herself the daughter of two black slaves, she said, 'I shall always hold it as a beacon for anything that I may be able to do in the future. I sincerely hope I shall always be a credit to my race and to the motion picture industry.'

The sad reality was that by the time she died, in 1952, she had played a maid seventy-four times. Big roles did not come her way after her Oscar win: 'It was as if I had done something wrong.' Her dying wish was to be buried in the Hollywood Cemetery alongside the great stars of the golden age, but that was also denied by a 'no-blacks' policy. It would be a further seven years before racial discrimination was outlawed in California. The controversy over recognition for black actors continued into Meghan's lifetime.

Discrimination was rife in Tennessee when Doria's ancestors moved further north and settled in Chattanooga, a deeply racist town little deserving its place in musical history as the title of the jaunty Glenn Miller classic, 'Chattanooga Choo Choo'. As recently as 1980, five black women were murdered there by members of the Ku Klux Klan in a drive-by shooting.

Meghan's ancestors did not face such life-ending hatred but they still had to battle for a better life for themselves and their families. Meghan's great-aunt Dora, for instance, was the first Ragland to go to college and became a teacher. Dora's elder sister Lillie ran a successful real-estate business in Los Angeles and was listed in the African–American *Who's Who*. She was married to Happy Evans, a famous black baseball player in the 1930s, a time when that sport was still segregated and there were separate 'negro' leagues.

Doria's grandmother, Netty Arnold, worked as a lift operator at the upmarket apartment block called the Hotel St Regis in Cleveland, Ohio, where she met and subsequently married James Arnold, a bellhop. They were both black, working in a place where only whites were allowed to live.

In Cleveland, one of their daughters, Jeanette, married twice. First to a local man, Joseph Johnson, a professional roller-skater, then, following her divorce, to Alvin Ragland, who would become Meghan's much-loved grandfather. The surname Ragland is actually one that his family took from their slave owner following emancipation.

Growing up, Meghan Markle was constantly fascinated by her family history, trying in vain to untangle its web and confessing that she was in 'awe of her past'. Her principle problem in trying to cast light on the 'blurred lines', as she called them, was that black slaves were not properly documented until they officially registered. In 1870, a sharecropper called

Stephen Ragland, Alvin's great-grandfather, had become the first black Ragland.

Meghan gave a different account of that important landmark in her family history when she spoke to *Elle* magazine in 2015 – before she met Prince Harry: 'Perhaps the closest thing connecting me to my ever-complex family tree, my longing to know where I came from, and the commonality that links me to my bloodline, is the choice that my great-great-great-grandfather made to start anew. He chose the last name Wisdom.' He may well have done so informally but genealogists poring over Meghan's ancestry have failed to find a thread linking the last name Wisdom to her family tree. Often family histories become confused by the telling and the retelling.

The Ragland family's life changed forever when they made the 2,300-mile trek from Cleveland to Los Angeles soon after Doria was born in September 1956. There were five of them in a borrowed car: Alvin, Jeanette, her two children from her first marriage – Joseph Jr and Saundra – and baby Doria. While it wasn't exactly an epic story matching the trip west of the Joad family in Steinbeck's magnificent novel of the Great Depression, *The Grapes of Wrath*, the trip did become the subject of countless stories told to Meghan as a little girl.

Uncle Joseph, who was some seven years older than Doria, was chief storyteller. One of the most vivid of his tales was when they pulled into yet another small redneck town in the middle of nowhere. There was a blizzard of biblical proportions and, rather aptly, they were searching for a room for the night. They had no luck, sent packing back to the highway by the locals who would not welcome any blacks on their white-only streets or, heaven forbid, in their white-only beds.

And then there were the countless times when they stopped for food at a diner and had to use the back door for 'coloureds'.

This was practically a daily occurrence as they shuffled in, trying not to draw attention to themselves.

Eventually they made it to Los Angeles, which, while not exactly the Promised Land, gave everyone a chance of a better life. Jeanette found work as a nurse, while Alvin, who had a strong entrepreneurial streak, started off working for his Aunt Lillie before finding his niche buying and selling bric-a-brac and curios in flea markets. Eventually, he opened his own antique shop called Twas New. By all accounts, he loved the objects for sale more than the money he might make from them. His pride and joy was his collection of vintage American cars.

Alvin was also a charismatic man whose company women enjoyed. His marriage to Jeanette did not last long in the California sunshine. They divorced and she became a single mum to the three children while he moved in with Lillie in the prosperous LA neighbourhood of View Park–Windsor Hills. The family remained close, however.

Meghan's maternal line is full of strong women, and Doria was no exception. She grew up with a committed sense of social justice, perhaps an understandable reaction to the hardships her family had faced down the generations. She went to Fairfax High School in Hollywood, which during her teenage years was still a hotbed of racial tension.

At that age, Doria, known as Dodi at school, was a member of the Apex Club, a class for exceptionally smart pupils. She was a purposeful teenager, a trait she would pass on to her daughter. She was also part of a group of black students who would protest rigorously about the continued injustice and inequality faced by their communities. One of her friends from those days, Jennifer Caldwell, recalled, 'She was a beautiful girl both inside and out. She had this beautiful afro hairstyle she was very proud of and she was always into fashion. She was whip smart, always smiling and sociable.'

Her parents may not have made a fortune but they were certainly comfortable. Doria lived a typical teenage life. She was the designated class driver when she passed her test and could borrow her mum's car. They would all head off, with Marvin Gaye songs blaring out, to their favourite hangout place, called Tico's, where they joined the queue for one of the restaurant's famous tacos.

Doria was a free spirit and didn't rush to engage in a career after school, preferring a relaxed, bohemian lifestyle in northern California for a while before she returned to LA. She found work as a temporary secretary, then as a trainee makeup artist at the Sunset Gower Studios in Hollywood, where they filmed the long-running soap *General Hospital*.

There she met a lighting director called Thomas Markle.

2

LOVING DAY

———

Doria couldn't miss Tom Markle. He was six foot three, well-built with a shock of red hair. She, on the other hand, was slim and striking. Meghan would later comment, 'I like to think he was drawn to her sweet eyes and her afro, plus their shared love of antiques.'

He had also come from a relentlessly white background in his home state of Pennsylvania. Meghan described it as a 'homogenised' community where the 'concept of marrying an African–American woman was not on the cards'.

Coincidentally, his ancestors had also made a dramatic move in search of a better life. In their case, they left their mining community in Yorkshire during the reign of Queen Victoria, in 1869, in pursuit of the American Dream. His great-grandmother, Mattie Sykes, was just a baby when they crossed the Atlantic.

News that Meghan may have had British connections caused a flurry of interest in her family tree when she was first linked to Prince Harry. It was even worked out that the couple were themselves seventeenth cousins, due to a tenuous link she had with King Edward III, who ruled England for fifty years from 1327 to 1377.

When she joined Harry on an official visit to Dublin in July 2018, it was established that she had an Irish connection as well. Highlighting the family tree of an important visitor to Ireland has become a common practice. Meghan was presented with documents showing she was descended from a Belfast girl.

The American connection began in the mining community of Mahanoy City, which despite its grand name has a population of less than 4,000. It's a bit in the middle of nowhere, some eighty miles from Philadelphia, and not exactly a step up from the north of England in Victorian times. It was a harsh environment and Mattie's father, Thomas Sykes, died from heart failure at the age of 43, leaving his widow to raise five children.

Meghan's ancestors hadn't moved far by the time Tom Markle was born, in July 1944, as World War II was drawing to a close. He grew up in the borough of Newport, Pennsylvania, seventy miles away from Mahanoy City, where his father Gordon worked for a time at an air force base in nearby Harrisburg before winding up in admin at the local post office. Tom's mother Doris worked at the J. J. Newberry's five and dime store in Newport. She would eventually be acknowledged as the matriarch of the family and someone loved and respected by Meghan.

The royal author Andrew Morton, who wrote the groundbreaking *Diana: Her True Story*, described Tom's childhood as being like something out of Mark Twain's classic *The Adventures of Tom Sawyer*. The family, including his two older brothers, lived in a modest white clapboard house on Sixth Street that was conveniently near woods and a river where the three boys would fish for catfish. Doris was a superb cook, filling her sons with homemade pies and making jam from the blackberries they picked in summer.

Such an idyllic-sounding youth was not enough to persuade any of the brothers that they wanted to stay in Newport, however.

They all moved away. Meghan painted a less sentimental view of her dad's roots, who, she said, 'came from so little in a small town in Pennsylvania, where Christmas stockings were filled with oranges and dinners were potatoes and Spam.'

The eldest of the three brothers, Mick, joined the United States Air Force and worked for many years in communications for the government, prompting speculation that he in fact had a job with the CIA. Understandably, he's never confirmed that rumour but he would prove helpful to his niece in the world of diplomacy some years later.

The middle brother, Fred, moved to Florida and found religion. He became the self-proclaimed leader of a little-known order called the Eastern Orthodox Catholic Church and was known as Bishop Dismas F. Markle. The unusual 'Dismas' comes from the Greek and is generally acknowledged to be the name of the good thief, the man who repented on the cross next to Jesus. It's not clear how many followers his church actually had, but some reports suggest it was about forty. Bishop Dismas has seen little of Meghan over the years – apparently she was aged six the last time they met – but to his credit has had nothing to say to journalists and very little to his friends about his family connections.

Tom, meanwhile, had grown into a strapping young man, but even he could not match his giant grandfather Isaac 'Ike' Markle, who stood 7 foot 2 inches tall and worked as a fireman on the railways. Tom was a popular figure at Newport High School. One of his contemporaries there, Loretta Strawser, who also lived on the same street as the Markle family, recalled that he was 'a nice person to be around.' Others remembered him as being laid-back and down to earth. He took an interest in the visual arts but it was only after leaving school that a hobby became a career.

First, though, he drifted from job to job, earning some going-out money. He set up the pins in a local bowling alley while he decided what to do next. He soon realised that he was never going to amount to much in Newport and needed to try his luck elsewhere. Although he didn't go on to college, Tom spent the equivalent of his gap year in the Poconos, the mountainous resort area in the north of the state. He found work at a local theatre where he had to muck in helping with everything, including the important technical tasks backstage.

Tom didn't return to Newport. Instead, he tried his luck in Chicago and found a job as a lighting technician at the WTTW television studios. He had to manage one potential problem with his career; he was colour-blind. It was testament to his dedication that he succeeded in keeping that hidden.

Instead, he thrived in his new direction in life, climbing his way up the ladder from the bottom rung. As well as his work at the TV station, he did extra shifts at the Harper Theater on Chicago's South Side in the Hyde Park neighbourhood of the city, ten minutes down the road from where the family home of Barack Obama has become a tourist attraction.

Tom's particular skill was lighting, and his flair soon grabbed the attention of the Harper's new owners, newspaper proprietor Bruce Sagan and his wife Judith, who was particularly influential in the world of dance. It was a golden age for the playhouse and as well as prestigious productions of Chekhov and Pirandello, Tom was on hand to help with the first Harper Theater Dance Festival, which swiftly became one of the highlights of the arts calendar in Chicago.

Tom worked hard, but it was the sixties and he liked to play hard as well, hanging out with college and television friends and enjoying a free and easy lifestyle. He was nineteen when he met a young clerk at the Illinois Railroad Company. Roslyn Loveless was an elegant eighteen-year-old and they clicked immediately. She thought him 'tall and handsome' with a 'great sense of humour and charming smile'.

Roslyn was soon expecting her first child and she and Tom moved into a one-bedroom apartment, got married and celebrated the birth of a daughter, Yvonne – who would later change her name to Samantha – in November 1964. Cracks in their relationship appeared soon after.

Roslyn gave a devastating account of those days in an interview with the *Daily Mirror*, a version of events that Tom has strongly denied, describing her accusation as 'not valid'. According to Roslyn, he had a bad temper: 'He would scream, "Fuck you", "Fuck off", "Leave me the fuck alone", or "Get the fuck out of here." Everything was fuck.'

An addition to the family, Tom Jr, in December 1965, did not improve things between the couple. For a while she moved to Newport, Pennsylvania, and lived with Tom's mum and dad, Doris and Gordon, who were very kind but could not meet the financial demands of supporting a young mum and her two small children.

Back in Chicago, Roslyn claims that Tom lived the life of a single man, mixing in circles where cocaine was commonplace and enjoying the company of other women. She said he did not give her the money she needed even to feed the children properly and she was reduced to shoplifting in the local store just to get enough food.

A friend came to her rescue and said she could stay with her, so Roslyn and the children took flight from the family apartment. She refused to sign divorce papers in which it was said he had been a 'true, kind and affectionate husband'.

They were eventually divorced in 1975, although by this time Tom had made the journey across country in pursuit of his personal dream to work in Hollywood. While he continued to work hard to make progress in his career, Roslyn and the children moved to Albuquerque in New Mexico to start a new life, encouraged by her brother Richard, who already lived in the city.

Tom didn't completely forget his Pennsylvanian roots, returning every year for family and high school reunions in Newport. After struggling for eighteen months to get a start, he had carved out a good life for himself as a lighting director on *General Hospital*. The famous daytime soap began in 1963 and is the *Coronation Street* of American television, so it was a prestigious job.

He was living close to the beach in Santa Monica where his daughter Yvonne, a restless and ambitious teenager, joined him when she was fourteen. She had her sights set on a Hollywood career as an actress or model, or both.

When he became a teenager, Tom Jr joined the household as well. He had decided that high school in laid-back California would suit him better than New Mexico. They moved to a large and very comfortable four-bedroom family house on Providencia Street in Woodland Hills; down the road from an exclusive country club, it was a property that would probably fetch more than $1 million if sold today.

Yvonne and Tom Jr were typical teenagers – bickering and squabbling and preferring the company of their own friends and social lives. Their father kept out of things, immersing himself in his work. And then he met Doria on the set of *General Hospital*. She was undoubtedly a ray of sunshine in his life, a thoughtful and calming presence in the household, except, it seemed, for Yvonne, who apparently referred to her dad's new girlfriend as 'the maid', which at best was the sort of casual racism that masqueraded as a joke, or at worst was blatantly racist.

Doria was twelve years younger than Tom, so, ironically, she was much closer in age to Yvonne, but that did not encourage any bond between them. One highlight in the uneasy household was when Doria invited them all to join the Raglands for Thanksgiving dinner at her parents' house. Jeanette, Alvin, Joseph Jr and Saundra were all there and Tom Jr was impressed by the sense of family they had, something that seemed to be missing from the Markle clan.

Six months after they met, Doria and Tom married, two days before Christmas in 1979. She chose a venue and ceremony that reflected her growing interest in yoga and alternative religions. The Self-Realization Fellowship Temple on Sunset Boulevard stood out with its faux Moorish entrance, including gold orb-topped turrets and stone elephants. The Fellowship was founded in 1920 by the charismatic Paramahansa Yogananda, regarded by many as one of the twentieth-century's most important spiritual figures and described by the *Los Angeles Times* as the first superstar guru.

He embraced the value of meditation and of Kriya yoga – influences that help give Doria an inner strength that has been of huge benefit to her daughter. Perhaps his most famous follower was the late Steve Jobs, the billionaire co-founder of Apple who would read Yogananda's book *Autobiography of a Yogi* at the start of each year. He made sure everyone attending his memorial service was presented with a copy.

Doria and Tom's ceremony was presided over by Brother Bhaktananda, a much-respected Buddhist priest in Los Angeles who followed Yogananda's philosophy for a simpler, more thoughtful life. In 1979, an interracial marriage was still a big deal in the US. While in the UK, the drawbacks might have been based on social stigma and entrenched attitudes, in America there was a long history of legislation to overcome. Amazingly, that had only happened in 1967, little more than a decade earlier, when The Beatles were singing 'All You Need is Love'.

In the US, what was really needed was 'Loving', the name of the couple that bravely took on racist laws and won. They had married in Washington, DC, in 1959 but were arrested when they returned home to Virginia, pleading guilty to 'cohabiting as man and wife, against the peace and dignity of the Commonwealth'. They were offered one year in prison or a suspended sentence if they chose to leave their home state.

They left but were rearrested in 1963 when they visited family, triggering a legal battle which they eventually won four years later at the Supreme Court. The Chief Justice concluded, 'To deny this fundamental freedom on so unsupportable a basis as the racial classifications … is to deprive all the State's citizens of liberty.' Now there's a national Loving Day every June in the US to celebrate the end of this absurd prohibition.

On her wedding day Doria wore a simple white dress with flowers in her hair, while the groom put on a sports jacket, shirt and tie and carried a bunch of orange blossoms. It was a lovely afternoon and Doria, surrounded by her family, looking like a teenager in love, sparkled with happiness.

They had been married for eighteen months when their daughter, Rachel Meghan Markle, was born before dawn on 4 August 1981 at the West Park Hospital in Canoga Park, a suburb in the San Fernando Valley just north of where the family lived in Woodland Hills. She was and will always be a California girl.

Tom, now thirty-five, was at the hospital and was 'thrilled to tears' when his baby was handed to him to hold for the first time. This time round he threw himself enthusiastically into the role of dad. She was, he declared, his 'pride and joy'. His son, Tom Jr, confirmed that he was a changed man: 'Before then, Dad's work took priority over everything, but she became his whole world. She was her daddy's princess.'

He was still working all hours, though, a dedication that was more than paying off when his work on *General Hospital* was being more widely recognised within the industry. After being nominated twice, he and his fellow crew on the soap won a daytime Emmy for 'outstanding achievement in design excellence'. This was big news. Before his retirement, Tom would end up being nominated nine times, testament to his ability in a crowded marketplace.

Meghan was a very cute baby and her delighted father was always happy to be the first to pick her up if she was crying. One big difference to becoming a dad now than when he was a younger man back in Pennsylvania was that he was making good money and could properly afford a child. She became the 'most special thing in his life'.

3

PEOPLE ARE FIGHTING

———————

Doria, twenty-three when Meghan was born, was not faring so well. She had to cope with not only looking after a small baby but also maintaining the peace in such a fractious household. The two older siblings, who have been paid many times for interviews, have often changed their accounts of life in the Markle household, but one fact is clear: they were teenagers and Meghan was a newborn.

Woodland Hills was a pleasant, middle-class, predominantly white neighbourhood in the Valley, as it was called. Meghan summed it up: 'It was leafy and affordable. What it was not, however, was diverse. And there was my mom, caramel in complexion with her light-skinned baby in tow, being asked where my mother was since they assumed she was the nanny.' While they have never publically acknowledged how difficult it was for them being an interracial couple in Woodland Hills back then, it's easy to imagine it was a constant battle. Meghan herself has said that she was too young to understand that they were living with institutional prejudice. With hindsight, this was not the best location for them.

The Markle household was one where everyone seemed to have their own set of friends. Doria relied on her own mother,

Jeanette, who had been at the maternity hospital with her, as well as friends interested in practising yoga, which had become a passion that would last a lifetime. When he wasn't working, Tom liked to socialise with his TV circle and would bring his little daughter downstairs to proudly show her off when they went back to the house.

Elder daughter Yvonne was often out on the town with other budding actors. Her father had helped her secure a walk-on, uncredited part in *General Hospital* but her career wasn't going anywhere and she didn't seem at all interested in helping with Meghan. Tom Jr was happy to smoke weed with his pals, although his father insisted they didn't indulge around the new addition to the family.

Perhaps inevitably, the presence of a young baby in such a fraught environment put a strain on Tom and Doria's relationship. Some family friends have hinted that Tom found fault with everything – something a strong-minded woman like Doria was not going to tolerate for too long. He admitted that he just wasn't home enough.

Doria moved back to her mother's house and took Meghan with her. For the sake of their young child, they stayed on reasonable terms and there was never a question of Tom not being fully involved with their Flower's upbringing. Meghan proudly states, 'I never saw them fight.' Although Meghan was just two when they split up, her parents did not divorce until 1987, when she was seven and at primary school. Whatever their feelings towards each other, they were determined that their daughter's world would be a safe and happy one.

Tom tried his best to ensure she felt no different from any other little girls her age. Meghan revealed in her now-famous blog, The Tig, that when she was seven she had her heart set on a family set of Barbie dolls for Christmas. They were called the

Heart Family and consisted of a mum, dad and two children, but there was a problem: the 'perfect nuclear family', as Meghan described it, was only available in all black dolls or all white ones.

Tom was not happy with that so he marched into a Toys "R" Us store in West Hollywood and carefully customised a set just for his daughter. As he saw it, he was not going to allow her to be disadvantaged by the colour of her skin, even if it was just a Christmas present.

Meghan recalled Santa's gift: 'On Christmas morning, swathed in glitter-flecked wrapping paper, I found my Heart family: a black mom doll, a white dad doll and a child in each colour.' The new family 'echoed her reality'. It was a sweet gesture for his daughter but also a serious one that she never forgot. The question of her racial identity was one that would absorb Meghan as a child and as an adult.

Meghan's first school was well-known and an important influence on her even at such a young age. The Hollywood Schoolhouse was founded in 1945 as a private nursery school that welcomed and encouraged ethnic diversity during the post-war years when many other private schools did not.

The renowned founder and first headmistress, Ruth Pease, had her own inspiring story. She herself was the only child of deaf parents and from a very young age would communicate with the hearing world for her parents. She would be teased about it by other children and grew up understanding the hurt-fulness of casual and thoughtless remarks and prejudice.

During the war, she and her husband took in a little boy whose father was Chinese and mother was white. His parents had trouble finding day care for him, almost certainly because the locals thought he was Japanese and the US was at war with Japan. Ruth's daughter, Debbie Wehbe observed, 'My mother wanted no part of that attitude. To her, children needed someone to take care of them: Period.'

The school just off Highland Avenue was originally known as the Hollywood Little Red Schoolhouse simply because Ruth's husband Robert painted the original building that colour. They added a distinctive bell tower that made the school's appearance seem like something out of a fairy tale or nursery rhyme. It was welcoming to nervous children and uncertain parents.

At Ruth's school, all children were accepted and nurtured for who they were as individuals. It was a perfect fit for Meghan as far as Tom and Doria were concerned. Ruth had officially retired in 1970 and her daughter had taken over, but she was still part of the furniture of the place, living to the grand age of 96. She would wave to the children from her balcony as they came into school and they would call up 'Good morning Miss Ruth' or 'Hello Grandma'.

Back in the early days the most famous former pupil at the school was the fifties' bombshell Jayne Mansfield. Now, it's Meghan Markle, although in Hollywood terms it remains to be seen whether Johnny Depp's daughter, the actress Lily-Rose Depp, becomes a household name. Despite one or two well-known alumni, this was not a celebrity or elite school.

Doria had moved into a spacious second-floor apartment on South Cloverdale Avenue, three miles from the school. It may not have been as leafy as Woodland Hills but the street was wide, clean and tidy with small front lawns dotted with flower borders and palm trees. It was a pleasant, safe neighbourhood in midtown LA.

To help pay some bills and also because she didn't want to be stuck at home all day, Doria started looking for work. Under the terms of the divorce agreement, Tom had joint custody and agreed to pay $800 a month towards Meghan's upbringing.

While Tom could afford the school fees at the Hollywood Schoolhouse, pupils whose parents could not meet them could apply for assistance grants. The school was quite liberal-thinking in its attitudes at a time when it would not have been derided as 'woke'.

Intriguingly, it was during her time at elementary school that the first signs of the two passions in Meghan's life began to form: standing up for what was right and wanting to be a performer. For the former, Debbie Wehbe, who was headmistress while she was a pupil there, gives credit to both Tom and Doria for encouraging her 'belief systems'.

Meghan's love of performing was evident at the annual end-of-year shows when all the children were encouraged to make the best use of their talents. When she was five, Meghan took centre stage to sing the old favourite, 'The Wheels on the Bus'. Right from the start, Tom would be there proudly taking photos of his daughter. He literally took pictures of her every day.

Importantly, Meghan found a best friend at the school. Ninaki Priddy, known as Niki, would turn out *not* to be a friend for life, but growing up they shared many memorable moments. For Niki's ninth birthday party, Meghan took a leading role in a jokey, spontaneous show where she pretended to be a queen surrounded by her servants. The whole thing was captured on video by Niki's mum Maria and was just some back-garden fun, but it did reveal how much the camera loved Meghan and, even at this age, she could be the centre of attention in any group. Over the years, Niki collected almost as many shots of Meghan as Tom Markle did, diligently sticking into albums happy photographs of the two girls at home, at school or on trips abroad.

From an early age Doria encouraged Meghan to be aware of the whole world and not just her little patch of Los Angeles. She was working for a travel agency that opened up opportunities to take her daughter with her on some wonderful holidays. While there was sun and beaches, culture and laughter, there was the occasional more sobering experience of those less fortunate.

She took her to see the slum areas of Jamaica, a genuine eye opener for a little Californian girl who could scarcely comprehend the unbearable poverty of what she was seeing. Her mother had soothing words: 'Don't look scared, Flower. Be aware but don't be afraid.'

In Oaxaca City, in southern Mexico, she saw for herself poor street children selling sweets to earn a few pesos to buy food. It was a stark dose of reality that illustrated the unfairness in the world. Doria had taken Meghan there for the famous Day of the Dead Festival – 'Día de los Muertos' – which is nothing like as grim as it sounds. The celebration, which begins on Halloween, marks the three days when the spirits of lost loved ones visit the living and is infused with a sense of fun and a carnival atmosphere: truly a party spirit.

Meghan fell in love with Mexico – the people, the culture and, perhaps best of all, the food. But she never forgot her mum's life lessons. In one of her essays for *Elle* magazine, she wrote, 'My mum raised me to be a global citizen with eyes open to sometimes harsh realities.'

Doria also encouraged Meghan from about the age of seven to join her for 'mommy-and-me' yoga sessions. Meghan was not keen: 'I was very resistant as a kid but she said, "Flower, you will find your practice – just give it time."' As with many things, Doria would be proved right in the end.

It's too easy to say that it was Tom who encouraged her acting while Doria was more serious. She spent most of her time with a mum who had more boundaries and limits in place, but Doria still liked to have fun and would dance carefree around the apartment to her favourite music. She loved the mellow soul of Al Green. And Tom was there when needed to lend a hand and support her ideals. Generally she would spend the week at her mother's and weekends with her father. When he dropped her back, the three of them would usually sit down, eat dinner from a tray on their laps and watch the game show *Jeopardy!* together.

Both parents strengthened her social awareness and they were both givers, much more so than takers. They would deliver meals to people in hospices, dig out the coins in their pockets for the poor living on the streets and at Thanksgiving they would buy a turkey or two for the homeless shelters. These gestures helped to form Meghan's character.

A grim period in modern Los Angeles history also had a lasting effect on her. In 1991, when Meghan was ten, police officers in the city were caught on film giving a savage beating with batons to a black motorist called Rodney King. His injuries included skull fractures, broken bones and teeth and permanent brain damage.

The following April, a predominantly white jury with no African–Americans found four police officers not guilty of using excessive force, even though the beating had continued for fifteen minutes. Los Angeles erupted into five days of rioting and violence. It seemed that everywhere in South Central LA something was being set on fire and the whole area resembled a war zone. There was nothing remotely Hollywood about this.

Meghan and her schoolmates were sent home for their safety. She remembered there was ash everywhere, settling on lawns and porches. Meghan shouted, 'Oh my God, Mommy, it's snowing.' Doria responded firmly, 'No, Flower, it's not snow. Get in the house.'

Meghan's social conscience was well-developed for her age. The current headmistress of the Hollywood Schoolhouse,

Ilise Faye, observed: 'She had a voice. She was one of those children that would stand up for the underdogs. She would stand up for what she believed in, and she was the leader among her friends.'

That leadership was evident when she heard that one of her classmates was upset about the Gulf War. The boy in question was in tears because his elder brother was in the military and was due to fly out to the Middle East. Meghan helped to organise a protest at her school against the conflict, carrying a homemade placard that stated, 'Peace and Harmony for the World'.

The following year, at the age of eleven, Meghan's class had a social studies assignment that involved watching and commenting on various advertisements. First up was one for Robitussin cough syrup, which suggested it was 'Recommended by Dr Mom'. Meghan's response was what about 'Dr Dad'?

The commercial that had the biggest effect on her, however, was for Ivory clear dishwasher liquid, a kitchen product from corporation Proctor & Gamble. She couldn't help but notice that it began, 'Women are fighting greasy pots and pans ...'

She was angry at the blatant sexism: 'I said "wait a minute, how can they say that?!"' She was even less impressed when two boys in the class piped up, 'Yeah, that's where women belong, in the kitchen.' That evening she told her dad all about it and he suggested that she write to the company in person. She sat down and composed a letter in her already immaculate handwriting urging them to change the wording of the commercial to 'People are fighting greasy pots and pans'.

Tom also suggested that she write to some powerful people as well, so she sent a letter to the new First Lady, Hillary Clinton, the renowned civil rights lawyer Gloria Allred, and to broadcaster Linda Ellerbee, host of *Nick News W5* on the Nickelodeon cable channel. The long-running news programme for school-age children had only recently started in 1992.

Meghan secured a famous victory and the advertisement wording was changed to 'People are fighting …' just as she had hoped. She appeared on *Nick News* to talk about it: 'I don't think it's right that kids grow up thinking these things – that mom does everything.'

And she had a message to other children: 'If you see something you don't like or are affected by on television or any other platform, write letters and send them to the right people and you can really make a difference – not just for yourself but lots of other people.'

Linda Ellerbee did not forget the gap-toothed, freckly, articulate youngster and recalled, 'It was absolutely clear that this young woman was strong in her belief. It didn't matter that she was eleven years old. She believed in women and in her own power. She wasn't afraid to reach out and say "I want my power. I want my rights."'

Not everything worked out that well. Sometimes she would send a letter of injustice and be 'rewarded' with a bag of sweets or candy in the post. She would usually take them into school, which at least helped with her popularity rating.

Meghan was never a latchkey kid returning to an empty house. Her grandmother Jeanette would look after her if her parents were working – although when she was old enough she would visit Tom at the ABC Studios a mile from the school and wait for him to finish work. He had secured a second significant job as a lighting director on *Married … with Children*, a slightly risqué sitcom that was first broadcast in the spring of 1987 and ran for ten years. She would later recall, 'There were lots of times my dad would say, "Meg, why don't you go and help with the craft services room over there? This is just a little off-colour for your 11-year-old eyes."' Ironically, Meghan wasn't allowed to watch the show at home, even if she had been in the studio during recording. Her mum would call her to watch the end credits, though: 'I could give the screen a kiss when I saw my dad's name go by.'

Meghan was more interested in the show's dog than in guest stars such as the renowned former porn star Traci Lords. The hound in question was a shaggy coated Briard called Buck, a canine superstar and arguably the most popular character in the show – appearing in 177 episodes. One Friday night before the show was being recorded, she noticed Melba Farquhar, the wife of one of the producers, feeding Buck some leftovers.

The next Friday, Meghan turned up with her own leftovers. Melba remembered, 'She had saved some of her dinner to give to him and wanted to know if it was ok if she fed the dog this time. She was just so sweet.' Meghan doted on Buck and would always seek him out for a pet and a cuddle. The dog's trainer, Steven Ritt, remembered her gentle manner with Buck: 'Meghan was always kind of an old soul, a little more mature than some of the children around the set at her age.'

Her maturity for someone still at elementary school was evident in her kindness to a girl called Elizabeth McCoy, who was one of those unfortunate pupils who was shunned and bullied principally because she suffered from petit mal seizures, a mild form of epilepsy characterised by a fleeting loss of consciousness. They are better described these days as 'absence seizures'. She stood out as different, which often makes the child an easy target for other children – the 'mean girls', as Elizabeth called them.

Sometimes Elizabeth would be just sat there as if in a daydreaming trance. If Meghan saw her, she would be the first to go over, hold her hand and sit with her until she was sure she was ok. Meghan was a couple of years older but would happily chat to the younger girl about the things that she found important and interesting. Elizabeth thought she was very cool.

Portraying the young elementary school Meghan as a serious-minded geek intent on saving the world is simply not how she was, though. She could enjoy herself as much as any other sociable young girl, like the time she dressed up as Elvira, the Queen of Halloween, complete with black wig, and pretended to try out various coffins for size.

For one end-of-year school show she joined her classmates to give an exuberant performance of one of the cooler seasonal songs, 'Christmas in Hollis' by the New York rap trio Run-DMC. She also narrated a performance by her friends of *How the Grinch Stole Christmas!*, the Dr Seuss story that had become one of the most popular films of the time, starring Jim Carrey with narration by Anthony Hopkins. The show ended with everyone singing the Spanish Christmas song 'Feliz Navidad' before a rousing rendition of 'Jingle Bells'. The concert was a snapshot of the school's diversity.

The shows often had a theme: one year it was Dick Tracy, when the Madonna and Warren Beatty movie was doing the rounds. Another time, a show was based around Japan. In June 1992 Meghan and her friends performed 'Broadway comes to Hollywood' at the annual end-of-term show, dancing to 'Greased Lightning' from the musical *Grease* and to the show-stopping 'America' from *West Side Story*.

The absolute highlight, though, came a year later at her graduation. She was still a couple of months short of her twelfth birthday when she put on a white mortar board to receive her 'Elementary Diploma'. Then she stood in front of the school, watched by teachers and beaming parents including both Doria and Tom, and introduced the entertainment that she and Niki had devised. She told them, 'We're here to thank all the people who have made us feel really special over the past nine years.'

She and her friends then launched their entertainment tribute. Meghan wore denim shorts, a stripy t-shirt and *Easy Rider* shades for some enthusiastic moves to Chuck Berry's timeless 'Roll over Beethoven'. Perhaps the highlight was the class's rendition of the 1957 doo-wop hit 'Mr Lee' by The Bobbettes. They changed Mr Lee to Mr T to show their appreciation of a favourite teacher, Mr Teryl.

And so it was time to cut the graduation cake and say goodbye to her first school, where she had been a big fish in a small pond, as the old cliché goes. Now, she would have to navigate the demands that middle and high school made on a teenage girl. She had shown some promise on stage and demonstrated a mature social conscience in someone so young. Moving forward, could she successfully marry the two?

4

WITH A SPARKLE

———

Just like any other day at the Immaculate Heart High School for girls, the morning began with a prayer. The students did not have to cram into church or kneel in corridors, they just had to stop what they were doing, stand still even if they were late and hurrying to class and think quietly for a minute or two, listening to the words coming from the loudspeakers dotted about.

The greeting was familiar. 'Good morning Immaculate Heart!' It was the voice of Christine Knudsen, who chaired the theology department. Occasionally she would recite a formal prayer that might end with an Amen – after all, Immaculate Heart had been founded as a Catholic school – but more often than not she would choose some words of inspiration. Sometimes she would talk about a film or an important sporting event; she might mention Gandhi if it was 2 October, his birthday. She used an Eleanor Roosevelt quote to great effect: 'You gain strength, courage and confidence by every experience in which you really stop to look fear in the face. You must do the thing you think you cannot do.' She encouraged the girls to think of the qualities that mattered in life, such as compassion, acceptance, fairness and personal integrity.

And she would always conclude with a rallying cry. If it was the start of the week, she would declare, 'MAKE IT A GREAT

MONDAY!' 'The idea is that we just take a moment to compose ourselves and reflect. It's a great way to stop and be free to start class,' explained the current school president, Maureen Diekmann.

On one particular morning, census forms were being handed out to the seventh graders in middle school during their English lesson. It was the usual kind of thing – just tick the box and move on. But for twelve-year-old Meghan Markle, it immediately presented a problem. There were four choices for ethnicity: white, black, Hispanic or Asian.

Meghan didn't know what to do. She asked the teacher, who looked at her light-toned skin and told her to check 'caucasian' because that was how she looked. But Meghan was uncomfortable with that advice because, in her eyes, it was choosing one parent over another. Imagine looking Doria in the eye if she had done as suggested. She told *Elle* magazine, 'I put down my pen; not as an act of defiance but rather a symptom of my confusion. I couldn't bring myself to do that, to picture the pit-in-the-belly sadness my mother would feel if she were to find out.'

Instead she just left it unanswered, heartbreakingly: 'I left my identity blank – a question mark, an absolute incomplete – much like how I felt.' That evening she told her dad what had happened. Tom was clear and clearly angry: 'If it happens again, you draw your own box.'

The school prided itself on its diversity. Neither race nor religion was of paramount importance. Although it was founded by the Sisters of the Immaculate Heart of Mary in 1906, little more than fifty per cent of the pupils were Catholic by the time Meghan enrolled. She would have been thought of as Christian while other groups included Buddhists, Muslims and Hindi, as well as those who didn't have a religion at all.

Even in the early days when all the teachers were nuns, the mindset was to be as welcoming as possible. The girls who did not share the Catholic faith were never told they were wrong. Despite being on one of the busiest junctions in the Los Feliz neighbourhood – Franklin and Western – the campus of Immaculate Heart was a tranquil urban oasis with plenty of space for conversation, laughter or some private moments. In the centre of the grounds was an inviting swimming pool that would have graced many of the movie-star mansions of Beverly Hills. Across the road was the building that housed the American Film Institute, just in case the pupils needed reminding that Hollywood was near.

Although the fees at the private school were expensive for those that could afford to pay the full amount, Immaculate Heart was not full of the children of millionaires; nor was it packed with celebrity offspring. Kim and Kourtney Kardashian, for instance, went to Marymount High School, another all-girl Catholic school on Sunset Boulevard; Jake Gyllenhaal and Ayda Field attended the Harvard-Westlake School in Studio City.

You can usually find at least one notable celebrity at any school in LA. Immaculate Heart was no exception. Until Meghan featured as an alumna, the best-known actress through the gates was probably the much-loved television and film star Mary Tyler Moore, who died in 2017.

Following her death, the president of the Screen Actors Guild, Gabrielle Carteris, said, 'At a time when independence for women was not the social norm, both the fictional Mary and the real-life Mary set an example, showing that women could take control of their lives and their careers.' It was an example that Meghan Markle would follow.

Mary Tyler Moore was a role model for the girls at Immaculate Heart, although more so probably for the mothers and grandmothers of Meghan's generation. An alumna more relevant to Meghan was Tyra Banks, who had graduated just a couple of years earlier. Tyra had shot up by three inches when she was eleven and had to contend with negativity and name-calling from bullies who would call her 'giraffe' and 'light-bulb head', but she had the last laugh. While she was still at the school she embarked on her successful career as a supermodel.

Tyra launched her TV career in 1993, just as Meghan started at Immaculate Heart, playing Will Smith's childhood friend Jackie Ames in seven episodes of his popular sitcom, *The Fresh Prince of Bel-Air*. She was only nineteen when she found fame. Meghan would have to wait far longer.

In some ways, Tyra has become a younger version of Oprah Winfrey, branching out into the world of broadcasting and philanthropy, and boasting a fortune estimated to be more than $90 million. As long ago as 1994, when Meghan was in eighth grade, Tyra started the Tyra Banks Scholarship so that disadvantaged African–American girls could attend Immaculate Heart. She recognised at a young age that not every girl of colour was going to become a supermodel.

In 1999, the year Meghan graduated, Tyra also founded TZONE, an annual seven-day camp designed to improve the leadership and life skills of similarly underprivileged girls in and around Los Angeles. Tyra wanted to build the self-esteem of pre-teen and teenage girls and help them to overcome gender stereotyping and body issues. The concept went nationwide in 2005 as the Tyra Banks TZONE Foundation.

For Meghan, her own confusion about her identity was not something that was going to disappear overnight. Despite the worthy philosophy of the school, she had to confront basic problems every day, including where to sit in the canteen at lunchtimes. Inevitably, there were cliques. Should she spend the hour with the black girls or the white girls, with the Filipino or Latino girls? Mostly she avoided the issue by joining every group or society going, making do with a sandwich during French club or giving her views on the next important question for the student body. It helped that she was intelligent and articulate, although there was a chance she was becoming a little earnest.

The girls at Immaculate Heart were encouraged to get involved in the community. In these early teenage years they were educated in the school's ideology values 'to become women of great heart and right conscience through leadership, service, and a life-long commitment to Christian values.'

In middle school, they were expected to volunteer for worth-while projects in the Los Angeles area. Meghan, aged thirteen, chose a particularly challenging one, working at a place that was on Doria's radar as something worth supporting.

The enterprise in the heart of downtrodden, downcast, down-town LA was run by a remarkable couple, Jeff Dietrich and Catherine Morris, a former nun, who is in her eighties now but still turning up two or three times a week to do her bit at the 'Hippie Kitchen', as the locals named their community kitchen back in the day.

Skid Row, fifty-four blocks of relentless misery, is not a place for a night-time stroll past the trolleys full of crumpled clothes and cardboard boxes, past the homeless men and women huddled round an oil-drum fire waiting for the sun to rise on another day; waiting for the soup kitchen on the corner of 6th Street and Gladys Avenue to open.

Jeff and Catherine met as volunteers there in 1974, four years after the kitchen opened in an old Victorian house. They were part of an organisation called the Catholic Worker movement that aims to help the most vulnerable members of society. The three hundred or so homeless people queuing for their only meal of the day were not fed religion as part of the deal.

Instead they were treated to an hour or so of respect where they could eat some freshly cooked food – vegetables, rice and beans or some salad with hunks of bread – in the tranquil, sunny courtyard dotted with palm trees and parrots, and chat about this and that and nothing in particular before stepping back into the harsh reality of their world. Perhaps best of all, it was a place of safety where they knew your name.

The kitchen was open in the mornings and the police were never too far away, patrolling the sidewalks where crack cocaine and bad alcohol were in competition to drag the Skid Row residents down even further. Meghan had been apprehensive, even fearful, of volunteering. She had seen the grim streets of Mexico and Jamaica, but here she was making a connection and becoming personally involved: 'The first day I felt really scared. I was young and it was rough and raw down there, and though I was with a great volunteer group, I just felt overwhelmed.'

Meghan was more her confident self when she gave her first serious speech; she spoke at her middle school graduation cere-mony at Immaculate Heart in June 1995. It was a masterful effort for someone not yet fourteen. Wearing the traditional white cap and gown, she showed no sign of outward nerves when she began, 'Good evening parents, friends, faculty and fellow classmates ...'

She thanked the school graciously for the previous two years, singling out the religious lessons that had helped her and others to 'develop spirituality in our lives' and the classes that had taught them 'a deep compassion to those who suffer from the Aids virus'.

She concluded in a mature way: 'We will graduate from high school in 1999 and begin college in the next century, taking many different paths. Some of us will go into politics, finance, entertainment, education and many other fields. But no matter what field we choose, we will always carry the spirit of Immaculate Heart with us. And always and forever as women of great heart, dedicate ourselves to making it a better world.'

Not for the last time in her life, a Meghan Markle speech was greeted with a rapturous round of applause. The last sentiment was one she has endeavoured to follow throughout her life and that she could have included in almost any speech she has made since.

Doria continued to nurture her daughter's empathy by taking Meghan with her to weekend meetings of her church, the Agape (Greek for unconditional love) International Spiritual Center in Santa Monica. These were very popular across a wide spectrum of ages and ethnicity. Dismissing these gatherings as an exuberant, exclusively black gospel event is completely wrong.

Of course the hall resonates with some glorious, uplifting singing, accompanied by the Agape house band of musicians, but there's also the chance to meditate, spending time in soothing silence and quiet reflection, that particularly appealed to Doria and her embrace of yoga culture.

The centre was founded in 1986 by the Rev Dr Michael Beckwith, a charismatic advocate of the New Thought movement that promoted positive thinking as a modern way of dealing with the universal problems of today – feeding the homeless, preserving the environment and helping children whose lives have been shattered by war and disease. They are the virtues that Doria and Meghan already followed and ones that would become even more important to them in the years to come.

These were religious gatherings and God did not take a backseat, but they were a world away from a draughty Sunday service at Crathie Kirk, next to Balmoral. A celebrity or two might drift in, happy that they were not going to be photographed or disturbed. The Oscar-winning actress Hilary Swank was a particular devotee and would often be there when Doria and Meghan attended.

In the school holidays, when Meghan was thirteen going on fourteen, Agape started a summer drama camp for some of the members' children. The camp, which met every day, was called Agape's 38 Flavours, because that was the number of children who signed up for it. They were from different cultures, all encouraged to share their experiences of life.

Meghan was one of thirteen or fourteen young teenagers, alongside a pocket of pre-teens and a group of little children. Another girl was known as Meg so Meghan adopted her own special jingle: 'Meghan Markle with a Sparkle' and everyone called her that.

Generally, Doria would be the morning taxi, dropping her off at 8am, then Tom would pick her up at 4pm. Meghan's domestic arrangements had changed. Tom and Doria had swapped roles to a certain extent. One of the popular myths about Meghan's childhood and beyond is that her mum and dad remained great friends. That was not the case, but like many parents, they made the best of it for the sake of their child.

Meghan was faced with the tricky dilemma of keeping both parents happy and including both in her life. During the week she lived with her father. The Woodland Hills home had proved far too large for one person after both Yvonne and Tom Jr had moved out, so instead, he found a second-floor apartment in an unassuming West Hollywood street called Vista Del Mar, conveniently near his work and the school.

At weekends she was back with Mum. Doria was following in her own dad's footsteps by setting up in business for herself and becoming a store owner. She found premises for two businesses in a modest shopping mall on La Brea Avenue, just a five-minute drive from home; one was a gift shop called Distant Treasures and the other, catchily named A Change of a Dress, included some of her own designs. Understandably, the stores required a lot of attention so there was little time for the school run, so Tom's place seemed a sensible option for Meghan during the week.

Tom didn't go to the Agape church but he was happy to do his share of parental chauffeuring for camp. This was the first time the teenage Meghan had come into contact with boys. She went to an all-girls school so the opportunities had been thin on the ground. That changed when she met Joshua Silverstein, a year older than her and just as keen on theatre.

Like her, Joshua was mixed race. His father David was Jewish and his mother, Beverly, African–American. His parents, who divorced when he was eleven, went to high school with Michael Beckwith. Some years later David bumped into Michael, who invited him to come along to Agape. He loved the sense of community there and would take his son to the services, often twice a week.

Joshua did not need to see which box Meghan might or might not have checked to understand her ethnicity: 'When I saw Meghan, I saw a lighter-skinned brown person with curly hair and freckles and fuller lips. And I was like, that person is a person of colour.'

Meghan and Joshua got together in a time-honoured way. He recalled, 'It was very typical of what kids do at that time. A friend told me Meghan thought I was cute and then I told my friend I thought she was cute. That was really the impetus we needed to become a couple. I took a day to think about it and figure out what to do. It was camp and we would be seeing each other every day so it was a big commitment to show up as a couple.

'So the next day I made my move and we just fell into it. It was very innocent and very cute. And everyone took it that we were together. If she was doing anything acting-wise, I was very focused on it and very, very interested in what she was doing.' Even though they were young, they talked about the black experience from the perspective of someone who had a white parent. They weren't overly serious conversations but ones in which they discussed what it might be like to be a person of colour in the entertainment industry.

The new couple also had the more traditional teenage problem – how to find any privacy. They would sit together at lunch but the other campmates would always be around. Joshua explained, 'It was this awkward and uncomfortable thing – like you are sitting with us and infringing on our space. But they were like – "Are you guys going to kiss? Kiss now."' They did kiss, making sure they practised a lot at every opportunity during camp.

Having been together most of the day, Meghan and Joshua would spend much of the evening on the phone to each other. He would be on the floor of his mother's bedroom and she would be in a closet upstairs – both of them trying to keep the conversation away from parental ears.

Camp was an enjoyable way of spending the summer holidays. The Agape theatre programme was different in that it combined theatre games and practice with a sense of spirituality. There was nothing overtly serious but it just seemed natural to take a break with some guided meditation or 'visioning', where you think about your goals for the future, or to end a day of fun with a prayer.

Meghan celebrated her fourteenth birthday at the beginning of August and was given a rousing chorus of 'Happy Birthday Meghan Markle with a Sparkle' at the camp. Her memorable summer ended with a spectacular show in the Sanctuary, Agape's main hall on Olympic Boulevard in Santa Monica. It was a culmination of all the various stories and presentations, improv games and sketches that they had worked on for six weeks. They each had to perform a monologue in which they created a new and totally original character. Meghan made sure her hair was at its wildest, smeared lipstick on her face and wore clothes that didn't really fit. Joshua remembers it as being 'quirky'. She loved the applause – the cheering, screaming and laughing that stays with you. The big finale was a huge, choreographed dance number entitled 'Agape's 38 Flavours', in which every boy and girl took part.

After camp was over, the group got together and met up at the promenade next to Santa Monica beach. Everyone was relaxed, just hanging; Megan and Joshua held hands as they walked along before they all went into the local cinema to watch the film *Clueless*, a big summer hit in 1995.

The movie, set in Beverly Hills, is loosely based on Jane Austen's classic novel *Emma*. The heroine, Cher Horowitz, played by Alicia Silverstone, is a high-school matchmaker who eventually falls in love with the Mr Knightley character (Paul Rudd), who in the film is rather coincidentally called Josh.

Unfortunately, the other, real-life Josh was unimpressed. He observed, 'I wasn't a fan. I was a young African–American boy watching a film about white women. It revolves around a shopaholic white woman and I was not relating to any of that.' When his guy friends said they were leaving, he went too and told Meghan that he would see her outside. He left just before the tender kiss between the two lead characters: 'I left my teenage, romance-driven beautiful girlfriend in a theatre while the kissing scene happened. What a dummy! I didn't understand back then that you don't do that. You don't leave – that's when you kiss the girl in the movie theater.'

That evening, Meghan let Joshua down gently during their long evening phone call. She explained to him why he shouldn't have done that. She was, he acknowledges, a little ahead of him in understanding how a relationship works. He recalled, 'I listened to her and I understood and I felt bad.' Meghan also observed, sensibly, that they were both moving up from middle into high school next term and would inevitably see little of each other. She told him she wanted to enjoy the high school experience, the next stage of growing up. 'So it was like "Oh heartbreak – but you are probably right,"' observed her now ex-boyfriend.

And that was that, although Meghan always remembered Joshua and she told chat show veteran Larry King in 2013 that he had been her first kiss.

They didn't keep in touch, although over the years he would still see Doria at Agape. When the church moved to new premises in Culver City, the entrance hall would be filled with various book, bric-a-brac and clothing stalls. Doria had one for her vintage lines and Joshua would stop to chat and discover how 'Meg', as her mother called her in public, was doing.

Joshua has become a well-known name in Los Angeles performing arts. He mentioned Meghan in his one-man show and later was a resident performer, the expert beat-boxer, on the Drop the Mic spot that proved so popular on *The Late Late Show with James Cordon*. As Meghan would also do, he has given back to the community; in his case with workshops and residences in local schools that have provided a safe and non-judgemental environment for boys and girls to realise their creative potential.

Meghan had enjoyed her first romantic interlude, but perhaps just as importantly she couldn't wait for the next show at Immaculate Heart; another step on her Yellow Brick Road.

5

STAR-TO-BE

Meghan could still be found most days after school on the set of *Married with Children*. She was part of the furniture, but she herself was becoming more aware of the world of television. Her interest in performing that had been nurtured at elementary school, inspired at the Agape camp and encouraged by Immaculate Heart, was becoming increasingly important. She wasn't just turning up to give Buck a cuddle – the much-loved dog retired in 1995 – but to watch what was going on and study the actors. One of them, Amanda Bearse, who played Marcy in the show, remembered Meghan as 'quiet' and 'respectful'.

Life at the studios, however, wasn't all about acting. Meghan became fascinated with food and the beautiful dishes that were served every day to the cast and crew. Sometimes Tom, who was popular on set, would suggest she help out in the craft services department where all the food was prepared. She explained, 'That's where I started to learn about garnishing and plating. I saw the appreciation of the food. I started to learn the association between food and happiness and being able to entertain.' She was happy to take over the cooking duties back at the apartment on Vista del Mar.

Meghan's first job as a young teenager involved food but there was nothing to interest Michelin at the wittily named Humphrey Yogart, a frozen yoghurt store in the Beverly Connection shopping mall on La Cienega Boulevard. The owner, Paula Sheftel, shrewdly realised that the youngest member of staff was a big asset, popular with the customers who appreciated her 'outgoing personality'.

Although she didn't earn much – just four dollars an hour – Meghan had her own money for the first time. Of more long-term significance was an encounter in the car park next to the parade. She was taking out the bins when she spotted an off-duty Yasmine Bleeth, famous for playing Caroline Holden, one of the swimsuit-wearing babes in *Baywatch* – not exactly a show at the forefront of female empowerment.

Meghan, however, was star-struck and blurted out, 'Oh my God, I loved you in the Soft and Dri commercial.' The ad for an anti-perspirant was all over the television screens at the time and featured Yasmine purring into the camera, 'What's the most important thing you put on?'

The star smiled at Meghan, shook her hand lightly and said, 'Ok, thank you!' She made a point of asking Meghan her name. Her gracious reaction would set a benchmark for how Meghan would react to her own fans and well-wishers in the future – look them in the eye and be kind. She never forgot Yasmine.

Meghan's own acting career at school was progressing steadily. In many ways it would mirror the path of her professional career – a collection of minor roles while waiting for more recognition. When younger, she had no expectation of becoming the next Shirley Temple. She did, however, strike lucky – a real-life former child star was in charge of the drama department. Her name was Gigi Perreau and she had a star on the Hollywood Walk of Fame.

From the beginning in middle school, she noticed that despite being 'very green', Meghan was one of those students who could absorb ideas. Gigi had plenty of them, as well as a lifetime of experience in Hollywood that began when she was just two years old and was cast as the baby daughter in the 1943 biopic *Madame Curie* that starred Greer Garson as the famous Nobel Prize-winning scientist. She clinched the role because unusually for someone so young, she could speak both French and English; or at least, gurgle in both languages. Gigi called it a 'beautiful film'.

She had made thirty-six films by the age of twenty. Her favourites, other than *Madame Curie*, are *Enchantment*, a war film in which she played the role of Lark as a little girl – portrayed as an adult by Oscar-winner Teresa Wright; and *The Man in the Gray Flannel Suit*, in which, more grown up as a teenager, she acted alongside screen legends Fredric March and Gregory Peck. She was awarded her star on Sunset Boulevard in 1960.

In between making movies, Gigi – short for Ghislaine and pronounced with a hard g – attended Immaculate Heart, so always had affection for the school, wanting to give something back to her alma mater. She returned as a member of the faculty in 1986, only forty-five and still acting. 'It's kind of wonderful to share,' was her simple philosophy, although it always made her laugh when she told friends about her career change. 'What are you teaching?' they would ask. 'Nuclear physics,' was the reply.

The drama group at Immaculate Heart is known as the Genesians, named after Genesius of Rome, the patron saint of actors. Gigi had been happy for Meghan to become involved in drama in middle school even though most of the roles in school productions went to older pupils. 'Meghan was just so eager,' she recalled. 'She had such a really dynamic personality, even as a child, that she just kept growing and growing – each play, each class, everything.'

Immaculate Heart was not a renowned theatre school, so Gigi was given carte blanche to shape classes as she saw fit. Her idea wasn't to make drama lessons just about plays and musicals: they were also about speaking and presenting yourself in the best possible light; and about listening. They would act out one-to-one scenes just as you might in real life at a job interview or an audition.

Singing was the one aspect of drama class that Meghan did not enjoy. For someone so very open in the other aspects of performance, she was shy about singing and not too keen on auditioning for any of the musicals. Right from the start, Gigi told her she had to push herself a bit and try out for one.

Gigi cast her as a porter in the production of *George M!*, the show based on the life of the legendary Broadway star George M. Cohan. Meghan was on stage for the showstoppers 'Give My Regards to Broadway' and 'The Yankee Doodle Boy'. The title role was played by Joseph Leo Bwarie, later to become an acclaimed Broadway performer as Frankie Valli in the Tony award-winning *Jersey Boys*.

Joe, as everyone called him, handled most of the choreography for Gigi's productions even though he was still at high school himself. Typically, she insisted that he audition for the role of Cohan even though it was his original idea to do the show. He had a quality that Gigi would also recognise in Meghan – an inbuilt professionalism. When they went off stage they weren't grabbing a soda and reading *Variety*; they were running lines with other people.

Gigi cast Meghan again as Delilah in *Back County Crimes*, in November 1995. The drama with music was written by the prolific post-war American playwright Lanie Robertson in 1980.

It's the story of life in a small town called Duty as told by the local doctor and features love affairs, sordid murder, comic misunderstandings and tragic events – quite grown up for a school production.

Meghan shared a place on the cast list with Luis Segura, a pupil at St Francis High School, in La Cañada Flintridge, a city in Los Angeles county, about fifteen miles from Immaculate Heart. These cities, such as Malibu and Pasadena, are dotted all around LA. Meghan and Luis dated on and off for a couple of years.

It was common practice for Immaculate Heart to call on all-boys schools if there were male roles that needed to be filled. The arrangement was reciprocal and girls could audition for female roles at St Francis and other similar schools in LA. Luis was a couple of years' older, which might have been an attraction for a teenage schoolgirl. Meghan was already a mature, well-travelled young woman. She had enjoyed a trip to Europe in the summer holidays with Ninaki Priddy, her parents Dalton and Maria and sister, Michelle. While Niki was not involved in drama, she was in Meghan's class at school and they remained close.

This was a dream trip for anyone, taking in Belgium, Switzerland, Paris and London, where the two girls posed for photographs in front of Buckingham Palace. Much corny signif-icance would be made of this picture many years later when Meghan actually met the Queen, but for now she was just another tourist taking in the sights of the capital as millions of others have done. At this point in recent history, by far the most interesting and charismatic person within the Royal Family was Princess Diana, who was much loved in the US.

Meghan was readily accepted by the Priddy family, a common theme throughout her life – until she met Prince Harry. She was also well liked by the Segura family and was a regular visitor to their Pasadena home while she was dating Luis. It helped that his sister Maria was at Immaculate Heart, in the year below. Meghan also got on well with his younger brother, Danny, encouraging him to try his hand at acting, too.

Meghan's own acting was progressing; she came more into her own in her next role in the perennial favourite, *Annie*. She played two parts – the quiet orphan, July, and Star-To-Be, an up-and-coming Broadway performer, which was exactly what Meghan hoped to be. In the latter role, she had a small solo in the song 'NYC'.

For each production, Gigi would audition something like fifty girls for maybe no more than twelve roles. She was what she termed 'colour blind' in that she cast on the basis of ability and audition – not on ethnicity or the colour of someone's skin – a way of thinking that TV and the motion picture industry is only now coming around to. The role of Annie herself, for instance, was secured by Meghan's friend, Danica Rozelle, a young African–American girl.

Gigi kept it as professional as possible, with proper callbacks before she made a final decision. For Meghan, it was good prac-tice for what would become her life as a working actress. After she had cast each role, Gigi checked to see if any of those who missed out would like to be in the crew. Everybody involved would then be called for a reading – the cast on chairs around a long table with the crew sat right behind, listening so that they too would really get to know the play or musical.

Gigi gave all her girls with acting ambitions one important piece of advice – she told them that there were no small parts. Gigi explained, 'I wanted everyone to know that they were part of the whole. If they just had three lines, they needed to know that those three lines were very important.' Meghan would remember that advice during the years when she struggled to get substantial roles.

After casting, it was six weeks of intensive learning of lines, songs and then rehearsing. Meghan's dad turned up to watch one evening and was swiftly enlisted as Gigi's technical advisor. She observed, 'I am very grateful to him. Very honestly, he was my right-hand person for many years.' Tom's involvement was an encouragement for Meghan during high school. 'Theirs was a very warm and very special relationship,' continued Gigi.

The week before opening night was a frantic one, with rehearsals starting right after school at 3.30 and continuing until 6pm. Tom would slip out to McDonald's to fetch much-needed fuel for the troops. He was at the helm for tech run-throughs while the musical numbers came under the watchful eye of Joe. On the Thursday before the Saturday opening, the all-important dress rehearsal would go on late into the evening. This was crucial for Tom, because the lighting was different after dark.

Annie ran for four nights in March 1996 when Meghan was fourteen. As a school tradition the programme had lots of thanks and little notes and best wishes. Meghan's 'biography' said 'she loves singing, smiling and dancing, and hopes to shuffle off to Broadway some day. Meghan is proud to have two roles in this year's musical and wishes to thank everyone who helped and supported her (especially Ashley, Danica and, of course, Yasmine).'

Tom received special thanks for 'parental sweat'. He wrote, 'To my 'Star-To-Be' and the cast and crew of *Annie*. I'm proud of you all. BREAK A LEG. Love Tom Markle (Daddy).'

As part of Gigi's preferred policy of alternating a musical with a more conventional drama, Meghan was cast as one of the would-be actresses in a production of *Stage Door*, the successful play that had been a memorable film in the thirties starring Katharine Hepburn and Ginger Rogers. Luis was in it, too, which was a bonus.

Meghan had the role of Judith Canfield, played in the film by Lucille Ball who, coincidentally, had donated to Immaculate Heart the stage on which they performed. Her daughter, the actress Lucie Arnaz, is another former pupil of the school; fittingly Meghan's favourite TV show as a child had been Lucille's classic comedy *I Love Lucy*.

It was time for Meghan to make more of an impact. She had her most substantial role yet in the Stephen Sondheim musical, *Into the Woods*, the clever interweaving of favourite fairy tales. Meghan was cast as Little Red Riding Hood and, in Gigi's opinion, 'just stole the scenes that she was in; she was really adorable'.

Meghan worked very hard in rehearsal, especially singing 'Hello, Little Girl'. She needed to; Gigi would sit at the back of the hall during run–throughs and bellow out that she couldn't hear her, encouraging her to project her voice to the four corners of the auditorium.

The spring term production ran for four nights in late March 1997. This time the programme notes made fascinating reading: 'Meghan is happy to be skipping on stage as Little Red Riding Hood. Meghan wants to pursue acting at Northwestern on her way to Broadway. Meg wishes to thank her supportive parents, her loving boyfriend, and the always encouraging Becca and Michelle. I love you all so much.'

Her father gushed, 'Congratulations and Best Wishes to my Wonderful Daughter Meghan and the entire fantastic and hard–working cast and crew of *Into the Woods*. You are all just great! Break a Leg ... Tom Markle.'

Meghan may have been only fifteen but she was already clear about what lay in store for her – Northwestern University in Chicago followed by the bright lights of Broadway. In her junior year, the conventional play was *The Women*, the famous all-female comedy of manners by Clare Boothe Luce that was first performed in New York in 1936. Renowned as a passionate public speaker, the writer was a figure to inspire any ambitious schoolgirl – the first American woman to be appointed an ambassador abroad when she headed the US Embassy in Rome.

The film had become one of the most famous films of the thirties, starring Norma Shearer, Joan Crawford and Rosalind Russell as Sylvia Fowler, the role that Meghan would play. She followed that with the part of Maisie in the Sandy Powell musical *The Boy Friend*, a vivacious homage to the 1920s. Meghan had gradually worked her way to close to the top of the cast list in school productions. This time the Segura family was represented by Danny.

Drama at school was very much Tom's domain. He even continued helping after Meghan had graduated. Gigi only remembers meeting Doria once or twice during the whole time that Meghan was involved in productions at Immaculate Heart. Her mother was still encouraging her caring side, however; she supported her decision to return to Skid Row and help at the Hippie Kitchen, three years after her first visit.

Meghan was inspired by Maria Pollia, who had been her theology teacher as a junior. They talked about the teenager's misgivings. Maria, who herself volunteered at the kitchen, was able to reassure her that those feelings were perfectly acceptable and understandable but that she should remember 'to put the needs of others above your own fears'. Maria was herself an alumna of Immaculate Heart and had been given the same advice when she was a student.

Meghan went back to dish out plates of food and clear tables with fresh resolve. She remembered the names of the people she served. She began to properly understand the meaning of community spirit – something that would serve her well when she connected with the women of The Hubb Community

Kitchen following the Grenfell Tower fire of 2017. She was continuing to develop her personal empathy.

That became even more apparent when she was the first to be chosen as a team leader at a Kairos Retreat organised by Immaculate Heart at the Holy Spirit Retreat Center in the upmarket neighbourhood of Encino. These four-day breaks were popular throughout Catholic schools and colleges in the US. While Kairos originally comes from the Greek for the 'right time', in biblical terms it is better translated as 'God's time'.

The principle purpose of the four-day retreat was to build empathy, giving the young women time and space to talk openly about their problems and concerns without having to worry about dashing off to the next class or what grade they might be given for their homework.

Meghan was one of six seniors leading groups of eight in daily discussions, trying to make sure every girl had the chance to express themselves. She also had to give a half-hour presentation in front of everyone in which she talked in a mature way about her own life journey. It was a chance to share some personal feelings about her parents' divorce.

Theology teacher Christine Knudsen, who organised the retreat, observed, 'Any young person struggles when their parents are divorced, even though I think she knew that both of them loved her, and they were both in her life.' Meghan was an ideal choice to be a leader because, added Christine, 'she had a lot of depth, probably because of her own experience of her parents' divorce. She'd take conversations to a deeper level.'

Meghan's ability to share thoughts and feelings was of particular benefit to one girl, who struggled with her shyness and was the quietest and most reserved of her group. Meghan wrote her a note in her distinctive and immaculate handwriting: 'You are so strong and so wonderful – your courage and strength in times of hardship is as admirable as your optimism and friendly nature. Never stop sharing your beautiful spirit and always remember how special you are.' She ended the letter: 'I am here if you ever need me. I love you. Meghan.'

Meghan was fortunate that three of her classmates and closest friends were also team leaders: Susan Ardikani, Erin Carr and Michelle Blade, who would go on to become one of the best-known artists on the West Coast. As well as their responsibilities to the Kairos Retreat itself, the classmates had the chance to talk late into the night about their aspirations. Meghan was aiming big, declaring that she was going to be president one day.

6

AT THE
HOLLYWOOD BOWL

———

Like many teenage girls, Meghan was finding life with dad a little constricting. He seemed to be always around – at home, obviously, but also at school, and not just for drama; he was the man called in to help with sound and lighting for important events. Having dad lurking in the background changing a light bulb was not the ideal scenario. He still doted on her but perhaps she needed a touch more freedom.

He was involved, naturally, in what would turn out to be her last show at Immaculate Heart. She had to dust off some of the tap-dancing steps she learned when younger for *Stepping Out*. Originally a London stage play, it was transformed into a star vehicle for Liza Minnelli in a 1991 movie in which she played a former dancer teaching a weekly tap class to a group of women. Meghan was the abrasive Vera, memorably portrayed in the film by Julie Walters.

Meghan wanted to stretch herself dramatically, so she decided to audition for a role in a play at St Francis High School. It would give her more independence. Luis had left school by this time and they had drifted apart. He would have a startlingly successful career as a realtor in and around Pasadena and has never talked about their teenage times together. Danny was still at the school, though, and they continued to be the best of friends.

The first production she went up for was also the first involving the new director of drama at St Francis, Manny Eulalia. He wanted to come in with a bang and stage something demanding so he chose *Oedipus Rex*, the Greek tragedy by Sophocles, which his English class were already studying. This was a million miles away from *Annie* and she was the only girl from her school auditioning, hoping to be cast among forty or so other budding actresses.

Meghan tried out for the leading female role of Jocasta, the Queen of Thebes, who marries her son Oedipus and subsequently hangs herself in the last act. Manny saw a lot of hopefuls but Meghan stood out: 'There are people who just walk in and they have that presence.' Manny was also impressed with the work ethic that Meghan brought with her from Immaculate Heart. As it was his first production, he wanted the process to be disciplined and she did not disappoint him.

Meghan encouraged Danny to audition as well and he was cast as Creon, Jocasta's brother, another of the leading roles. In return, Danny nominated Meghan to be Homecoming Queen at St Francis, a big deal in US school culture. Usually, co-ed schools or all-boys schools hold Homecoming Dances on the same weekend as the Homecoming Football Game (American Football). Since all-girls high schools like Immaculate Heart don't have football teams, they don't hold the dances.

At seventeen, she had blossomed into a stunning young woman who cast a spell over the boys of St Francis. By now the gradual process of sorting out her teeth had paid off. Dental work was a rite of passage for American teenagers. Gone was her trademark gappy grin and in its place she had a million-dollar smile.

The competition to be Homecoming Queen was fierce. Such a contest did not sit easily with Meghan's feminist views, but she was a teenager enjoying her social life and the attention of boys. The first stage was an essay listing her achievements and accomplishments to date. Meghan sailed through that, largely due to her impressive charity work on Skid Row. Next she was interviewed by four boys, the committee, who were members of the student body. They were impressed.

The winner was announced in November 1998 at a special red-carpet ceremony during the Homecoming game between St Francis and another school team called the Chaminade Eagles from neighbouring West Hills. A school football game is a raucous event so, at half time, the Homecoming court was greeted with much hollering and cheering as they made their way onto a makeshift stage in the middle of the field.

The girls were given a guard of honour onto the red carpet by boys brandishing swords. Each one was announced over the loudspeaker and then Meghan was declared the winner. After she had been crowned by last year's Queen, Carla Suarez, the entire court was applauded as they were driven away in a fleet of classic convertibles.

Danny was Meghan's escort for the big dance that night. Meghan loved dancing and wasn't usually much bothered about posing for official pictures. This evening she was a little more careful because she was wearing her Queen tiara and didn't want to send that flying across the dance floor.

Dressed in an elegant strapless ivory ballgown and carrying a bouquet, she already looked like a Hollywood star. Her broad smile was entirely natural, however, and not one of those weary ones celebrities manufacture for the cameras as they are snapped for the thousandth time that night in the name of publicity. Danny stood proudly at her side with his hand resting lightly on her shoulder. They never dated – she had, after all, been dating his elder brother.

Meghan's popularity was boosted by becoming the Homecoming Queen of an all-boys school. They could all see how attractive she was. One of her admirers was Nema Vand, a year younger than her and very handsome. He admitted, 'Meghan was amazing, a woman among girls. Everyone was in love with her. She was sweet and very kind.'

Nema, who would later become one of the stars of the reality show *Shahs of Sunset*, still enjoys telling the story of the time when he was at the same party as Meghan and she came over and sat on his lap. Then she spoke to him in the Persian language, Farsi: 'You are so beautiful, she purred. Nema recalled, 'I asked her, "How do you know Farsi?" She said, "I learned it for you." Then she walked away. She played with our hearts masterfully,' he sighed

When word got round that Meghan was in it, tickets for the three-night run of *Oedipus Rex* in early January 1999 sold out rapidly. Manny Eulalia remembered that Meghan's first entrance on stage was greeted with a round of applause, which was not exactly in keeping with such a moving and powerful tragedy.

The play was held across the road from St Francis in Flintridge Preparatory School. Its theatre held 250 people so the standing ovation the cast received was quite something. Meghan was exceptional in the role of the despairing mother who eventually kills herself when she realises she has committed incest with her son.

She did not have Tom in her corner – or more precisely, in the wings – which was perhaps a blessing as she was now seventeen, but she thanked him in the programme notes, alongside 'Mommy', Danny Boy, the 'beautiful, amazing sweeties of St Francis' and one boy in particular called Gabriel Stewart, known to everyone as Gabe. He and Meghan dated a few times and kept in touch for a year or two until, as he put it, 'her life took a different direction'.

Her school stage career was not over. The best was yet to come. She auditioned for the annual musical at the Loyola High School in downtown Los Angeles, another all-boys school with close ties to Immaculate Heart. She was cast as the devil's side-kick Lola – Señorita Lolita Banana – in a production of *Damn Yankees*, a dream role for Meghan.

The Adler and Ross musical from 1955 had practically swept the board at the Tonys, winning seven awards including one for the legendary Broadway star Gwen Verdon as Lola.

The show, a rough reworking of the Faust legend in a baseball setting, ran for more than a thousand performances on Broadway. Gwen had the stand-out number 'Whatever Lola Wants', which she reprised in the Hollywood version of the film. She was a tough act for anyone to follow.

Meghan didn't disappoint. Though experienced in school drama, it was still a big step to parading around the stage in a sequinned leotard, suggestively purring the lyric 'I always get what I aim for'. She was still at high school, so it wasn't exactly Pussycat Dolls but, as the idiom goes, Meghan brought the house down.

Gigi Perreau was in the audience, sitting beside Tom Markle. She was impressed, 'I was so thrilled to see her because it seemed like everything she had worked for. It was very exciting, I must say.'

Meghan was now in her final year, twelfth grade, at Immaculate Heart. She had her first taste of modelling on a catwalk at the annual mothers and daughters fashion show in March 1999. Meghan showed off her legs in a short skirt and some very high heels that would become something of a trademark in her acting career.

As Gigi observed, 'She was a cute little kid in eighth grade and then by the time she was Lola she was absolutely gorgeous.' Understandably, she attracted a degree of envy from the other girls. Gigi noticed it, 'There were some girls who were very jealous of her. It happens in a high school situation.'

That situation might have been even worse if Meghan had been crowned Prom Queen at Immaculate Heart in April 1999. She had to settle for being one of a very glamorous prom court, alongside friends including Niki Priddy and Susan Ardakani escorting the Queen, Camille Townsend. The event, called that year Midnight Masquerade, was held at the swish InterContinental Hotel in downtown Los Angeles.

Her date this time around was a handsome young student at Loyola called Giancarlo Boccato. They looked like a Hollywood couple and dazzled on the dance floor. The pictures of the night showed just how much the camera loved Meghan. It always had. The hundreds of shots that her dad took of her growing up revealed that she lit up any photo and one's eye was always drawn to her in a group picture.

The Immaculate Heart photographer John Dlugolecki wasn't at all surprised, therefore, when Meghan turned up at his studio in Burbank for her official school senior portrait meaning business. Most of the girls would just have the required white cap and gown shot and then disappear, not Meghan. She drove out in her mum's station wagon with the personalised number plate 'MEGNMEE' with a bag of clothes on the front seat.

Normally it would be just ten or fifteen minutes and a good-bye, but John allocated her an hour. She brought a black v-neck sweater and wanted to pose for an atmospheric shot against a black background. It was her first proper professional session. John was delighted to have a subject keen on trying something different. He decided to use rim lighting to highlight the edges around her hair.

While she posed, they chatted about her plans after leaving high school. John was an alumnus of Notre Dame, the prestigious university in Indiana. Meghan wanted to broaden her horizons away from Los Angeles and told him she was keen to go to college in the Midwest, so he encouraged her to try for his alma mater, although it had no special connection with Immaculate Heart.

Meghan had talked many times with John's wife, Vicki Conrad, who usually accompanied him as co-photographer on important school nights to share the load. Meghan had one big concern that played on her mind: 'What can you do with a degree in theatre?'

Vicki was herself a theatre major, so was speaking with authority. She told her, 'You can do anything you want.' Meghan was uncertain so Vicki added, 'You learn how to act with people. You learn teamwork; being on a budget; being on time; meeting deadlines. That's what jobs in the world involve.'

Vicki was an example of what she was explaining. Her 'day job' was as the manager of one of the largest shopping malls in southern California. She strongly encouraged Meghan to try the Chicago university Northwestern, whose drama department had a growing reputation in the late nineties. Vicki told her she would give anything to go to Northwestern right now.

Meghan still wasn't sure. She won a place at Notre Dame, even earning a small scholarship. But in the end she chose Northwestern, which had been her preferred choice throughout her teens. Unexpectedly, her intention was to major in English and concentrate on developing her own writing skills. She was an avid reader and had been totally absorbed studying some of the great writers at school – it was one of the reasons why she had auditioned for *Oedipus Rex*.

She studied classic English literature including Shakespeare and the Brontë sisters, as well as some of the greats of twentieth-century American literature, such as Steinbeck, F. Scott Fitzgerald and Salinger. For the present at least, drama was on the back burner. She did not want to become that cliché – the Los Angeles teenager who dreamed of becoming a Hollywood star. Her earlier intention to tread a path to Broadway also seemed a distant dream.

She still had one pleasant task to undertake before closing the chapter on her school days – graduation at the Hollywood Bowl. Immaculate Heart was one of only two schools in the Los Angeles area allowed to hold their big day at the iconic venue that normally played host to some of the biggest stars in music. The only time the school's graduation was 'bumped' in recent years was when they had to change their date because it clashed with a Paul Simon concert – although, inevitably, in 2020 it was cancelled owing to the coronavirus pandemic.

Traditionally, the girls wore white satin dresses that were rather plain and unflattering, so they would all frantically try to custom-ise them into something a little more Givenchy. They stood in line, each carrying a bouquet of red roses, to have their name called to enthusiastic applause. Meghan collected many awards that afternoon in June 1999, testimony to Maria Pollia's opinion that she was one of the top five students she had ever taught. They included one for drama, a service award for mentoring younger students, the Bank of America Fine Arts award, the Notre Dame Club of Los Angeles achievement and perhaps, most interestingly, she was commended in the National Achievement Scholarship Programme for outstanding black students – a recognition of her identity at last.

After the ceremonial duties were concluded, she joined the others to sing John Lennon's 'Imagine' and 'I Will Remember

You', the timeless and poignant break-up song by Sarah McLachlan. It was a day never to forget.

Meghan's graduation photograph hangs with all the others in one of the main corridors at Immaculate Heart. To accompany it, she chose an empowering quote usually attributed to Eleanor Roosevelt, 'Women are like teabags; they don't realize how strong they are until they're in hot water.'

Meghan intended to earn some money in the summer break before travelling to Northwestern, at least to make sure she had the right wardrobe – not just for looking good but also keeping warm during the bitterly cold Chicago winters. She sent off the best headshot from her session with John Dlugolecki to various casting agents in the hope of finding some work as an extra.

She soon struck lucky with a tiny part in a video for a new single by Tori Amos called '1000 Oceans'. The singer-songwriter is one of the most thoughtful of modern avant-garde artists: Meghan's tastes were more traditional, preferring old-school performers such as Joni Mitchell, although she did have a soft spot for Mark McGrath, the lead singer with US rock band Sugar Ray, who she thought was 'hot'.

'1000 Oceans' is a haunting ballad about love and loss, crying a thousand oceans to come to terms with grief. Blink and you miss Meghan. She is seen briefly at thirty-nine seconds and fifty-nine seconds, one of a crowd staring at Tori in a glass container that is reminiscent of an exhibit in a museum or a zoo. A day spent filming in a far-from-glamorous disused car park was worth it to be able to pop a couple of hundred dollars in cash in her purse at the end of it.

Another shoot, this time for a new Shakira single, promised to be even more lucrative: $600 for two days' work. The Columbian singer was on her way to becoming one of the biggest-selling artists in the world. Meghan had to audition to be one of the crowd dancing wildly to the track, 'Ojos Asi'.

The day of the audition was chronicled on film by her friend Niki Priddy as the young women drove around Beverly Hills shopping for outfits in a station wagon with the number plate signature 'Classy Girl'. As they make their way to the famous shopping street, Melrose Avenue, they point out some of the stores they wouldn't be visiting on Rodeo Drive – Chanel, Prada, Gucci, Louis Vuitton, Valentino and Tiffany.

The girls drive down Santa Monica Boulevard in West Hollywood and point out that it is known in this neighbourhood as Boystown because of the local homosexual community. Meghan observes, 'We could walk around naked here and they wouldn't care.' Before the audition, they stop off at Meghan's house for chocolate croissants and iced milk and to cuddle her mother's cats, Bella and Maria.

She had moved back in with Doria because she wasn't getting along with her father. She had given up popping in to see him or even collecting her mail. She admitted, 'My dad and I are not on the best of terms.' She still had a picture of him on the fridge, though, taken during last October's fathers and daughters picnic at Immaculate Heart, so perhaps it was a temporary falling out. The photograph was a lovely shot of Tom with his arm around his smiling daughter but, like a million and more young women, Meghan was no longer Daddy's little girl.

The audition, which we don't see, went 'pretty well', she thought. She had to dance crazily. Afterwards, driving over to Niki's house, she admitted that her principal worry during the audition was that she was going to fall out of her top. She didn't get called back for filming, which was disappointing, but it was something she would get used to in the future.

The day ended with her trying on some of the outfits she had bought during the day. The film was by no means a masterpiece and Meghan could never have imagined that Niki would store it away and make it public for the whole world to watch. That would be many years later. In the immediate future, Meghan was leaving her safe and secure world in Los Angeles and setting out on the next stage of her life.

7

NORTH BY NORTHWESTERN

Meghan was the first to put her hand up. Her fellow new 'sister' at Northwestern's Kappa Kappa Gamma Upsilon chapter, Liz Kores, had asked if anyone would like to volunteer with her for the Glass Slipper Project, a Chicago-based charity that helped provide new and nearly new prom dresses and accessories for girls who could not afford their own.

The prom, as Meghan already understood from her own experience, is one of the key rites of passage for teenage girls in America, and to be denied that moment because you came from a poor family was unthinkable. Meghan jumped at the chance to be one of the fairy godmothers who could help Cinderella go to the ball.

Meghan and Liz joined other volunteers at the designated 'boutique' for the day setting up the racks of eye-catching, colourful dresses and arranging the tables of jewellery so that every girl could be a star for the evening and nobody would ever know they hadn't been shopping in Bloomingdale's.

They would then help choose a dress for the excited teenagers, who had stood patiently in line, anxious about their big day. Towards the end of the day Meghan and Liz were frustrated at not being able to find anything suitable for one girl in particular.

Liz recalled, 'Meg wouldn't give up and so we started looking in all the size racks, in case maybe a dress had been racked wrong. Eventually we found a dress and the girl put it on. And she cried. And then we cried!'

Liz Kores, who runs a successful PR firm in Chicago, has maintained her links with the Glass Slipper Project ever since and is now on its board of directors. In twenty years, the non-profit organisation has helped provide dresses for 20,000 prom students – that's one thousand every year.

For her part, Meghan has not forgotten the importance to women of any age to feel happy and confident in what they are wearing. She is a patron of the inspirational UK charity Smart Works, which provides interview clothes and training for un-employed women in need. She explained, 'It's not just donating your clothes and seeing where they land, it is about being part of each other's success stories as women.'

Meghan always seemed to have plenty of clothes and was happy to lend them to other members of her sorority. Each university has a number of sororities and the new students in their freshman year would tour round the various chapters to discover if they would be a good fit. Friendships formed and connections made might last a lifetime and be of huge benefit in future careers, too. The activities, the rituals and the initiations are all kept secret. Not all of them have a secret handshake or code but each sorority has its own rules for its members, who are not supposed to discuss them with outsiders. The recruit-ment process of finding the right chapter on arrival at university is known as 'rushing'.

After meeting, then chatting informally and formally with the recruitment committee, the new students have to wait to hear if they are being invited to join a particular chapter. Meghan was more accomplished than most at this sort of audition process because of her theatre work at Immaculate Heart, not to mention her Kairos experience and mixing in adult circles with her parents.

Meghan's rush took place over several days in January 2000. She immediately impressed. One of the KKG sisters, Coulter Bump, who was in the year above Meghan, recalled, 'We just wanted to make sure we secured her interest in our sorority. Myself and most of my sisters agreed that Meghan is a really lovely person. She was respectful and polite. She always had this manner to her of being dignified and poised, just very appropriate in every circumstance. A person like that is what I wanted to ensure we had in our house and luckily, she liked us back.'

Meghan chose KKG as the best match for her. Thank goodness she did not have to face any 'hazing' – the humiliating initiation practice favoured by some sororities that sets new arrivals a task specifically to humiliate them. Instead she was simply given a t-shirt, inspired by the popular 1980s all-female animated cartoon *Jem and the Holograms*. She wore it when she joined her new sisters to celebrate at the local Chuck E. Cheese fast-food joint in Evanston close to the Northwestern campus, which was actually situated some twelve miles north of downtown Chicago.

Sorority is not for everyone but Meghan decided to embrace its culture rather than strike out to make her own friends. It was an interesting decision to join KKG as this particular sorority was overwhelmingly white – there were other chapters that were predominantly black and Meghan had just won an award at Immaculate Heart that was only given to black students. She didn't seek to identify as a white woman or as a black woman – a continuing dilemma for her.

In any case, she was already in the minority at Northwestern, where only five per cent of the students were black and even fewer were biracial. Meghan was still just nineteen and discovering her racial identity in a wider world than Los Angeles. She was, as she called it, 'navigating closed-mindedness'.

She found herself facing that in her very first week at university when another resident in the North Mid-Quads dorm asked her if her parents were still together. When Meghan replied that they weren't, her new 'friend' continued, 'You said your mom is black and your dad is white, right.' Meghan smiled weakly and nodded, wondering what was coming next. It was a question: 'And they're divorced?' When Meghan nodded again, the girl continued, snarkily, 'Oh, well that makes sense.'

Meghan didn't really understand what the narrow-minded girl meant exactly but she understood the implication that an inter-racial marriage was doomed to failure. She chose not to be confrontational and open a 'Pandora's box of discrimination.' She held her tongue. It was not the time … yet.

This exchange remained in Meghan's memory but did not prevent her making new friends and joining in some rewarding university experiences; far from it. She met friends for life. She has admitted that she enthusiastically embraced the concept of the 'freshman fifteen'; the fifteen pounds in weight first years were traditionally expected to gain by eating too much fast food, drinking in a favourite local dive bar called The Keg of Evanston in Grove Street and rounding off an evening out with a trip to the 24-hour Burger King in Orrington Avenue.

Like the majority of her student friends, Meghan had a fake ID because you needed to be twenty-one to drink legally in Illinois. The girls could pick one up easily enough in Chicago. The Keg was notorious for underage drinking and fights, eventually closing in 2013 after a protracted battle with the authorities, who frowned on its activities.

She found a new boyfriend, Steve Lepore, who was quite a catch and greatly enhanced her standing among the sisters of KKG. He was the epitome of tall – very tall – dark and handsome. At 6 foot 5 inches, he was nearly a foot taller than Meghan, who measured 5 feet 6 inches in her bare feet. Originally from Cleveland, Ohio, he was a celebrity on campus having won a gold medal as a member of the USA Basketball Junior World Championship Team in 1998 and a silver medal the following year. He played in the position of shooting guard and both years he was the leading points scorer on the team. His sport was his number one priority.

They weren't really a good match. Steve was an ambitious and dedicated young sportsman using college to gain a foothold on a career as a professional basketball player. He was in his sophomore year when Meghan enrolled at Northwestern. She was enjoying the freedom of being away from home for the first time. Steve was much more likely to get an early night than enjoy a drinking session followed by a flame-grilled Whopper.

While they were one of the more striking couples around campus, their relationship never really had the chance to develop into anything serious because after his sophomore (second) year he accepted a transfer to Wake Forest University in Winston-Salem, North Carolina. The move would enhance Steve's prospect of a professional career in basketball. But it was 700 miles away from Chicago, so there seemed little point in he and Meghan making a go of things.

Steve never made it as a big-time NBA player but he did spend a season with the Brighton Bears team in the British Basketball League. Most recently he is proving a great success as an assistant coach at Eastern Kentucky University in Richmond, Kentucky, and is married with a young daughter.

It seems strange to highlight the fact that Steve is white, but throughout her life race is a constant thread for Meghan. Because of her light skin, some of her fellow students didn't seem to understand her ethnicity. She was invisible to them when they made casual racist jokes or unappealing comments. They might refer to the 'black guy' working in Burger King – not the guy with the wonderful smile.

Northwestern was not an especially racist community, just another stop along the way for Meghan that was unaware of its prejudice. There would be many such stops. As she would later say, 'Most people can't tell what I'm mixed with and so much of my life has felt like a fly on the wall. And so some of the slurs I've heard, the really offensive jokes or the names, it just hit me in a really strong way.'

She had a more blatant encounter with the revolting face of racism on a college break back home in Los Angeles. Her mum was called the 'N' word to her face. This wasn't Hicksville USA but cosmopolitan LA. The memory has never left Meghan. She was in the passenger seat while her mother was driving her silver Volvo. Doria wasn't pulling out of a parking space quickly enough for another driver who shouted the most offensive of all words at her.

Meghan could not believe it as she looked over at her mum, welling up with 'hateful tears'. In her now famous essay for *Elle* magazine, entitled 'I'm More than an Other', Meghan wrote movingly, 'I shared my Mom's heartache but I wanted us to be safe. We drove home in deafening silence, her chocolate knuckles pale from gripping the wheel so tightly.'

Meghan's friends at university continued to be impressed by her calmness, perhaps a defence against the sense of rage and outrage she might otherwise have felt. She found herself following Doria's example and turning more to yoga, not as a bored seven-year-old but as a young woman waving her teens goodbye and welcoming a new decade.

Her mother had given her a book entitled *The Four Agreements* by Don Miguel Ruiz, which was first published in California in 1997. Simplistically, it is a self-help book on how to become a better person. Meghan was inspired by its thoughtful message. From a small beginning the book became a classic best-selling guide to combating stress and promoting wellbeing in the modern world.

The four agreements are made with yourself as an individual. They are: 1. Be impeccable with your word; 2. Don't take anything personally; 3. Don't make assumptions; and 4. Always do your best. Meghan's copy was well thumbed and of considerable help to her: 'I constantly circle back to the Don Miguel Ruiz classic for the simplest ways to simplify your life.'

Bearing in mind Meghan's future treatment by the press, the first assumption is of particular interest in that Don Miguel warns against gossip, lies and empty promises and other ways by which we cause problems with our words. If you're not careful with what you say, you can cause damage.

Her daily yoga practice and a page or two of Don Miguel's book helped Meghan to achieve a calmness that was appreciated at Northwestern. She was not the least bit aloof, however, and would throw herself into any community project, whether it was painting houses for the Habitat for Humanity charity or taking part in the famous annual Dance Marathon.

The year Meghan participated, more than half a million dollars was raised for the cancer support group, Gilda's Club Chicago. She joined her friends for the thirty-hour dance at the Norris University Center, the students' union of Northwestern. Meghan admitted, with more than a little understatement, that the whole session was 'difficult'. Students had to stay on their feet for forty-five minutes every hour, urged on by Ginger Harreld, who was the first woman to be the event's MC.

As Meghan navigated her way through college, she was the ideal choice to become the recruitment chairwoman for her sorority chapter, able to make it as warm and welcoming as possible to new arrivals and to help them overcome their nerves. One of the perks of the role was that she could claim her own room in the Kappa Kappa Gamma house itself. It wasn't exactly luxurious but it did afford privacy, if not much space, and there was a cooking staff and a housekeeper known as the 'house mom' to take care of everything.

On many days as she walked around campus, Meghan would pass an unassuming plaque that commemorated the most famous visitor to Northwestern: Princess Diana spent three days in Chicago in early June 1996, helping to raise close to $1 million for the university's cancer research programme.

Meghan made lifelong friends at Northwestern. Two of them in particular, Genevieve Hillis and Lindsay Jill Roth, have been key supporters of Meghan through some of the most significant events in her life, including her marriage and pregnancy. In some ways they represent two of Meghan's separate passions – politics and entertainment. Neither seemed obvious friend material for a young woman from California.

Meghan met Genevieve at KKG. She is the daughter of a wealthy businessman from Milwaukee called Bob Hillis, who in 1985 founded Direct Supply, a company that specialised in maintenance and healthcare before concentrating on fulfilling the needs of the elderly – or 'senior living', as it is called in the US. After university, Genevieve worked her way up the political ladder, becoming an influential lobbyist and fundraiser working for, among others, Wisconsin state Governor Scott Walker, before taking on a new role as head of Governmental Affairs at her father's company.

At first meeting, Lindsay seemed the polar opposite to Meghan – she was a petite, blonde, Jewish girl from New York who had attended a co-educational Quaker High School on Long Island called Friends Academy. Her well-off parents were both attorneys but Lindsay did not intend to pursue law as a profession. Instead, she was studying for a degree in journalism and theatre with ambitions to work in the world of entertainment. Lindsay had already been 'bitten by the bug', as she called it, by working as a radio producer as a sixteen-year-old schoolgirl on the WOR station in New York City.

Meghan got to know Lindsay when they sat next to each other for a literature class and discovered a mutual love for the work of the acclaimed Pulitzer Prize-winning American writer Toni Morrison. The novelist, who died aged eighty-eight in August 2019, is widely recognised as being one of the most influential of modern times, bringing black literature into the mainstream.

When Meghan and 'Linds' sat down to talk about her work, Morrison was the only African–American and one of only a handful of women to have been awarded the Nobel Prize in Literature. She wasn't published as a young woman. Instead, she worked as an editor at the publishers Random House and could not help but notice how few novels spoke to her. She wanted to reach other black readers, weaving stories that resonated through the generations.

Morrison stayed at Random House as a senior editor many years after writing her first novel, *The Bluest Eye*, which was published in 1970. She was proud of her achievements as an editor, helping to develop a 'canon of black work'. She explained, 'We've had the first rush of black entertainment, where blacks were writing for whites and whites were encouraging this kind of black flagellation. Now we can get down to the craft of writing, where black people are talking to black people.'

Meghan was a huge admirer of the woman described by the *New York Times* as a 'towering novelist of the black experience.' She included Morrison in her list of the ten women who had changed her life, which she revealed in the pages of *Glamour* magazine in 2017. She had been especially drawn to her debut novel, which Morrison had written while holding down a full-time job and being a single mother to two young sons.

The Bluest Eye is the painful and overwhelmingly tragic story of Pecola Breedlove, who, growing up in an America obsessed with cute images of Shirley Temple, believes the only thing that can save her from her perception of her own ugliness is a pair of blue eyes. Meghan had read it and thought 'Wow!'. She added, 'She creates this world for you that you get to feel part of.'

Morrison's work reached a wider audience in her later years, thanks to recommendations on Oprah Winfrey's TV Book Club. Oprah, who coincidentally would become one of Meghan's closest friends, had starred in the film adaptation of Morrison's most famous work, *Beloved*.

Chatting with Lindsay reminded Meghan that while she enjoyed reading and had ambitions to become a writer in some shape or form in the future, she still adored the theatre and acting. It was time to change her major from English to Theatre. She was still reluctant to be the cliché girl from LA who wants to be a Hollywood star, so she opted for a dual major, combining theatre with international relations.

Her theatre classes introduced her to a new social circle, including Larnelle Quentin Foster, another student with designs on an acting career who would also become a good friend. He was extrovert and dramatic; a man always described as flamboyant or larger than life as people tried to dance around the fact that he was gay.

Meghan was not remotely concerned by Larnelle's sexuality. She may not have been fully aware at first because he wasn't 'out' in the larger world and had yet to tell his parents. They lived locally and were both successful professionals. Larnelle would invite Meghan to the family house at weekends and they would attend a church service together and cook a special Sunday meal, which for Meghan was an ideal way of passing the time. She particularly loved preparing curry, fast becoming one of her signature dishes.

Larnelle's mum, Lona, welcomed Meghan and would have loved her son to become more romantically involved. He observed, 'If my mother had her way, of course I'd be with Meghan. She would say, "Oh I love Meghan so much." I was like "Yes, Mom, I do too" but it was never going to happen. I obviously knew she was a beautiful woman, but it was just not on my radar.'

From Meghan's point of view, they could enjoy a lovely friendship, go out to shows and theatre performances in Chicago without the bother of any taxi awkwardness on the way back to campus. Larnelle would prove to be a very loyal friend, declaring that Meghan is 'very kind, very genuine and someone who cares deeply about her family, her friends and the world.' He was another who appreciated Meghan's calmness: 'I never saw her mad.'

Meghan loved Larnelle's company because he was one of those people who made life fun. It's all very well embracing worthy causes but, as she would later touchingly observe, 'You have to thrive', and university was the place to do that.

8

A SENSE OF SELF

Meghan had an Achilles' heel. It was the same one that would trouble her most famous fictional character, Rachel Zane, in the TV drama *Suits*. She didn't test well in exams. That wasn't significant when she was racking up credits towards her degree based on diligent homework and intelligent assessments. But it mattered hugely when it was time for her to sit her Foreign Service exam.

Her dilemma as to which of her majors would be her chosen career seemed to have resolved itself in favour of the diplomatic path when she secured an internship at the US Embassy in Buenos Aires during the summer break of 2002. The posting was arranged at the last minute with the help of her uncle, Mike Markle, who apparently knew the ambassador and was able to put a word in for his niece. She may only have been a junior in the press office but it carried prestige for an ambitious young woman of twenty and was a great career start.

For the most part, Meghan's daily routine was one that millions of interns know only too well: answer the phone, prepare standard acknowledgements of letters and fetch coffee. Her tasks were not the least bit demanding but she was experiencing an entirely different world to that of lecture halls, soap opera sets and yoghurt shops. She also witnessed first-hand the grim reality that the US was not universally respected and being an American was not necessarily a passport of popularity.

The eye-opener came when she saw for herself the reaction on the streets to the visit to the Argentine capital of US Treasury Secretary, Paul O'Neill. His visit to Brazil, Uruguay and then Buenos Aires was part of a whistlestop tour to reassure governments throughout the region that America still had their interests at heart.

Meghan had turned twenty-one the previous weekend and after celebrating with new friends, including apparently a rather handsome marine, she was handed the birthday treat of travelling in the Secretary's motorcade on its twenty-mile journey from Ministro Pistarini International Airport in Ezeiza to Casa Rosada, the executive mansion of President Duhalde in Plaza de Maya. Today the palace is best known for the balcony scene from *Evita*, when Madonna steps out to address the crowd as Eva Peron.

A motorcade was perhaps not the most 'diplomatic' gesture when the US was being held responsible by many for an economic disaster that included debt default, devaluation of the peso and a twenty-two per cent unemployment rate. Many blamed the Argentina's worsening poverty levels on a free market system favoured by Washington. Since the beginning of the year, more than 1.5 million people had been plunged into poverty.

About 1,500 protestors clutching placards and shouting anti-American slogans marched from the downtown headquarters of Congress to the presidential building. This was not an occasion to practise your wave to the crowd and Meghan would later describe what happened as one of the 'scariest moments of my life'.

When the motorcade pulled up, the protestors burnt a photo of Secretary O'Neill as well as a paper American flag. They banged their placards down on his limousine when it pulled up just before sundown, but the police were able to disperse the crowd and send them home before things got out of hand.

O'Neill, who died in April 2020, would be dismissed from his job by the end of the year after repeatedly clashing with President George W. Bush over financial policy. For many, his time as Treasury Secretary is best remembered for his tour of some of the poorest areas of Africa with U2 singer Bono.

They were the odd couple: Bono, the rock superstar with the trademark blue wraparound shades and Paul O'Neill, a hard-nosed financier renowned for his suit and tie and all-around neatness. He observed of their incongruous trip, 'It is possible for the two of us to see life through each other's eyes.'

They visited Ghana, South Africa, Ethiopia and Uganda, countries in which the U2 singer wanted to show Secretary O'Neill the threat of Aids as well as each region's chronic lack of fresh water and levels of poverty – all causes that Meghan would enthusiastically espouse later as she became better known.

For the moment, however, she was preparing for the all-important exam, the Foreign Service Officer Test, which she sat in the embassy in the Avenue Columbia, Buenos Aires. And just as Rachel Zane failed her LSAT test, in real life Meghan could not pass her key exam. Perhaps it was the maths element that ruined it for her. The subject had always been her weak spot and it remained so. In Meghan's defence, she was in the youngest bracket of candidates applying for a career in the Foreign Service, and the pass rate was less than fifty per cent.

When her six-week internship came to an end, she still had the next part of her summer adventure to enjoy – a trip to Spain. She took part in a three-month programme in Madrid organised by the Institute for the International Education of Students, a Chicago-based organisation better known as IES Abroad. One of the principal benefits was that the majority of the course was taught in Spanish, so that Meghan could proudly state on her CV that she was fluent in the language. She enjoyed finding out about drama in a foreign country and would discuss the local theatre scene at length with the local IES director, Javier Martinez de Velasco, who found her intelligent and articulate company.

Meghan could have re-sat the Foreign Service test but perhaps the moment had passed for a career in international diplomacy, especially when she returned to the United States and went to ABC Studios in Los Angeles to audition for a small part in *General Hospital*. She had actually already starred in a soap opera, albeit a student venture, written and filmed at Northwestern. Called *University Place*, it was a fictionalised slice of campus life. One of her co-stars, Shaun Zaken, would move to Hollywood and become a good friend while pursuing a career as a comedy writer.

General Hospital was entirely different from a student venture but the casting director, Mark Teschner, was impressed enough with Meghan's audition to give her a very small role in two episodes. In one she wore pink hospital scrubs and in the other turquoise ones. Her dad may have had a word to help but she would have got nowhere without making it past the audition herself. She was even given a name, Nurse Jill, although her part was classified as an under-fives role, which meant she had fewer than five lines.

Meghan's first acting words on national TV were 'Wait a second'. She followed that up by speaking on the telephone: 'I have her chart right here, Doctor Lambert. I don't see the notation anywhere.' It was a start. Mark Teschner thought she did 'a nice job' and that she had poise.

Meghan was now in her senior year and it would only be a matter of months before she graduated from Northwestern.

During her time at the university she had taken a number of classes, including one on human sexuality and another about industrial engineering, which was a great deal more interesting than it sounds. One of the required books for reading was *Who Moved My Cheese?* by Spencer Johnson, M.D.

The short book published in 1998 is a motivational work about how best to deal with change in your life. Meghan was impressed by its advocacy of self-empowerment, albeit with a light-hearted approach and has acknowledged that she has applied some of its thinking in her own decision-making over the years.

On her return to Evanstown from Los Angeles for her final semester, she joined a history and criticism seminar led by the new chair of the Theatre Department, Harvey Young. Twice a week, eight students, including Meghan, would gather in a circle to discuss with him works by African–American playwrights and how theatre could mirror society.

Under the umbrella of 'Studies in Black Performance', they looked at the work of some of the most influential black writers of the twentieth century, including Alice Childress, Suzan-Lori Parks and Lorraine Hansberry, who died from cancer at the age of thirty-four in 1965. She was the first African–American woman to have a play performed on Broadway when *A Raisin in the Sun* opened in 1959, with Sidney Poitier playing the lead character. For the first time, a predominantly white theatre audience in New York could glimpse the harsh reality of life for a black family living in a desperately poor Chicago ghetto. Lorraine was the inspiration behind the Nina Simone classic 'To Be Young Gifted and Black'.

One advantage of a small group discussion was the opportunity for everyone to express their opinions. Professor Young recalled Meghan's thoughtful contribution: 'She was intelligent and shared her honest reactions. All the class had smart, incisive comments that pushed the conversation forward.'

Among many they discussed, the students looked at two plays: *Color Struck* by Zora Neale Hurston and *Dutchman* by Amiri Baraka. The former was first published in 1926 and tells the moving and tragic story of a black woman, Emma, who is plagued by crippling insecurity within her own racial community. Colorism, as it has been called, reflects the preoccupation within the black population about the shade of the colour of one's skin.

Dutchman is a more modern one-act drama, written under Baraka's original name, LeRoi Jones, and first performed in 1964. The shocking tale about racial stereotyping unfolds in a railway carriage and chronicles the encounter between Clay, an articulate young African–American man, and Lula, an older, flirtatious white woman. She goads him into launching a bitter soliloquy about the challenges he faces as a black man. She stabs him to death and orders the other passengers to throw his body off the train.

Both plays reflect concerns about racial identity and finding a place in society. Meghan was particularly keen to talk with Professor Young, who was African–American, about her experiences as a biracial woman and finding her place in both white and black communities.

Professor Young was impressed with her insight and sophisticated understanding of what it meant to be perceived and treated differently:'The fact that a person who is twenty-one could have such experiences around race, and such an awareness of what it means to be biracial or a raced person really stuck with me. She was quite aware of how people respond to race and was very clear about the need to think about the experiences of people who are not only biracial but also people of colour.'

Professor Young, who is now Dean of the College of Fine Arts at Boston University, continued to follow Meghan's progress, her passion not just for theatre but also for women's rights. He is not surprised that she continues to speak out so eloquently about issues that matter. He observed, 'She had a self-confidence you could see helping her weather the storms of the professional world.'

Professor Young appreciated what he called Meghan's 'sense of self' – a woman who knew who she was: 'She had a very clear sense of herself as a biracial woman with a sincere interest in Black history. We talked about the echoes of racism and also colorism; and, in particular, the offhand comments that someone says that are hurtful and remind you that they don't really see you or understand your experience.'

That last observation from a distinguished academic perfectly illustrates the profound ignorance of so many people.

Meghan didn't need to sit finals. She graduated by completing the required number of credits and was soon back home in Los Angeles, impatient to make a start as a proper actress. Professor Young expected her to choose acting as her career. He observed, 'She's a lovely woman with drive – it's the latter that's the key component for success.'

He wasn't the only one from Northwestern following her progress. The young women of her sorority cheered when Meghan's first movie scene came up. They were sat in the cinema in Evanston watching *A Lot Like Love*, a rom-com starring Ashton Kutcher and Amanda Peet. Meghan was nowhere near the top of the cast list, of course. Her credit read 'Hot Girl #1'.

Her audition itself was like a scene from a satire on Hollywood. The British director Nigel Cole, whose recent credits included *Saving Grace* and *Calendar Girls*, was sitting in and said to her,

'Can you say "Hi"?' Meghan responded, 'I can. However, I've read the script and I really respond to this other role and I'd like to audition for that.'

That was not how auditions worked. She observed, 'This panic spread across the room because who does that? Who takes that sort of risk?' She didn't get the part she wanted but she did secure Hot Girl #1. The one small consolation was that she said a few more words than 'Hi', although that was her first. She sits beside Ashton on a plane and says her 'Hi' but then has a brief exchange with the passenger sitting across the gangway and tells him her name is Natalie. Lindsay Roth, who had also travelled west after university, had told Meghan about the audition, but her walk-on part did not make the final cut.

The film is one of those light and airy passages-of-time romances that sprung up following the success of *When Harry Met Sally* and *Serendipity*. The film was not a complete flop, largely owing to the popularity of Ashton Kutcher, whose star was on the rise after *Dude, Where's My Car?* These days, it's mainly remembered as Meghan's film debut.

Back on television, she was cast in a legal series for the first time, as Natasha in *Century City*, billed as a science-fiction drama set in 2030. At the audition, Meghan was economical with the truth when she was asked if she was in an actors' union, which was a prerequisite for any actor seeking employment in the industry. She explained her fib: 'And I got there, and they're like – so you're union. And I'm like, "Of course, I'm union. I mean, yeah, absolutely." But then I wasn't.'

She appeared in an episode entitled, 'A Mind is a Terrible Thing to Lose'. Nine instalments were filmed and this was broadcast as the fourth, but it turned out to be the last when the studio abruptly cancelled the entire run because of dire ratings. Once more, Meghan had just a few inconsequential lines but it did mean she could build a proper, if slim, CV that included all her high-school roles to make it seem more substantial.

One of the show's stars was Viola Davis, who would become the first black actor to win the triple crown of acting – a Tony, an Emmy and an Academy Award. Brought up in abject poverty where she stole food from rubbish bins, she is a powerful advocate for women and the eradication of child poverty. Her success has given her the voice to address Hollywood's problems with black actors and the limited roles they are offered.

At this time of her life and career, though, Meghan was more concerned with making some progress as an actress than campaigning for good causes. That would come later.

PART TWO

ACTOR TO ACTIVIST

9

PITY PARTIES

Meghan was running on empty – tired and miserable as she went from one audition to the next. It seemed she had done a million of them. Her looks seemed to guarantee that she would get to try out for a role and then, perversely, ensure that she didn't get the part. Even her car, a beat-up Ford Explorer Sport that 'rattled like a steamboat in the morning' was on the point of giving up.

On yet another try out for a 'Hot Girl' casting, the long-suffering vehicle decided it didn't want to play ball anymore. Meghan couldn't open the doors. She was trapped inside and about to miss her date with rejection. She had only one course of action – to crawl out through the trunk. She wasn't so much 'hot' as hot and bothered.

After yet another no, Meghan had the ignominy of hoping nobody would notice her unlocking the boot of the car and sliding in so that she could drive home as if this was the most natural thing in the world.

Meghan's dilemma was keeping going, maintaining her drive when setting off in the morning to audition for another nothing part in a bad film or TV show. Acting is a hazardous profession for young women. Back at Immaculate Heart, Gigi Perreau had been absolutely clear about the moral standards her girls should maintain: 'They would say to me, "I was at the mall and someone came up and said could I go to their apartment because they were in the movie business" – you know the sort of thing. I told them there were too many scam artists out there and that they should ask me first and I will find out what is going on. My advice to them was never do anything that you would be embarrassed for your children or grandchildren to see.'

The downfall of Harvey Weinstein and the rise of the #Me Too and Time's Up movements has hopefully led to greater protection and respect for women in the world of entertainment, but Hollywood's sexist treatment of young women in the noughties was proving problematic for Meghan and others trying to advance their careers. And, even if an actress did land a half-decent role, she would be judged on the red carpet by her hair and the designer dress she was wearing.

That was some way off for Meghan, who was still trying to navigate the bottom rungs of that ladder. She explained her dilemma: 'I was in my early twenties, still figuring so much out and trying to find my value in an industry that judges you on everything that you are not versus everything that you are – not thin enough, not pretty enough, not ethnic enough, while also being too thin, too ethnic, too pretty the very next day.'

And so Meghan would go for forty auditions where the average twenty-something hopeful might go up for ten. Very occasionally, it was good news. She had a small role in an episode of *Cuts*, a comedy show on the UPN network set in a hair salon. As far as Meghan was concerned, she had been nominated for an Emmy and invited friends around to help her celebrate.

Five years later she was able to re-evaluate her perceived success: 'I remember freaking out and celebrating over getting one line on a shitty UPN show. At the time, that was a big success. It was phone calls of congrats, and flowers and celebratory dinners with wine glasses clinking. It was a landmark of more work to come, and a glimmer of hope that said, "holy shit, you're really doing this."'

That would prove not to be the golden ticket to success. If anything, it just led to more auditions and more disappointments. Promisingly, she had a decent part in a one-season sitcom called *Love Inc.* that followed the ups and downs of a dating consultant in New York. In the ninth episode, entitled *One on One*, Meghan played Teresa Santos, who worked on the New York subway and had to deal with attention from two possible admirers, including her boss. In the small world of Hollywood, the writer of one of the other episodes, Aaron Korsh, would later be a hugely significant figure in Meghan's career.

Meghan's own love life seemed to be as topsy-turvy as the characters in *Love Inc.* When she first moved back to Los Angeles from college, she would hang out with Shaun Zaken. He was finding it even more difficult than Meghan to make a breakthrough, although he was cast as a waiter in an episode of *Sex and the City*. Eventually he would find his niche as a writer.

Meghan went out with another aspiring actor, Brett Ryland, for a while; he too was struggling for roles and moved into writing. Her most newsworthy 'date' was with Simon Rex, an actor who she met on the set of *Cuts*, in which he played a character called Harrison in a couple of episodes.

He is always listed as one of her exes, principally because it gives the tabloid press the chance to snigger that he was once in some gay porn films with titles including *Young, Hard & Solo*. He and Meghan had lunch. Simon set the record straight on the *Hollywood Raw* podcast when he recalled, 'Nothing happened. We never even kissed. We hung out once in a very non-datey way. She was just someone I had met on a TV show and we got lunch. That was the extent of it.'

More disturbing than the flimsiness of the stories was Simon's claim that he was offered money – as much as $70,000 – by two tabloid papers to lie about an affair with Meghan: 'I said no to a lot of money because I didn't feel right about lying and fucking up the fucking Royal Family.'

A proper relationship for Meghan sprung up in the unlikely surroundings of a dive bar off Sunset when her eye was drawn to a gravelly voiced film producer holding court in an unmistakable New York accent and a liberal use of the F-word. Trevor Engelson was one of those characters who could take over a room; he was witty with a self-deprecating manner that made him stand out among Hollywood egos.

Trevor, who was nearly five years older than Meghan, was from a wealthy Jewish family living in Great Neck, a prosperous commuter village on Long Island. The writer F. Scott Fitzgerald lived there with his wife Zelda in the early 1920s and is said to have modelled West Egg in his famous novel *The Great Gatsby* on the well-to-do neighbourhood. Trevor's father David was a successful orthodontist and his mother, Leslie, was a speech-language pathologist, more commonly referred to as a speech therapist. They were both well-respected members of Great Neck society.

Trevor always wanted to be in Hollywood; one of the most famous directors of all time, Francis Ford Coppola, went to his school, Great Neck North High School, and he toyed with following in his footsteps when he went to the University of Southern California (USC) in Los Angeles.

That ambition didn't last long: 'I wanted to direct but when I went to USC I realised you needed talent to do that.' Instead, he would spend his summer breaks taking low-paid internships on any film or TV show that would have him, although he did once spend some time on *The Tonight Show with Jay Leno*.

His first job after graduating was as a PA on the shark movie *Deep Blue Sea*. One of the stars, the rapper LL Cool J, another New Yorker, gave him the nickname Trevity Trev. It was one that stuck. He became fascinated with the world of producers: 'They didn't look like they were working that hard, they were making a bunch of money and they had the cutest girls on set. And I was like "I want to do that".' One of the movie's producers, Alan Riche, advised Trevor that he needed to make progress as an agent before he could branch out into the world of production and helped secure him a start at the Endeavor Talent Agency on Wilshire Boulevard. In the late nineties, Endeavor was a boutique agency concentrating on television, but it soon branched out into films and is now one of the giants of the entertainment world.

Trevor was in the mail room, which was a start. He moved up in the world, to the 'motion picture literary desk', working under the high-flying agent Chris Donnelly. Trevor was very keen, too enthusiastic to make gradual progress. He sent out uncommissioned scripts, known as specs, to actors and directors using the official Endeavor letterhead. He admitted, 'I was doing some stupid shit.' Chris was on holiday and didn't know anything about it. Trevor was promptly fired.

Realising that he was not suited to working at a big company, Trevor found work as an assistant at a small start-up called O/Z Films, run by two former USC students, Nick Osborne and Jeffrey Zannow. In 2001, when Trevor was just twenty-four, he and Nick founded Underground Films. He liked to bring a touch of hustle to the world of expensive suits and air kisses. He sold his first spec entitled *The Road to Freaknik*, about a road trip to the famous black street party in Atlanta, to Fox Searchlight for $25,000. 'I partied my ass off,' he recalled. He may have played hard but he also worked hard.

After a morning workout at home, he would stand in his steam shower reading scripts covered with a plastic sheet, making marks with a waterproof pen. If he didn't like the story after ten pages, he would toss it aside and start on something else. Meghan was instantly attracted to his energy and his philosophy that the next big thing was just around the corner. He told her, 'Hope is the greatest currency that we have in this business.'

Trevor seemed to have a number of one-liners for every occasion. 'Every day is a fucking adventure,' he would say, and that's how he treated life: 'If I'm on a plane somewhere, I'm working. When I land, I'm working. When I'm drinking, I'm working. But I'm always having a lot more fun than most people I know.'

The Hollywood agent Toby Guidry recognised a winning characteristic that Trevor possessed: 'He was a straight-shooter. He wasn't one of those producers who you would never hear from; he would always get back to you whether it was business or personal. I liked him very much.' Toby also recognised that beneath the bravado, Trevor was intrinsically a 'very private person'.

When Trevor left a party, a meeting or just drinks at the bar, he wanted to have made a lasting impression. He was the person you would remember in the morning. In Meghan's case, that was true, but she still needed to apply herself to more pressing matters, including paying the bills. Toby, who also became friendly with her during her Hollywood years, recognised that there was no 'crystal path' for ambitious actors; it could take years just to get an agent.

Like many Hollywood hopefuls, Meghan had to take on extra work to make ends meet. She worked as a restaurant hostess in Beverly Hills, showing diners to their seats. Her second job utilised her skill as a calligrapher. Meghan has exquisite handwriting, so it seemed a perfect 'resting' job and was apparently 'super lucrative', especially working on correspondence for the fashion house Dolce & Gabbana. The best technique, she confided, was to be patient, use fluid strokes and to wear a white tube sock on your hand so you didn't get any oils smudging your work. Her expertise led to her teaching informal classes on the art of calligraphy at the Paper Source stationery store in Beverly Hills. She also taught a class on how to achieve the best gift wrapping.

If you were lucky enough to be a guest at the wedding of singer Robin Thicke and long-standing actress girlfriend Paula Patton in June 2005, your souvenir place card and envelope were written by Meghan. She's still proud of her work, although the marriage itself ended acrimoniously nine years later.

Paula, incidentally, was also a biracial actress from Los Angeles, five years older than Meghan and just making her breakthrough in films with a small part in the Will Smith comedy, *Hitch*. She was definitely doing better than Meghan, who was trapped on the annual pilot-season lottery. This is traditionally the annual rite of spring when new shows are put together for one sample episode in the hope of attracting the attention of the big networks in the autumn.

The pilot is usually shot in April after camera crews have finished the previous season of established shows. The month of June is when fingernails are bitten while networks decide what they pick up. Meghan would go five straight years making pilots that never amounted to much.

At least she was now getting roles where the character had a name. She appeared in one episode of a sitcom called *The War at Home* that starred the comedian Michael Rapaport as Dave Gold, the head of a dysfunctional Long Island family. The show ran for two seasons and Meghan popped up towards the end of the first series in an episode entitled 'The Seventeen Year Itch'.

She played Susan, who Dave believes has a crush on him. It turns out she was just checking him out for her mother. The part was just an extension of the generic Hot Girl role, for which female actors were required to look good rather than deliver lines compellingly.

Meghan proved adept at the light comedy, but it didn't lead anywhere. Instead, she had to make do as literally thousands of hopefuls did with a bit-part in the ubiquitous *CSI* franchise. She was cast in the spin-off *CSI: NY* that starred Gary Sinise as New York crime scene investigator, Mac Taylor. She had a name, Veronica Perez, but, frustratingly, it was yet another variation on the Hot Girl role. This time she had to wear a skimpy basque, suspenders and a pair of Marigolds to play a maid who cleans for businessmen at a seedy hotel. She becomes a suspect when one of her clients is found dead.

A TV movie called *Deceit* went nowhere, too. Meghan was Gwen, a friend of one of the lead characters. The star, Canadian actress Emmanuelle Chriqui was an example for Meghan, if she needed one, of another beautiful actress who had taken every role under the sun to become noticed.

Meghan's merry-go-round continued – one step forward, one step back and just enough work to keep going. A daily run, yoga and watching her weight by not eating too many French fries was her routine. Occasionally she would treat herself to a facial – something she had been doing since she was a teenager. And then there were the pity parties – the evenings after she realised that all her scenes had been cut – a 'tailspin of sobbing in bed with a bottle of wine and a box of cookies.'

She understood that it was 'part of the game'. She was used to going up for roles where she wore next to nothing and said even less, so perhaps it was time to try for something with a more regular pay cheque.

10

YOU'RE ENOUGH

Meghan hated *Deal or No Deal*. It pretty much represented everything she disliked about Hollywood and the entertainment industry. How could she talk about the empowerment of women while wearing a dress that was far too tight and tottering about on a pair of killer heels that made her feet ache? Pure and simple, she was eye candy on a mindless game show. She didn't even have a name – she was briefcase girl number 24 and she wasn't allowed to sit down until a contestant chose her.

Deal or No Deal was originally a Dutch game show that became popular in many countries including the UK where it was hosted for more than ten years by Noel Edmonds. In the States, the Canadian comedian Howie Mandel was in charge. He didn't notice Meghan and when asked about her after she had become world famous, he simply said he didn't remember her.

The basic idea of the game was risk and reward. Twenty-six beautiful young women held briefcases containing anything from one cent to a million dollars. Contestants could end up with practically nothing if they chose the wrong case. Meghan first auditioned to be one of the twenty-six in 2006, but only became a fixture on the show after *CSI*. She needed the money.

She explained, 'I would put the show in the category of things I was doing to try to make ends meet.'

Trevor's career was not exactly in the fast lane at this point either. His first feature film production, a superhero action movie called *Zoom*, was a complete bomb, making an estimated $12.5 million on a budget of $75 million. It also received a number of nominations and wins in the various bad film of the year awards, including being named Foulest Family Film in the Stinkers Bad Movie Awards.

At least the pay for *Deal or No Deal* was good, certainly the best wage Meghan had earned so far. The girls were paid $800 an episode and might film as many as seven episodes in a day. In all, Meghan appeared in thirty-four shows in 2006 and 2007. Howie Mandel made an estimated $75,000 a show.

The charitable way of looking at the show is that the briefcase girls were like glamorous beauty contestants. The less charitable view is that it was a ghastly cattle market in which they all wore the same dresses, customised to show off as much leg and cleavage as possible – a vulgar combination that fashion-conscious Meghan thought too much. She explained, 'It's the golden rule that when you're showing décolletage or cleavage, then your skirt needs to be at your knee. If your hemline's a little higher, put on a fitted turtleneck or have a higher neckline.'

There were no turtlenecks on *Deal or No Deal*. For a Christmas edition, they wore little Santa suits. Sometimes the dresses were so tight that the women could not even bend over to put on their shoes. An assistant would be on hand for that specific job. As a final humiliation, the girls were advised if and when they needed to stuff their bra with silicon enhancers, known in the trade as chicken fillets, or just tissues to boost their cleavage. Meghan's private opinion would not have been popular: 'When sexiness is forced, it never translates in the same way – and I also don't think you're taken seriously in the same way.'

Even Meghan, by now an experienced actress, had trouble sustaining a plastic smile throughout the show. She confided, 'I would end up standing up there forever in these terribly uncomfortable heels just waiting for someone to pick my number so I could sit down.' She was seldom chosen and she recalled that she never held the briefcase containing the $1-million jackpot.

In four years, Meghan had gone from working in the US Embassy in Buenos Aires to holding a briefcase on a popular game show. She did not believe, however, that she was in any way superior to the other girls on the show. They were all in it together – trying to make a living.

One of the other 'briefcase babes' was a young model, Chrissy Teigen, now a famous face in American entertainment and married to the singing star, John Legend. She recalled Meghan, 'I remember her just being very quiet and sweet. Just really kind and I don't say that about anybody.'

Sweet is the adjective that the majority of the other women on the show have used to describe Meghan. More insightful, Claudia Jordan, briefcase number one, observed, 'I didn't feel she loved it. It was just a step along the way.'

One step she didn't want to take was to have anything to do with Donald Trump, who turned up a couple of times to promote his own show, *The Apprentice*. He tooled round the girls, offering his card and inviting them to play a round of golf. One of them, Tameka Jacobs, told Andrew Morton, 'He was a creep, super-creepy, but some girls were attracted to money and power and took his number.' Meghan was not one of them.

For some reason it seemed she couldn't persuade Trevor to cast her in any of his ongoing projects. She did have an up-and-coming agent, though – Nick Collins, who was with the

Gersh Agency on Wilshire Boulevard. Originally from Boston, he had started off as an assistant at the agency in 2005 but had moved up to agent by the time he sent Meghan along to the audition for a new pilot two years later. Nick's star in Hollywood was rising faster than Meghan's, though.

Nick may not have been an actor, but he understood the struggle to pay the bills while hoping for that break. He had been waiting tables at a restaurant in Brentwood when he secured his first job at Gersh. But from Meghan's point of view, the important consideration was that she did not give up. She adopted and adapted one of Trevor's favourite expressions: 'Don't give it five minutes if you're not going to give it five years.'

She insisted that Nick continue to put her up for auditions. She reflected, 'Working on *Deal or No Deal* was a learning experience, and it helped me to understand what I would rather be doing.' The line of approach continued to be scattergun – go for as much as possible in the hope that something might hit the target. She had high expectations for *The Apostles*, a pilot for a TV police series that seemed to have substance. At last she had a role that was more than just a 'hot girl'. She wasn't a cop herself – she was Kelly, the wife of the lead character, John Preacher Calhoun, played by Keith Robinson.

Her character, Kelly Calhoun, was a former stripper and hooker who had been 'saved' by her sanctimonious husband. This was one of those dramas where the private lives of the police were just as important as the action of their day job. For once Meghan didn't seem to mind showing off her physique in a scene where she teaches the other wives how to strip seductively for their man.

Keith enjoyed working with Meghan, observing that it was 'all about the work' with his co-star and that she was not in any way a diva. He also noted that she was very beautiful and that 'it was not hard to kiss a beautiful woman'.

For everyone, it was a crushing disappointment when Fox decided not to develop the show as a series, choosing instead to put out the feature-length pilot as a stand-alone film. Her dad had even sent her a congratulatory note when she was first cast. Meghan summed it up: 'A pilot is like your baby. It's a huge amount of work and a huge commitment, then you wait and see if it gets picked up and it's a hard thing to let go of.'

One small consolation was that the casting director for *The Apostles*, Donna Rosenstein, was impressed by Meghan and cast her again for another TV pilot, a comedy called *Good Behaviour*, about a family of criminals trying to go straight. Keith Robinson was a welcome familiar face on set. He had a small role as a police officer. Of more significance, however, was one of the co-stars, Patrick J. Adams, who would be at Meghan's side for her big breakthrough. Meghan acknowledged that even though this was another pilot that died and went straight to TV, she and Patrick had instant on-screen chemistry. His career path was very much in line with Meghan's; auditions and some success, but still waiting for a break-through role. The wait for them both would be another three years.

Trevor, meanwhile, was doing much better, having recovered from the flop of *Zoom*. He was co-producer on a Robin Williams comedy called *Licence to Wed* and an executive producer on another comedy, *All About Steve*, that starred Sandra Bullock and Bradley Cooper. He had branched out into literary management and was building a stable of writers that could be part of any film package he put together. Proof that he had finally arrived came when he was included in the *Hollywood Reporter*'s 'Top 35 under 35' in the Next Generation Class of 2009. Meghan joined him for the awards party at the fashionable MyHouse lounge on Hollywood Boulevard.

Coincidentally, she had moved into his house – a small yellow villa in a street off Sunset Boulevard, not far from the famous Whisky-A-Go-Go nightclub and the more notorious Viper Room. They were very settled as a couple about town. While it was a fun neighbourhood to explore in your twenties, Meghan was just as happy staying home and playing host to their friends, who would drop by for a roast chicken dinner, one of her seafood creations or a lamb tagine – another favourite. She never saw creating dishes in her kitchen as a chore or woman's work; and wine was always a must with dinner. She loved a big Californian red, an Oregon Pinot or an Argentine Malbec, a wine she had become a fan of during her stay in Buenos Aires. For those warm evenings, she liked nothing better than uncorking a bottle of Sauvignon blanc or Sancerre.

Professionally, Meghan laboured on, ever hopeful of *the* break. Another pilot was for the reboot of *Beverly Hills 90210*, the hit 1990s show that made stars of Jason Priestley, Luke Perry and Shannen Doherty. In the new series, entitled just *90210*, Meghan played Wendy, who made it no further than episode two. Her character is first seen giving implied oral sex in a car. It's really nothing and we don't actually see anything at all – that's all left to the imagination, although it didn't stop the *Daily Mail* declaring 'Meghan Markle is seen performing sex act in a CAR ...'

Meghan, it seemed, was just stuck playing a series of variations on the theme of Hot Girl, this time hot high school girl. She was now twenty-seven. At least a rigorous exercised regime was paying off. That included regular classes run by her close friend Heather Dorak, a former dancer from San Antonio in Texas, who had taken up Pilates when an injury put an end to her dancing ambitions in her early twenties. The two women had met in LA in 2005 and Meghan has credited Heather with completely changing her attitude to working out through her Pilates Platinum studios.

Meghan's toned figure was on show again in an episode of the revived *Knight Rider*, the old eighties' favourite that starred David Hasselhoff and his car named KITT. She played Annie Ortiz, an ex-soldier investigating the death of her old drill sergeant. She spent most of her scenes in the episode 'Fight Knight' in a skimpy black crop top while cage fighting.

By one of those quirks of scheduling, Meghan was on TV the following week in October 2009, in an episode of *Without a Trace*, another long-running crime drama that every ambitious young actor had to appear in while seeking a bigger break, rather like *The Bill* in the UK. At least she did not have to learn her character's name for a small part in the sitcom, *The League*. She was a divorcee who flirts in a bar with the main character Pete, played by Mark Duplass. A TV commercial for Tostitos corn chips was just another small tick in her bank account.

Meghan needed something to change – not just getting that break, but a transformation in her attitude to the treadmill of her twenties. Her game-changing moment occurred when she went to see another casting agent, April Webster, who was looking after a new series called *Fringe*. Meghan had never met April before, although she was aware of her reputation as one of the leading players in her field, responsible for *Lost*, *Star Trek* and, coincidentally, the original series of *Knight Rider*.

Fringe was a drama, which, rather like *The X-Files*, combined the FBI with unsettling sci-fi mysteries. Meghan was reading for the part of junior FBI agent Amy Jessup in the opening episode of Season 2. Halfway through her audition piece, April stopped her mid-sentence and said simply, 'You need to know that you're enough.'

April, with so many years of experience, had identified self-doubt as a major stumbling block for Meghan. She declared, 'Less makeup, more Meghan.' Nobody had offered her this advice before. Meghan recalled, 'She saw all that self-doubt beaming through the self-tanner and excessive blush. You couldn't pay for a therapy session this good.'

That was the wake-up call that Meghan needed, sleepwalking as she was from one unsuitable role to the next. The 'enough' sentiment would become a daily mantra for her, the core of many inspirational speeches and interviews that she would give in the future when she became one of the most famous women in the world.

She got the part in *Fringe*, but it lasted only two episodes. Weirdly, Amy's character just disappeared with no explanation, although there were rumours of contractual disputes with other cast members that affected storylines. One unexpected bonus was that the series filmed in Vancouver, giving her a first chance to explore that beautiful part of Canada.

Meghan, though, had new resolution to be more than a pretty face flitting from one show to the next. She made a decision, aptly at New Year 2010, that she was going to rekindle her enthusiasm for writing. She started a blog, calling it 'Working Actress' – which is what she was. She decided to keep the posts anonymous, meaning she could be more honest and forthright in what she wanted to say.

How times have changed for Meghan. She described herself back then: 'I am a working actress. And I don't have an entourage. Not a star. Not in the tabloids: the kind of girl who is sometimes recognizable-ish.' The blog should be essential reading for all would-be stars, including the online interview the 'working actress' gave in which she described how she would go on set and discover a kissing scene that wasn't there before or that her outfit had been changed from jeans to a dress 'the size of a loincloth'.

She also confided how bothersome it was if the actor playing your boyfriend was 'grinding a little too hard into you during a love scene (oh yes, and with a big old chubby ... that's not awkward at all!!)'.

The working actress also revealed what she kept in her handbag for auditions in the early days. It was not a glamorous pot-pourri: a mini stapler, highlighter, pens, deodorant, breath mints, a hair clip to stop her hair falling in front of her eyes while reading a dramatic scene and a black tank top, which she could throw on and look a million dollars at short notice.

The realisation that she was 'enough' may have been a Damascene moment for Meghan but it did not coincide with an immediate change of fortune. Trevor, however, had come through at last with a small part for her as a bartender in his next feature film, *Remember Me*, starring Robert Pattinson, who had quickly become one of the biggest stars in Hollywood thanks to his recurring role as Edward Cullen in the *Twilight* franchise. Meghan's role may have been minor but she was paid a reported $180,000 for it – some proper money at last.

The romantic drama filmed in New York ended with a 9/11 storyline, which wasn't to everyone's taste but it did good business for Underground Films when it opened in March 2010, making $56 million on a budget of $16 million. Trevor wasn't as involved in the film as his partner, Nick Osborne, although he did observe Robert 'might not love all the fame that he had'.

Meghan thought Robert was a 'sweetheart' and a 'really lovely guy'. He's a Londoner, brought up in Barnes, West London, and had first made a name for himself, aged nineteen, in *Harry Potter and the Goblet of Fire*, in which he played Cedric Diggory. Meghan enthused, 'It's a great example to be able to watch someone who is young, whose stardom has really taken over his life in a big way, and yet he is still gracious, humble and cool. I think that is really endearing.'

He was already a superstar, even though four years younger than Meghan, while she remained just a working actress trudging through another spin-off of *CSI* – this time, *CSI: Miami*. At least she didn't have to strip to her underwear as a police officer, Leah Montoya, who is rescued from a burning building by crime lab boss Horatio Caine. She is seen coughing and tearful in the arms of actor David Caruso.

She didn't need to learn any lines in Russell Brand's wild comedy *Get Him to the Greek*. As partygoer Tatiana, all she had to do was snog Russell, a chore for which she didn't even receive a credit. She was much higher up the cast list in *The Boys and Girls Guide to Getting Down*, a sex, drugs and rock 'n' roll canter through a night of partying in LA. Meghan's task as Dana was to appear realistic while she snorted a line of two of cocaine.

Yet again, it was a pilot that wasn't commissioned as a series. 2010 was the last year that Meghan would be an actress in her twenties. Nine years had passed since she said her first lines in *General Hospital* and her CV was not exactly groaning with roles that Jennifer Lawrence or Emma Stone might have wanted.

At least Trevor provided another lucrative job. This time it was for a short thriller with a twist called *The Candidate*, written by two of his clients. Meghan had an undemanding role as Kat, the apparently loyal secretary to the main protagonist. The clever central theme was of a secret organisation that could use the power of collective thought to cause the death of someone, a candidate, not considered worthy of living. Meghan was third on the cast list and earned a reported $171,000, which seems a lot of money for a couple of minutes onscreen.

She didn't have much to do in *Horrible Bosses*, either, but she was happy to be in it because it fulfilled an ambition: she met Donald Sutherland, one of her film idols. Meghan is generally coy about being a fan of someone but she could not conceal her excitement at working with one of her favourite actors. She was chatting to her on-set hairdresser who assured her that debonair Donald was a gem and that she would fall in love with him by lunchtime.

Later, when they were introduced, she told him, 'Mr Sutherland, I hear I'm going to fall in love with you before lunch break.' He laughed, thankfully. The now veteran star of more than one hundred films was just one of the big names in a cast that included Jennifer Aniston, Jason Bateman and Kevin Spacey. Meghan played Jamie, a FedEx delivery girl who is chatted up by an account manager – comedian Jason Sudeikis – when she delivers a package to his office. He jokes that there must be a hidden camera because she is 'way too cute to be a FedEx girl'. The comedy was a huge box office success, grossing nearly $210 million worldwide. Meghan's thirty-second role was hardly a breakthrough, however.

Perhaps a new legal drama might be something. She was on her way to the audition for *A Legal Mind* when it occurred to her that she might not look the part. She was wearing a plum-coloured spaghetti-strap top and a pair of heels but felt too Hollywood casual and not enough chic lawyer. She dived into the nearest H&M store and bought a little black dress off the peg for $35, not even trying it on because she didn't want to be late. The change of outfit proved to be inspired because, sure enough, she was asked to put it on. And it fitted, which was a huge relief.

That was the only good thing about the audition … or so she thought.

11

I WON'T STAND
FOR RACISM

Meghan had no idea that behind the scenes the production team loved her audition. She thought it was the worst one she had ever done. She had even rung up Nick to tell him that he needed to get her back in for a second chance. He told her bluntly, 'It's my job to get you in the room and then it's your job to do your job. There's nothing I can do. Just focus on your next audition.' She was being too hard on herself – as usual – but she had a feeling right from the start that potentially there was more to the character of Rachel Zane than someone who was only in the show to provide office glamour.

She had totally misread the room. To her amazement she received a callback for a screen test and this time she was far happier about things. After she got the part, Meghan reflected, 'I think we are always going to be our worst critics.' *A Legal Mind* had been created and written by Aaron Korsh, who had come across Meghan before when she was in *Love Inc.* He had once worked in banking and originally developed a script based around a Wall Street company but wisely decided a New York law firm had more possibilities for storylines and character development.

Aaron, who had also written for the long-running sitcom *Everybody Loves Raymond*, was worried that the part of Rachel was going to be difficult to cast because it required a combination of toughness and likeability: 'We looked at each other after Meghan's test and were like, "Wow, this is the one!"' Meghan, it was clear, could act smart and sweet at the same time.

The director, Kevin Bray, who would be in charge of the pilot, recalled that there was some discussion about Meghan's ethnicity after her audition — was she Latina or perhaps Mediterranean? He told the others at the casting table that he could tell she was biracial, like himself.

The final responsibility for the new show rested with the production head, Bonnie Hammer, the chairman of the NBCUniversal Cable Entertainment Group. She thought Meghan was relatable and authentic, and perfect for the role. When Meghan received the phone call from Nick Collins confirming she had got the part, it was time to party — and this time without the pity.

Originally Meghan's character was called Rachel Lane, until someone pointed out there was already an actress in Hollywood with that name. Aaron didn't have to look far for new inspiration. The renowned casting director for the series was called Bonnie Zane, so Rachel Zane came easily to mind.

The pilot, filmed in New York in August 2010, featured the six actors who would become the regular stars of the series: Gabriel Macht, Patrick J. Adams, Rick Hoffman, Gina Torres, Sarah Rafferty and Meghan. She and Patrick had remained good friends over the years and it was reassuring to be in tune with an actor especially if a fictional romance was part of the script. She explained, 'We had great chemistry. It makes work a bit more like play when you can laugh at the same jokes and have a short-hand with each other, which we really do.'

The camaraderie between the cast was evident from the start. It helped that Gabriel and Sarah had also been friends for many years. Meghan too enjoyed a great rapport with Sarah, sharing banter off screen as well as on. 'We're very silly together,' said Meghan.

In the beginning, the plot focused mainly on Harvey Specter (Gabriel) and his brilliant, quirky assistant Mike Ross (Patrick), but gradually the personalities of the other lead characters were teased out. Meghan did not have much to do in the pilot – other than hint of a romance to come. She is introduced after thirty-one minutes and ten seconds wearing a tight-fitting white top, pencil skirt and expensive heels, which became a familiar look throughout the series, defining her eye-catching silhouette.

Rachel slaps down Mike when he first meets her in the office of Pearson Hardman, where she is the leading paralegal, and is assigned to give him his first day orientation. He blurts out, 'Wow, you're pretty.' She coolly responds, 'Good. You've hit on me. We can get it out of the way that I'm not interested' – signifying, of course, that this was TV and she would be. Amusingly, Mike is called Ross and she is called Rachel, which might have given everyone a clue that their relationship was going to be a long-running romantic saga in the style of the two much-loved *Friends*' characters. The additional edge to Rachel was that she was far too talented to be a paralegal but could not pass the LSAT, the law school admission test.

While she waited anxiously to see if the pilot would be picked up for a series, Meghan and Trevor decided on a late-summer holiday to the Caribbean island of Belize. It was idyllic and the perfect place for Trevor to produce a diamond solitaire ring and ask her to marry him. She was thrilled to accept but they decided not to set the date yet, preferring to wait until they knew what was happening with *Suits*, as it was now called.

None of the cast knew for sure if *Suits* was going to be more than just a pilot. But the lead actors were seasoned professionals who sensed there was a buzz around the show. Meghan described the sense of elation when it was given the green light in January 2011 for a whole series: 'There was a communal "Oh my God"!' Nobody could have realised that within a year of the first episode being aired on the cable channel, USA Network, in June, that *Suits* was being called the hottest show on television.

Although the pilot was shot in New York, the remaining eleven episodes of the first season were filmed in Toronto, masquerading as the Big Apple. They had to build a new set to exactly match the offices they had used in the opener, but overall the production would be much cheaper in Canada, where the tax situation was more generous. Meghan didn't know Toronto but she was a seasoned traveller who had been all over the world. She and Trevor loved travelling, particularly enjoying trips to Europe and, if time was tight, there was always the chance to swim in his parents' pool back on Long Island.

As she prepared to leave Los Angeles in March 2011, there was some sad family news when her grandfather, Alvin Ragland, died aged eighty-two. Doria's dad had fallen over when he got tangled up with his dog's lead, just yards from his home. He hit his head on the pavement and didn't recover from his injuries, dying in hospital nine days later.

Alvin had been a popular and sociable man all his life. He was a familiar figure at the weekend antiques market, the Melrose Trading Post held at Fairfax High School, which Doria had attended. He would drive up in his beat-up truck and spend an age unloading his merchandise. Some of his fellow stall holders thought he was homeless because of the state of his vehicle, not realising that he lived in a smart olive-green house in the upmarket suburb, recognised as one of the most prosperous African–American neighbourhoods in the whole of the US.

After he and Meghan's grandmother divorced, he married again, to a teacher, Ava Burrow, who was twenty-three years his junior. Although the marriage didn't last, Ava remained on good terms with her stepdaughter and step-granddaughter, who she called Meggie and described as being 'very clever and very pretty'.

Doria had moved in with Alvin in his later years. Her businesses had struggled and she had filed for bankruptcy in 2009. She decided to reinvent herself working as a yoga teacher and enrolling as a mature student, obtaining a psychology and subsequently a master's degree from the University of Southern California in 2011. She had plans to give back to the community, starting a late career in social work specialising in the mental health problems of the elderly.

When her father's affairs had been sorted out, she was able to stay on at the family home in View Park–Windsor Hills. It would prove to be an ideal location when she started work for the Didi Hirsch Mental Health Services in nearby Culver City. Her house would always be a welcome bolthole for her daughter, although Meghan was happy with Trevor ten miles away in their bungalow off Sunset. She was, however, preparing for the longest time they had been apart for seven years.

She didn't need to move to Canada permanently for the moment because one series did not guarantee a second commission. The good news, however, was that the ratings for the first 'rookie' season that concluded in September 2011 were excellent – top-rated in the key 18–49 age range in its Thursday evening slot at 10pm.

The reviewers, too, enjoyed the unashamed escapism. *GQ* magazine summed up the appeal: 'If you're trying to escape reality, you're in the right place. The people of *Suits* are more beautiful and much wittier than anyone you know.' *The New York*

Times was more cautious, noting a formulaic approach, although the paper did concede it had a 'snappy sense of its own fun.'

Unsurprisingly, a second season was given the go-ahead, which would again mean Meghan heading off to Toronto, a five-hour plane ride from Los Angeles and her home with Trevor. They decided this would be the right time for their wedding. Trevor had revealed they were about to get married on a live video podcast in LA.

He was swigging from a flask engraved with Trevity Trev, which did not go down well with her watching fiancée, who texted him curtly: 'Put that flask down, it looks incredibly unprofessional!' Trevor was a good interview, relaxed as ever as if he was chatting to chums in a bar. When one of the interviewers suggested that Meghan might go on the show, Trevor responded, 'She's a big deal, fuck off.' He was very proud of her and had posted on social media urging people to watch his 'bad-ass fiancée' in her new show.

Their September wedding party was a gloriously relaxed affair with a beautiful beach location in Jamaica. They had completed the legal paperwork in LA before travelling to the Caribbean. The bride and groom booked all fifty-five rooms at the exclusive Jamaica Inn in Ocho Rios, a boutique hotel made famous when Marilyn Monroe and the playwright Arthur Miller dined there during their belated honeymoon to the island in early 1957. Noel Coward, Errol Flynn and the James Bond creator Ian Fleming were just some of the celebrities to have sipped martinis in the bar. Bond himself would have been right at home in an immaculate white tuxedo watching the sun set over the ocean.

More than a hundred guests flew in for Meghan and Trevor's three-day party, the ultimate fun-packed, flip-flop slice of Californian culture – no stuffy protocol whatsoever. Beer and rum flowed generously during days spent on the beach. Meghan put on a bright yellow bikini for the wheelbarrow races across the sand, in which the women would balance on their hands while being pushed by men holding their ankles. In the evenings the night was well and truly danced away. Doria was there and happily joined in, although she wisely drew the line at wheel-barrow races – so did Tom Markle.

Ninaki Priddy was matron of honour and she would later tell journalist Rebecca Hardy that her oldest friend had 'shone with happiness'. Meghan changed into a simple yet stunning white dress for a short ceremony in which the couple exchanged a few words they had written for each other. As a mark of recognition for Trevor's Jewish heritage, they were hoisted up on chairs while the guests sang a rousing chorus of 'Hava Nagila'.

There was time to laze about, eat good food and wine – the type of break Meghan always enjoyed and she was sorry to leave for the reality of Los Angeles. She would later describe the place as 'very romantic'. Back home in LA, there was further sad family news when Grandma Markle, her dad's mum, Doris, died at a nursing home in Glendale She had been suffering from dementia and Meghan rallied round to support her father at a difficult time.

Trevor was right when he described Meghan as a big deal. She may not have been A-list yet but she was on her way. To prove the point, she was chosen as a host for the first time when she co-presented the Anti Defamation League Entertainment Industry Awards at the Beverly Hilton Hotel. The ADL, founded in 1913, is an international Jewish organi-sation opposing prejudice of all kinds. Trevor's mum Leslie was an enthusiastic fundraiser. While it has been a leading move-ment in the battle against anti-semitism, it has also been vocal in denouncing racism and the groups such as the Ku Klux Klan that perpetuate it.

In 2011, the evening's honouree was the renowned Hollywood executive Ryan Kavanaugh, producer of *The Social Network*, *Mamma Mia!* and *Despicable Me*. The Distinguished Entertainment Industry Award had been won three years earlier by Bonnie Hammer in recognition of her work spearheading the Erase the Hate public service campaign that won an Emmy for USA Network. The not-for-profit charity had been founded in 1994 to 'fight hate and discrimination' in America. Bonnie was one of its leading supporters.

Bonnie was an inspiration for Meghan, another key figure in her life who was committed to colour-blind casting and had seen an actress and not a biracial girl with freckles. Meghan later included Bonnie in a list of the ten women who had changed her life for the better: 'It's one thing to have respect for your boss, but it's another to have the kind of respect that comes with feeling comfortable.' They became long-standing friends and she considered Bonnie an 'absolute force' and a mentor.

The ADL awards night was the first time Meghan needed to shine on stage and not just look good on the red carpet. She chose a simple sleeveless peplum dress in black velvet by Stella McCartney, who would become one of her favourite designers. She matched it with a pair of black suede point-toe shoes that Rachel Zane might have worn. On her right wrist was a highly desirable gold Cartier love bracelet. The fashion commentator Alison Jane Reid thought it 'feminine and flattering' and a 'clever and safe choice' for Meghan's hour-glass figure.

Anything by Stella McCartney was a popular choice in Hollywood, especially a black dress that perfectly suited a woman of Meghan's height – 5 foot 6 inches – who could not wear the outfits that look good on a catwalk model. Alison-Jane observed, 'Sky-high pumps and heels and this form-fitting dress accentuate her tiny waist and slim her hips. It's a bit like a chic suit of armour.'

Trevor was there in a smart if slightly rumpled grey suit. He posed proudly next to Meghan, although all eyes were on her. This was perhaps the moment when the baton of fame and success subtly changed hands. She was on the verge of moving on from working actress to becoming one of the best-known faces on American television.

Encouraged by Bonnie, Meghan didn't waste any time finding her voice while filming the second season of *Suits*. She put on a crisp white t-shirt emblazoned with the slogan 'I Won't Stand for Racism' and spoke to camera about her experiences in another Erase the Hate initiative.

Speaking with sincerity and purpose, Meghan introduced herself as a biracial woman who wanted to be part of something important because it 'hits a really personal note'. She recalled the offensive jokes and names, her mum being called the 'N-word', her grandparents' journey across America where they had to go round the back of restaurants to get food for the family. She observed, 'I thought that was really isolated to *those* days that we had passed. Sadly, they are not.'

She believed that a campaign could have effect if everyone took part in however small a way – that people should not think a simple act like a wearing a t-shirt in solidarity with a cause would not change anything. 'But it does,' she implored. 'It raises awareness and it puts it under a consciousness that is bigger than just doing nothing at all.'

On a personal note, Meghan spoke of the struggle she faced with her own identity and how certain people did not see her as a black woman or a biracial woman: 'They treat me differently I think than they would if they knew what I was mixed with.'

Meghan had not lost her way with words, the ability to set the right tone as she spoke of her future hope for a more tolerant society: 'I am really proud of my heritage on both sides. I am really proud of where I have come from and where I am going. But I hope that by the time I have children that people are even more open-minded to how things are changing and having a mixed world is what it's all about. Certainly, it makes it a lot more beautiful and a lot more interesting.'

These words were spoken in February 2012. Her hopes would turn out to be in vain. It would be six years before she became a mother and two more before the killing of George Floyd roused the world from its complacent slumber.

12

NETWORKING

Meghan was becoming more famous – at least in Toronto. When she filmed the first series of *Suits* nobody seemed much bothered by another film crew outside the Bay Adelaide Centre in the financial district. Occasionally someone would come up and ask the cast what they were doing and nod politely in a 'that's interesting' sort of way, before walking on.

Now the show was a big hit, a few passers-by had become a rubber-necking crowd. 'It's crazy,' said Meghan, enjoying every minute of her success. The set for outdoor scenes was surrounded by police and security, but it was all good-natured and quickly became a safe tourist attraction among the skyscrapers. Meghan called it a 'sweet pride'.

The second series saw Meghan's character develop. Rachel Zane was more than just a quick-witted paralegal. She had what one reviewer described as the show's 'emotional heart'. She had aspirations and a back story of failed ambition that had disappointed her father, top lawyer Robert Zane. He is introduced in one episode, played by well-known actor Wendell Pierce, who had also been in the cast of *Horrible Bosses*.

The surprise to many was that Rachel's father was black, so she was biracial – just as Meghan was in real life. Mike Ross was taken aback and during a sharp exchange of dialogue, she tells him, 'You think this is an all-round tan.' Social-media fans of the show were as stunned as he was – not all of them in a positive way and, for the first time, Meghan had to contend with racist tweets. She responded simply, 'The reaction was unexpected.'

Wendell was less diplomatic: 'The ignorance that is racism is given. Like gravity, it's there, it exists. You should always be vigilant for it and be prepared for it.' Meghan would need to be watchful in the future.

Fortunately, the online comments did not cast a cloud over her enjoyment of *Suits* and the sense of achievement it brought. One of the unwritten rules of creating a publicity buzz around a TV show or a new film is to suggest a fictional romance spilling over into real life. *Suits* was no different, cashing in on the obvious on-screen chemistry between Meghan and Patrick J. Adams. The cast were all genuine friends but there were no illicit love affairs behind the scenes.

Patrick, for instance, was in a serious relationship with the actress Troian Bellisario, star of the long-running TV series *Pretty Little Liars*. They had met when they played opposite one another in a new play by American playwright Bill Cain called *Equivocation* in 2009 that ran for a limited time in New York and the Geffen Playhouse in Westwood, Los Angeles. Like Megan, Troian was biracial, with a white father and African–American mother.

Toronto was Patrick's home patch and at weekends he played host to his fellow cast members in his old family home. During this downtime, Meghan had struck up a great friendship with Rick Hoffman, who played Louis Litt on the show. She was impressed watching him develop his character's multi-layered, love-to-hate-him personality where, even though he was being nasty, it was apparent that there was a deep-rooted sadness and insecurity behind it all.

While Meghan was closest in age to Patrick, she was probably more in tune with Rick and Sarah Rafferty, who were nearly ten years older. She also forged a friendship with Abigail Spencer, who played attorney Dana 'Scottie' Scott, one of the recurring lawyers in *Suits*. They had first met when they were both struggling young actresses doing the rounds of shows like *CSI*. Even back then, Abigail thought Meghan had something about her. She recalled, 'I saw her and I thought "Who is this gorgeous girl?" She was so stunning.'

They had another reason to bond when they discovered they were both born on the same day in 1981. Abigail was originally from Florida, where her father, Yancy Bailey Spencer III, had been renowned as one of the leading figures of professional surfing around the Gulf Coast. After his death in 2011, a statue was erected in his honour on Pensacola Beach.

Abigail had a young son, Roman, but her seven-year marriage to businessman and producer Andrew Pruett had been in trouble for some time and they eventually filed for divorce in early 2012 citing 'irreconcilable differences'. Nobody realised at the time that within a year, Meghan's marriage would follow a similar path.

Both actresses had moved on from minor roles, but there was still a chance to catch pre-fame Meghan in *Dysfunctional Friends*, a movie in which she played a photographer, Terry, whose main scene was giving a hefty whack to a male model. Meghan had warned the actor Christian Keyes that she might 'improv' an extra slap. He was happy about it and now dines out on being 'pimp-slapped' by a member of the Royal Family. More seriously, he observed that Meghan was super-professional on set – a 'class act', he said.

In the hit whodunit show, *Castle*, she had a decent part as Charlotte who turns out to be the murderer, unmasked by the title character played by Canadian actor Nathan Fillion. During her many TV appearances, this was the only time she had been cast as a villain. Her role was still relatively small, although it was the last time Meghan's name was not near the top of the credits.

Meghan was still going up for roles during the hiatus from filming *Suits*, but her agent Nick Collins had moved her up several divisions from the Working Actress days. Back in Los Angeles, she was feeling less settled than in Toronto. Her home with Trevor seemed more like his bachelor pad now, perhaps more cluttered and chilled than her new mature style. She wanted something homelier and decided to get a dog.

Meghan set her heart on having a puppy. She hadn't grown up with dogs and this would be the first one she had owned. A pet would be the perfect companion for her when she went back to Toronto to film the next series of *Suits*. She went to a rescue centre and noticed two five-week-old puppies that had been found abandoned in the Downey district of South East Los Angeles. They appeared to be a sort of Labrador crossed with a German Shepherd. One of the litter brothers was black and the other golden.

Meghan was sat playing with the golden-coloured pup when Ellen DeGeneres walked in with her wife, the actor Portia de Rossi. The couple were well-known animal lovers providing a home for many unwanted cats and dogs. Meghan had never met Ellen but she recognised instantly one of the best-known faces in entertainment.

'Is that your dog?' asked Ellen. Meghan mumbled 'No,' whereupon Ellen told her forcefully, 'You have to take the dog. Rescue the dog!' The television host was just warming up and continued, 'Have you thought of a name for him yet?' Meghan, who was a little in awe of meeting such a big name so randomly, said she had in mind to call him Bogart after the movie legend.

'You're taking the dog home,' insisted the star. In the car park a while later, Ellen came up to her white Audi SUV, tapped firmly on the window and yelled, 'Take the dog.' Meghan was persuaded and went back into the centre to collect her new companion – because, as she would later admit, 'Ellen told me to.'

Meghan became devoted to her little puppy, who she nick-named 'Bogs', which was slightly less appealing than Bogart. Soon afterwards, the dog was installed in her new home, a three-bedroom detached house in Yarmouth Road, a sleepy side street in the Seaton Village district of Toronto. The neighbour-hood is named after John Colborne, 1st Baron Seaton, who distinguished himself at the Battle of Waterloo in 1815 and subsequently became a significant figure in the development of Canada in the nineteenth century as a military commander and acting Governor General.

Seaton Village is lovely, leafy, quite well-to-do and distinctly middle class. If this were London it might be Camden or Islington, fashionably trendy without the price tag of Hampstead. Although relatively modest considering her wage, the two-storey plum-coloured property was perfect for a single woman. She was renting but was allowed to decorate in what she called the style of a 'Californian bungalow', which meant it was light, airy and mini-malist. She filled it with vases of flowers and wanted to make her home as sunny as possible to contrast the harsh Canadian winters.

The garden was secluded and private, although there were garages round the back, which would make security problematic in the future. Nightlife was a short train ride away or just fifteen minutes in a taxi, while fashionable restaurants were within walking distance. Best of all was the park across the road where she could take Bogs for a walk, or a run if she was feeling more energetic.

Trevor had begun 2012 by urging his Facebook friends to watch *Suits*, adding, 'so proud of my girl'. A year later, in January 2013, he did the same thing, enthusing, 'so proud of my amazing wife.' The following month Meghan did not accompany him to the Oscars. Admittedly she was filming in Toronto, but this was the biggest Hollywood night of the year and not something she would have missed lightly. That may have been a clue, but the announcement in May that they were separating was a complete surprise to their friends. They had been married for just twenty months, although they had spent much of that time apart.

People often like to find a particular reason for a split that's more dramatic than just living separate lives with half a continent between them. In Meghan's case the finger was pointed at her brief friendship with a Canadian ice hockey player Michael Del Zotto, who was nearly ten years her junior.

Meghan had been introduced to the millionaire sportsman when his team, the New York Rangers, played a fixture against the Toronto Maple Leafs. He was a friend of Rick Hoffman, and she travelled down with her co-star to watch Michael play a home game at Madison Square Garden in New York. She posted a picture on Instagram that has appeared many times in the press. She is wearing sunglasses and a black coat and is posing between Michael and Rick; and that's the evidence.

Michael gave the rumours short shrift, stating that he was friends with Rick and that was it. Meghan had once posted that he was 'the best' but she deleted the throwaway line after her divorce and never mentioned him again. The press did approach Trevor and asked him directly, but he had nothing to say about it.

The divorce became official in August 2013, citing the usual 'irreconcilable difficulties'. Neither of them has spoken about each other or revealed the details of any settlement. Meghan stayed in Toronto and Trevor carried on with his life in LA, living in the bungalow they had shared. His parents liked Meghan and were particularly disappointed at the marriage's collapse. They kept in touch with Doria so were able to hear about their former daughter-in-law's progress.

Underground Films & Management is still going strong, although partner Nick Osborne has become a full-time writer, leaving Trevor in sole charge. Trevor was briefly linked with the actress and swimwear model Charlotte McKinney, who described herself as a 'curvier bombshell type of girl'. He posted a picture of them together with the caption, 'way out of my league here but loving it.' He would begin a more serious relationship with heiress Tracey Kurland, a nutritionist whose father is a former investment banker with a fortune reportedly in excess of $500 million.

They married in a million-dollar celebration at the swanky Miramar Resort in Montecito, California, in May 2019 in a Jewish ceremony with a rabbi; the men were in elegant black tie and the female guests wore fine dresses. This was far more *Great Gatsby* than Jamaica Inn. Professionally, arguably the most interesting project Trevor has been involved in as a producer was a TV film entitled *L.A. Burning: The Riots 25 Years Later* about the aftermath of the Rodney King beating – an event that still resonates strongly with Meghan, especially after the George Floyd killing.

One casualty of the split was Meghan's friendship with Ninaki Priddy. Her maid of honour was resolutely on Trevor's side after the divorce, believing he had the rug pulled out from under him. She eventually sold her story and her album of photographs chronicling their near thirty-year friendship for a six-figure sum, reputedly in the region of $200,000.

More positively from Meghan's point of view, the actress Abby Wathen, who starred alongside her in her next movie, *Random*

Encounters, recalled that they would talk about their divorces. 'I was destroyed,' revealed Abby, 'but she was empowered. She took her power back. It wasn't the right relationship for her, so she moved on.'

As evidence of that, Meghan slipped her engagement and wedding rings into an envelope and sent them back to Trevor. Much was made of this in the media as if this was some crime. Trevor had been an important part of her life as a struggling twenty-something but now she was entering an exciting new phase.

The romantic comedy *Random Encounters* bridged the gap between the working actress and the successful one. The director, Boris Undorf, did not have Meghan on his radar until she was recommended for the part by her friend, casting director Toby Guidry. Boris was unsure: 'She was a lot more beautiful than what I felt was right for the character, but it was clear that she had a good sense of comedic timing and a great energy on screen, which is what ultimately won me over.'

He was impressed with Meghan's professional handling of all the technical aspects of acting, particularly 'finding her light' – a skill she had learnt from her dad. Meghan wasn't the star – that was Abby Wathen. Instead, she played Mindy, her roommate and best friend, who says the memorable line: 'Random encounters is what we're looking for.' The film had a low-key digital release in 2013, but five years later, when Meghan was one of the most famous women in the world, it was rereleased on DVD in the UK under the title of *A Random Encounter*. Meghan's name was then centre stage and her picture loomed large on the cover. You could have been forgiven for believing she was the star.

Meghan was now a single woman looking to make friends and connections in Toronto. She loved lazing about on the sofa with her dog Bogs but she was also very sociable and enjoyed going out for a prosecco or two in the newly opened Soho House bar. As far as the fashionable Toronto residents were concerned, the cast of *Suits* represented Hollywood and they were happy to open doors to the top table of Canadian society. One of her new set was Jessica Mulroney, the daughter-in-law of the former Prime Minister Brian Mulroney. She was also half of one of the city's most glamorous couples – her husband Ben was a well-known face on national TV as host of entertainment shows, *etalk*, and *Canadian Idol*.

Jessica came from new Montreal money; her great-uncle Morton Brownstein, a Romanian immigrant, founded Browns, the fashion shoe empire. Unsurprisingly, both Ben and Jessica could often be seen wearing an elegant pair of shoes from the family firm. They were also parents to young twin boys when Meghan first arrived in Toronto.

Jessica was a perfect friend for someone new to the city. She knew all the best places, shared a love of yoga and fashion and was spearheading a charity initiative in Toronto called The Shoebox Project. For many years, her mother Veronica had been persuading her friends to fill a shoebox with small gift items, which she would then drop off at a women's shelter. Jessica and her sisters-in-law decided to do the same in Toronto, and when Meghan was getting married to Trevor, they started collecting the shoeboxes. They distributed more than four hundred in time for the Christmas holidays to shelters including the Red Door project that helped victims of domestic abuse and their children.

Meghan no longer needed to worry about paying the rent. She was making fantastic money in *Suits* – reported to be in the region of $50,000 an episode. That translated to taking home more than $450,000 a year. She happily financed her mother's further education. This was a perfect time to quietly resume volunteering.

She chose to become involved with the St Felix project in downtown Toronto. She worked diligently in the kitchen of the charity's centre in Augusta Avenue, providing meals for the homeless and the hungry – those suffering through extreme poverty or poor mental health; and pets were always welcome. The volunteering was a throwback to those teenage days in Skid Row, Los Angeles, when she helped out at the Hippie Kitchen.

According to those that worked alongside her, Meghan was 'always very humble during volunteering, keeping a low profile and working hard.' She was just one volunteer among many. By contrast, professionally the cast of *Suits* were encouraged to keep a high public profile, to increase their personal standing and that of the show. They were expected to look Hollywood glamorous at special 'An Evening with *Suits*' events that publicised each new series of the show. The format was usually a screening, followed by a discussion and a Q and A. Turning up to these ticketed events was part of the contract – something actors understood.

Volunteering, however, was entirely different. Meghan insisted on no publicity and no cameras. Only one picture exists of her days with St Felix and even that is a low-key affair where, barely recognisable in a pulled-down baseball cap, she is one of a group of a dozen men and women doing their best for those less fortunate. She never forgot the community charity, however, and was happy to give it a name-check when she was one of the most famous women in the world.

This was a low-profile experience and it reveals two sides of Meghan: the private woman, taking her dog for a walk before spending the morning doing her bit to help others; and the professional actress, keen to network to raise her profile professionally and draw attention to the causes that mattered to her.

She was, for instance, on the guest list at the Novak Djokovic Foundation Dinner, a star-studded New York evening that included an auction in the grand ballroom of the stylish Capitale venue in the Bowery. She had absolutely nothing to wear – or so she thought. In a panic, she called a fashion PR, Elizabeth Tuke, who she had met the previous month in Toronto. They immediately struck up a friendship, as Meghan often seemed to do easily. Elizabeth liked her because she wasn't like so many of the fashionistas she met.

Typically, Meghan had just the right outfit – a black Temperley dress – sitting in her hotel-room closet but did not have the right jewellery to accessorise. Quick as a flash, Elizabeth took off her own Bounkit semi-precious earrings and handed them to Meghan – job done.

She dazzled at the dinner, which was like an Oscar night without the awards for the super-rich and famous and raised $2.5 million for preschool children's programmes in Serbia.

Novak had lost the final of the US Open tennis champion-ships the day before but was in fine spirits hosting the event. Naomi Campbell, Goldie Hawn and Ricky Gervais were among the auctioneers for the night. One offer was for a week on a luxury yacht that sold for $300,000 – twice. Anna Wintour, the legendary editor of *Vogue*, who would become a good friend of Meghan in the future, donated one of the prizes – joining her to attend a fashion show. Meghan didn't bid but she did attend New York Fashion Week for the first time the following week. She seemed to be everywhere.

Meghan had to fly to Europe to shoot her next film, a British crime movie with the unappealing title *Anti-Social*, directed by Reg Traviss, who had been in a relationship with Amy Winehouse when she died tragically in 2011. Meghan played Kirsten, the model girlfriend of a street artist who gets mixed up in criminal gang rivalry. The story was inspired by three real-life crimes: the Graff Diamonds Robbery in 2009, the Brent Cross smash and grab of 2012 and the Selfridges Burka Robbery earlier in 2013. To lend it some credibility among a youthful audience, there were roles for London rappers Skepta and Devlin.

The high spot of the venture for Meghan was spending a month filming in Budapest. She loved exploring the beautiful Hungarian capital with her leading man, Gregg Sulkin. They kept warm while tramping the streets by eating delicious chicken soup and drinking mulled wine. Gregg, who was ten years her junior, had worked with Troian Bellisario on a few episodes of *Pretty Little Liars*. He was very complimentary about Meghan, who he called a 'well-educated human being'. He declared her to be his favourite of all the actresses he had worked with: 'She's such a poised, well-mannered, classy girl who takes work seriously.'

They had to finish the movie with scenes shot in London, which gave Meghan the opportunity for some UK networking. She may not have been a fan of the red carpet but she did not want to miss out on the world premiere of one of the biggest films of the year, *The Hunger Games: Catching Fire*, the second of the blockbuster films starring Jennifer Lawrence. She flew to London for the premiere at the Odeon, Leicester Square, and was duly photographed in a simple but very sexy Alexander McQueen LBD. Unusually for a brisk November evening, Meghan had chosen a short dress.

Meghan received her first UK exposure with a few lines of tittle-tattle in the *Sunday People* in November 2013. She had met Katie Hind, the showbiz columnist of the newspaper, for a glass of prosecco and a chat at the trendy bar of the Soho Sanctum Hotel. The informal meeting had been set up by a PR company in London, who faced the difficult task of getting Meghan a mention in a very crowded marketplace.

The two women, who were the same age, enjoyed several glasses of fizz and Meghan talked openly about her divorce and moaned about men as if she and Katie were enjoying a regular girls' night catch-up. Meghan had always been socially adept and, by this time, had no trouble talking to journalists. She was thirty-two, had been in Hollywood for ten years and was not an ingénue nervous of making a good impression.

At one point, Meghan produced her iPhone and showed Katie a picture of the England footballer Ashley Cole, who she said was trying to contact her on Twitter. Katie warned her off by retelling various stories of Ashley's former marriage to the pop queen, Cheryl. This, of course, would make a little story for Sunday.

Katie was nice about Meghan. Anything about Ashley Cole was newsworthy at the time so the five paragraphs focused on him targeting the actress as a replacement for his ex-wife. Under the headline 'Ashley has sparkle for Markle' she wrote, 'The Californian beauty is soooooo much nicer than the scraggy lot he has been pursuing with Cheryl in 2010.'

The story appeared next to a picture of Meghan wearing the McQueen LBD from the premiere, so that was worth doing. Tellingly, Katie didn't mention *Suits* at all, despite its popularity across the Atlantic. Meghan clearly had a long way to go to receive proper recognition in the UK, but it was a start and, in PR terms, it was job done. The two women parted on good terms, saying goodnight with a hug and a smile, which was always Meghan's preferred style.

A couple of days later she was on the red carpet again at the glitzy Global Gift Gala, a celebrity driven charity event backed by the Eva Longoria Foundation at the ME London Hotel in the Strand. Meghan was on presenting duty at the dinner and auction and posed for pictures with co-presenter, the top male model Oliver Cheshire. This was strictly business and Oliver was accompanied by his long-standing partner, the singer Pixie Lott.

The stars of the night were Eva herself and her friend Victoria Beckham. They both wore black dresses designed by the former Spice Girl but this time Meghan too was interviewed on the red carpet by the TV celebrity reporter Lizzie Cundy, who referred to her as the 'hottest girl in the US' and gave a big plug to *Suits*.

It was a polished minute of celebrity chatter. Meghan mentioned how cold it was in London, which was funny considering it was freezing in Toronto. More amusingly, she said she had never been called 'love' or 'darling' so much in her life.

13

THE TIG

Meghan posed happily for a photograph with her arm around Serena Williams. She didn't know the tennis superstar well enough yet to call her Rena, as her friends did, but she soon would. They had said a brief hello at an event in Miami a couple of years before but now they had the chance to chat properly.

They were on the same team for a game of celebrity flag football in New York, the day before the Super Bowl, the biggest event in the US sporting calendar. The big attraction of this variety of American Football was that there was no contact; instead of physical tackling, players had to rip away a flag from the opposing runner's belt. It meant that Meghan would not be covered in bruises when she flew off to Vancouver to shoot a new movie.

Meghan and Serena were on the blue team for the eighth annual DirecTV Celebrity Beach Bowl. There's no beach in Manhattan, obviously, so the organisers imported enough sand to create one in the SuperFan Stadium, a large heated tent at Pier 40 in the Hudson River Park on West Street.

The event on the first day of February 2014 was free, on a first-come first-served basis and was also televised, so good publicity all round. Meghan's team – sporting the logo of the

NYPD – won, although nobody paid too much notice to the score. One familiar face on the opposing team was the model Chrissy Teigen from her *Deal or No Deal* days, who, on the day, was the main attraction for the ranks of photographers.

During the game, Serena recognised Meghan and barrelled up to her to pal up so they could enjoy the afternoon together. They didn't chat about tennis, nor about acting, but, as Meghan confided, they talked of 'good old-fashioned girly stuff'. They were almost exactly the same age and shared a passion for hot sauce and fashion.

Like Meghan, Serena was brought up in Los Angeles, but she was a black girl from the notorious Compton area where her half sister was killed in 2003, an innocent bystander in a gangland shooting. She faced a media too keen to criticise her appearance: the *Daily Telegraph* columnist Matthew Norman once infamously wrote that her 'breasts were registered to vote in a different US state from the rest of her'. And then there was the familiar dismissal of racism by white observers. Former world number one tennis player Martina Hingis once said of Serena and her sister Venus: 'They can always say it's racism or something like that and it's not the case at all.'

This was not the day to talk about racism or sexism, however, although Serena was a shining example of how determination and talent could fight both. Instead they chatted about Serena's online presence. She used her global fame to expand her commercial empire while promoting the issue of female empowerment that was so important to Meghan. She was almost as fond of motivational phrases as Meghan herself, declaring that 'every woman's success should be an inspiration to another'.

Serena treated fashion seriously and not flippantly – just what Meghan wanted to do. The current slogan on her website declares, 'Be Seen, Be Heard.' Serena also exploited other aspects of social media, including Instagram and Reddit – the social news website co-founded by Alexis Ohanian, who she would eventually marry in 2017. Meghan had a long way to go to match the reach of the world's richest sportswoman, with a fortune estimated at more than $225 million, thanks not just to tennis but also to lucrative endorsements and investments.

Plans for her own online presence were now high on Meghan's list of priorities, but first she flew off to Vancouver to shoot a TV movie called *When Sparks Fly*. She had ditched her Working Actress blog – it had been a pleasing diversion while she was climbing Hollywood's greasy pole, but she was too successful for that now. Life was so busy when *Suits* was on a break that goodness knows how she found time to learn her lines.

She had made sure she kept in regular contact with her agent, Nick Collins, to discuss opportunities during the hiatus. With *When Sparks Fly*, finally she had the starring role in a movie. She played big city Chicago journalist Amy Peterson, who is sent to rediscover her roots and write a feature about growing up in a small town in Washington where her parents ran a local fireworks business – hence the slightly cheesy title. On arrival, she discovers her old boyfriend still lives there and is about to get married. She also finds out that love and life was better back in the day.

Meghan was quite an old hand at light comedies but this was a higher-profile venture for her, especially as it was for the popular Hallmark Channel in the US. Amy, she said, was much closer to her true personality than the rather polished and refined Rachel Zane: 'It was fun to eat ribs and get barbecue sauce all over my face and run around in jeans all day.'

The generic storyline of a big fish returning home to a small pond was not an original one but it would be released in timely fashion for Independence Day 2014 so that it could take advantage of the Fourth of July celebrations. One online reviewer said the film left you feeling 'all swoony' in the end, which was the perfect praise for this type of venture.

Before she could return to normality, Meghan was required to take part in the pre-season publicity for *Suits*, which this year involved a tour of seven leading universities. She was there for events at Harvard, which in the show had turned down Rachel Zane for a place, the University of Boston and a return to Northwestern, a particular highlight for her. She told the students packed into the Ryan Auditorium that she had forgotten what a schlep it was getting from one end of the campus to the other. She recalled the Burger King and the Dance Marathon, prompting co-star Rick Hoffman to spring up and bust a few moves.

Back in Toronto, it was time to take her plans for a new website more seriously. Hers would be an online destination to take advantage of her growing celebrity and promote the three Fs in her life: food, fashion and feminism. Her first task was to decide what to call it. Short, snappy and catchy – that was what Meghan needed.

She remembered an 'ah-ha moment', the time, or more precisely the moment, she had first tasted the gorgeous Italian red wine Tignanello. It's a relatively new blend, mainly Sangiovese, that Meghan tried on a trip to Tuscany where it was first produced in 1971 by the famous house of Antinori.

This is not a wine likely to end up in the bargain shelf of Tesco: you can easily pay £100 for a bottle, especially in a top restaurant. Meghan observed that one sip 'opened up her palate and perspective to wine knowledge'. In other words, she liked it. Such enlightenment would become a 'Tig moment'– the 'now I get it' time when something clicks. It didn't have to be wine, of course, it could be anything.

Tignanello as a name for the website didn't roll off the tongue, but shortening it to The Tig was perfect. Imagine sitting down and devising the very best glossy magazine – that was The Tig. The concept wasn't new but it was trendy at just the right time. Gwyneth Paltrow's famous Goop site had grown from a weekly email about wellbeing to a global lifestyle brand. Many others had jumped on the idea as well: there was Serena's, but also Ellen DeGeneres had ED; Reese Witherspoon's was called Draper James and Jessica Alba fronted The Honest Co.

It was a crowded marketplace and some websites were more overtly commercial than others. In fact, Meghan had first been approached by a company who wanted her to produce that sort of site – a meghanmarkle.com. She ditched that idea because she wanted it to be more than a catalogue. Instead she took advice from one of her new Toronto friends, the photographer Jake Rosenberg, who had been the co-founder of the successful digital media company, Coveteur. He would take many pictures of Meghan for her new venture, but first he linked her with his web designer.

The Tig turned out to be much more than a business venture. Meghan described it as a conversation among girlfriends. At weekends or back in her trailer between scenes on *Suits*, she would sketch out ideas that reflected an articulate, modern woman. She regularly wrote about the things in life that most interested her: as well as food and fashion there were features about travel, the places she had visited, the restaurants she enjoyed, the views that filled her with wonder – all with her personal take on life.

Meghan's ability to confide was a quality that raised The Tig above other online sites. For Father's Day in June 2014, she paid tribute to her dad, who had taken a backseat in her life since she moved to Toronto. She recalled the fishing trips to the beautiful

Big Bear Lake and Kern River in California where they would eat their catch for lunch; or the Saturdays when it was his turn to look after his young daughter and he would dutifully drop her off at ballet and tap classes before the obligatory smoothie treat on the way home; or the times when she was broke and he had filled her beat-up car with petrol so that she could make an audition.

They were the best of times that she was happy to share, describing Tom as a 'thoughtful, inspiring, hardworking Daddy'.

Meghan's blog was far more nuanced than just rose-tinted memories, though. Among the nice words about her dad, she mentioned the incident from school when, curly-haired and freckle-faced, she didn't know which ethnicity box to tick. That encapsulated the appeal of The Tig – an online magazine that was more thoughtful than superficial. She clearly understood that it was not just about having a voice – it's how you use it.

For the most part The Tig was a sunny stroll through Meghan's life – where the fashions were fabulous and the food heavenly. She featured heavily in the many pictures. One day she would be sharing her recipe for *spaghetti alla chitarra*, washed down with a bottle of 'Tig' and dreaming of the view from a terrace in Positano; the next it would be giving her five tips on getting the best out of your meditation time.

If she needed them, she could rely on some premier culinary tips from the new man in her life, Canadian chef and restauranteur, Cory Vitiello, who at this time was probably better known in Toronto than she was. They started dating quietly in May 2014 and were very much a celebrity couple.

Cory was handsome and successful. He was born and brought up in Brantford, a provincial town about a hundred miles south of Toronto where his father Gerry had been a PE teacher. Just like Meghan, he had discovered a love of cooking as a child when he watched his Italian grandmother prepare food and she would let him join in. While his friends were asking for an ice hockey stick for Christmas, he asked his mum and dad for an Easy-Bake Oven.

By fifteen he had decided that a career as a chef was his dream, but he also had an eye for business. He started his first catering company out of his parents' house as a teenager before training properly at the renowned Stratford Chefs School. He served his apprenticeship at the Scaramouche Restaurant, a Toronto institution which served classic European dishes and boasted peerless views of the city at night – not that the kitchen staff saw them.

Cory spent a year in Melbourne, Australia, as a sous-chef, which he described as 'absolutely gruelling', before landing his first senior job back in in his home country as head chef (chef de cuisine) at the chic and arty Drake Hotel on Queen West Street, boasting a stunning roof top terrace that was just the place for Meghan and her new set of friends. Cory's growing reputation in the city was cemented when *enRoute*, the in-flight magazine for Air Canada, named him the best new chef in Toronto in 2009. It was time to open his own restaurants.

One of his ventures was the trendy The Harbord Room, in the neighbourhood of downtown Toronto known as the South Annex, which soon became a magnet for celebrities visiting the city. The restaurant had a nice balance between cosy and cool and the back patio was the place to dine and be seen. Cory was also the chef in demand if there was a prestigious launch to organise. He provided the catering, for instance, when the luxury brand Jimmy Choo launched in the city.

Cory had made the jump from chef to chef-about-town. He was pictured at top social events with the heiress and politician Belinda Stronach before dating the Korean–Canadian TV presenter, Tanya Kim. He was there for the opening of the Soho

House, this time with another glamorous TV host, Mary Kitchen, the entertainment anchor for the local City TV. They shared top guest billing with Ben and Jessica Mulroney.

If there was a society magazine just for Toronto, Cory would have featured in its pages every week. Unsurprisingly, therefore, he was named by *Hello! Canada* as one of the country's most beautiful people, alongside Justin Bieber and Avril Lavigne. He would certainly have been on the radar of Meghan and the rest of the *Suits* gang as they became better known around town.

After a long day's filming, Meghan liked nothing better than to relax with her 'Suits sisters', as she called her friends Sarah Rafferty and Gina Torres, who was then married to the popular actor Laurence Fishburne, star of *CSI: Crime Scene Investigation*. Sometimes Gina, who shared Meghan's love of food, would cook a warming supper, a scrumptious Cuban hash called picadillo. She was born in New York but both her parents hailed from Cuba. Other nights, they would venture out to one of the trendy downtown bars or bistros.

Meghan could walk from Yarmouth Street to South Annex in little more than ten minutes and so one evening they chose to eat at The Harbord Room at a time when Cory was moving between tables, chatting easily to guests and making sure everyone was happy. He made a point of talking to Meghan, particularly when he discovered that they shared a favourite dish, roast chicken.

They exchanged numbers and quickly started dating seriously. Cory was genuinely well liked in Toronto and proud to introduce his stunning new girlfriend to the upper echelons of society, both at home and abroad. Through Cory, Meghan was very much on the social scene. He introduced her to other Soho House regulars, including, most importantly, the man in charge, Markus Anderson.

Meghan formed a long-standing friendship with the supremely well-connected Markus, who had worked his way up from waiter to becoming the membership secretary in London before taking on the role of global consultant. He knew everybody. Markus described his role to Coveteur: 'When Soho House decides to open in a new city, I'm one of the first people sent out to get to know the city, the creatives that live there, and determine who we want to involve in the house.'

Originally from the country town of Peterborough, Ontario, he relocated back to Toronto when that branch was opening in 2012 and the cast of *Suits* were getting to know the city. He was never romantically involved with Meghan but was the ideal companion with whom to share a glass of champagne. She wrote gushingly about him many times in The Tig and on Instagram: 'What would I do without you, my loving, supportive and endlessly fun friend?'

He was there when Cory hosted a party for Meghan at The Harbord Room to celebrate her thirty-third birthday. All her co-stars from *Suits* were there as well as the new friends she had made through Markus and her boyfriend. Perhaps more importantly than a party was Meghan's post on The Tig marking the day. Entitled simply 'Birthday Suit', it featured another Jake Rosenberg photograph teasingly suggesting she was nude. Underneath she had written about her search for identity, the school lunches where she felt she didn't fit in and the wise words from April Webster that changed her life: 'You need to know that you're enough.'

Her birthday wish was dedicated to the women who had become followers of her site. As ever, she addressed them as if they were having lunch: 'I want you to be kind to yourself. I want you to challenge yourself. I want you to stop gossiping, to try a food that scares you, to buy a coffee for someone just because, to tell someone you love them … and to tell yourself right back. I want you to find happiness. I did and it never felt so good.'

Meghan was used to interacting with The Tig readers, sifting through rafts of responses to something she had written. The 'Birthday Suit' was no exception, but the reaction to a post she had written a few weeks before on the Fourth of July would be more significant for Meghan moving forward. Entitled 'Musings on Independence Day', she invited everyone to raise a glass 'to the right to freedom, to the empowerment of the women (and men) who struggle to have it, and to knowing, educating and loving yourself.'

She quoted from a Ted Talk given by the Nigerian writer she much admired, Chimamanda Ngozi Adichie, in which she defined a feminist: 'The person who believes in the social, political and economic equality of the sexes.'

Amid the subsequent positive messages, one email stood out: it was from Elizabeth Nyamayaro, the Senior Advisor to the Executive Director of UN Women, praising her for using her site to highlight important messages for a female audience. The message suggested working together in the future, specifically in connection with their HeForShe campaign that was about to be launched. Meghan thought it was a hoax and had to get in touch with the UN to reassure herself that it was genuine.

She was very excited when she discovered it really was from Elizabeth. This was big news. UN Women was the abbreviated title for the United Nations Entity for Gender Equality and the Empowerment of Women. These were issues closest to Meghan's heart. The relatively new organisation was formed in 2011 when the UN General Assembly noted, 'Women in every part of the world continue to be marginalised from the political sphere, often as a result of discriminatory laws, practices, attitudes and gender stereotypes, low levels of education, lack of access to health care and the disproportionate effect of poverty on women.'

Meghan wanted to be involved but she also wanted to know more, fascinated perhaps for the future at how the corridors of power at the UN worked. She persuaded Elizabeth to let her shadow her in the New York office to see for herself – at her own expense. At least she didn't need to find a new outfit to look the part. She just popped into the costume department of *Suits* and told them she needed something to wear for the United Nations. Fortunately, Rachel Zane's clothes were just right.

The week went well. Meghan was completely absorbed in finding out about the priorities of the organisation, attending morning briefings with the Secretary General, Ban Ki-moon's team and planning how she might become involved. She sat in on a meeting with The Clinton Foundation in New York and another in Washington, DC, at the World Bank headquarters, where she was introduced briefly to Barack Obama. The President's charismatic smile would be duly recorded on The Tig.

The problem for Meghan was one of credibility – why would anyone want to listen to an actor who shared lifestyle tips? Confidence for moving forward came from Emma Watson, the female lead of the Harry Potter films. She gave the keynote address at the launch of HeForShe at the Museum of Modern Art (MoMA) in New York in September 2014. Meghan was sat in a semi-circle of presenters and important guests including the Secretary General, the first female president of Finland, Tarja Halonen and the Executive Director of UN Women, Phumzile Mlambo-Ngcuka.

Emma, already a Goodwill Ambassador for UN Women, gave the sort of rousing speech for which Meghan herself would become renowned. Meghan was impressed with Emma, just twenty-four, pressing the point that gender equality was not just a 'women's issue' but 'everyone's issue'.

The speech was an excellent template for how to construct and deliver a successful speech. It's one Meghan followed and still follows: begin by sharing something relevant and personal – preferably from childhood. In Meghan's case it might be writing to Hillary Clinton about a sexist commercial or the race riots of her childhood. Then, when the audience was onside, deliver some powerful arguments and sound bites that everyone would remember on the way home and the next day on the way to work. Emma left her audience with the emotive phrase 'If not me, who; if not now, when.'

Meghan's 'when' was happening.

14

EMBRACING THE
EXPERIENCE

―――――

Although they were part of the social whirl, Meghan and Cory were not a couple that existed solely for the pleasure of the gossip columns. There are very few pictures taken of them on the town, at some gala or important social function. They were just as likely to be seen strolling hand in hand near her house, walking Bogart or just shopping for groceries in a local supermarket.

After a day's shooting on *Suits*, she had the habit of dropping into The Harbord Room to see Cory. Occasionally she might join him at a dinner party. On days off, they would stay home and cook for each other. Meghan was a talented and enthusiastic foodie but Cory was a professional, passing on culinary tips and recipes for his girlfriend to try. Meghan even toyed with the idea that they could team up for a television cooking programme. She made sure she gave him plenty of name checks in The Tig, declaring that the food at The Harbord Room was 'out of this world'.

While Cory had been hugely helpful with networking in Toronto, Meghan's ambitions now stretched beyond Canada. She has often said that her mother Doria raised her to be a global citizen and that is what she intended to be. She hired her friend

Elizabeth Tuke, who had started her own PR firm Tuke Consulting, to promote her goals. Elizabeth described Meghan as 'a Renaissance woman who deftly juggled the demands of an acting career, her blog and commitments to various Humanitarian organisations.'

She also took on board a high-flying commercial agent from London, Gina Nelthorpe-Cowne. Gina appreciated Meghan's sharp eye for opportunity and astute business brain. She believed she could help build her image as an actor and public figure. She also enjoyed socialising with Meghan, which makes the job of being a representative so much easier. Having a strong roster of clients allowed the Kruger Cowne agency to mix and match them to boost each other as well as promoting special events that the agency was handling at the same time. Meghan was ideal because she brought an American TV presence and, just an importantly, The Tig, which could be of mutual benefit to everyone.

Gina's company was representing the interests of One Young World, a forward-thinking London-based charity that was established in 2009 to reach out to young people, to address global issues and talk about ways to accelerate social impact. It focused on the aspects of modern life that interested Meghan and was a perfect fit to raise her international profile. She was duly added to the panel for the organisation's annual conference in Dublin in October 2014.

The opening ceremony at the Convention Centre in the Irish capital was a rousing affair, more Olympics than sober-suited gathering. Delegates from all around the world entered the arena brandishing their country's flag to the sound of drums and U2. Meghan, in her now familiar crisp white shirt, was on stage with other panellists, including sportsmen Sol Campbell and Boris Becker, who were fellow Kruger Cowne clients. The former

Irish president Mary Robinson sat next to Bob Geldof, another star name on the agency's books, and they both gave keynote addresses.

Meghan was on two panels during the three days of debates. The first was a session entitled 'Bridging the Gender Cap' and the second addressed human rights, focusing on modern-day slavery. To begin with, One Young World co-founder Kate Robertson was unsure how good Meghan would be on a panel or speaking up in a question and answer session. She need not have worried. Meghan was well practised in connecting with a young audience, whether it was at junior graduation or at the Kouros retreat. She knew instinctively how to reach a crowd – displaying a natural empathy while making serious points.

She told the audience that she had become more empowered during her time as a star of *Suits* – so much so that she had rung Aaron Korsh and told him how fed up she was that every episode of the new season seemed to begin with the words 'Rachel enters wearing a towel'. Meghan was adamant that she wasn't going to do it anymore, telling him, 'It's just gratuitous; we get it, we've already seen it once.'

Meghan explained that she had reached the point where she was feeling empowered enough to just say no. She said, 'When you're an auditioning actress, so hungry for work, of course you're willing to do things like that. For me, speaking up and saying, "I'm not going to do that anymore" has been a big shift for me personally.' Aaron agreed with her and decreed no more towels.

She also argued that young women in music videos needed to have a higher value of themselves. She had a point – even the quickest of flips through MTV prove the case that in that world they are lucky to get the towel. Fame and money were giving Meghan a voice, although there was still some way to go. The *Irish Independent* described her as the '*90210* starlet'.

One of the insightful points she made was the need for men to stand up and empower women. It had been part of one of the discussions at the UN when she had been at the headquarters in New York. One initiative mentioned there was a group of CEOs in Australia who refused to speak at any conference unless four female CEOs were also invited to speak, because 'their voice is just as valuable.' Meghan observed, 'You need men to try to effect that change because at the end of the day what scares people is this idea that female empowerment is somehow threatening. No, it's not. You empower the women, you empower the community.'

'She was so eloquent, so erudite,' recalled Kate. 'It wasn't your average actress stepping up and talking about gender equality. It was the real deal – very forthright, very confident and very uncelebrity.'

For her part, Meghan was impressed by the palpable sense of energy among the young delegates, more than a thousand from all over the world who cared so passionately about changing the socio-political landscape for the greater good. The summit represented Meghan's first steps on a global stage – she was discovering that using fame and celebrity in a positive way was one of the best ways of speaking up about issues that really mattered to her.

As an introduction to the discussion on gender, there was a filmed message from Sheryl Sandberg, the chief operating officer of Facebook and one of the most successful businesswomen in the world. She was also the author of a book that Meghan had read called *Lean In: Women, Work and the Will to Lead*, a number one bestseller in the US when it was published in March 2013. Subsequently it has sold more than four million copies.

Sheryl used the phrase 'Lean In' to argue that women should be more assertive in the workplace. She also started the Lean In

Foundation, a non-profit organisation dedicated to 'offering women the ongoing inspiration and support to help them achieve their goals'. This was just the sort of ideal that inspired Meghan.

One of the women of high achievement quoted in *Lean In* was the former Secretary of State Madeleine Albright, who had said during a speech a year earlier, 'There's a special place in hell for women who don't help each other.' Meghan was a huge admirer of the woman who had navigated her way around the corridors of power in Washington to reach the highest echelons of the Clinton administration.

She included Madeleine in her list of the ten women who had changed her life. Meghan wrote, 'She was the first female Secretary of State for the US, the US Ambassador to the UN, an author, and a mom – and she seemingly juggled it all with finesse.' She also confessed that if she were put in a room with the formidable achiever: 'For once in my life, you'll find this girl with the gift of the gab unequivocally without words.'

Rather like the Olympics, cities were invited to bid for the honour of holding a One Young World summit. Before the Dublin event was over, the 2016 event was awarded to Ottawa, much closer to home for Meghan and an event with which she intended to become involved. By that time she was much better known, described by the organisers of the event as an actor *and* activist.

A couple of weeks later, she was still buzzing from her One Young World experience when she and Cory flew to Miami for the Art Basel festival, one of the most prestigious art fairs in the world. The three-day extravaganza is a huge social event in the international calendar, where you might rub shoulders with Tracey Emin or Marc Jacobs at the same party.

One-year-old Meghan is having a lovely time at a family picnic with mum Doria in the summer of 1982.

An early Meghan hug – for her favourite Rainbow Brite doll.

Meghan was always photogenic, even as a child chilling on the bed at home.

Even though her parents split when she was two, growing up she saw lots of her dad, Tom.

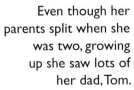

Meghan, aged twelve, out horse riding with her dad at Big Bear Lake, a resort ninety miles northeast of Los Angeles, in the San Bernardino Mountains.

Because of her natural empathy, Meghan was chosen as a team leader for the Kairos spring retreat during her senior year at the Immaculate Heart High School.

Meghan is joined by her proud mum to celebrate her graduation from Northwestern University in 2003 with a double major in theatre and international studies.

Fact: happy times with her first husband, Trevor Engelson, at their wedding in Ocho Rios, Jamaica, in 2011.

Fiction: in *Suits* the course of true love was not running smoothly for Mike Ross and Rachel Zane.

Fact: in the company of two of her favourite men; Meghan joins boyfriend Cory Vitiello (left) and Markus Anderson, the global consultant of Soho House, at a party celebrating Art Basel in Miami, 2014.

Fiction: enjoying a glass of red wine in the 2016 film *Dater's Handbook*.

Simply Meghan – her natural beauty is captured by the
Toronto-based photographer Janick Laurent in 2015.

Four of the best Meghan hugs: five-year-old Luke is treated to a Meghan squeeze at Dubbo Airport, New South Wales, Australia, in October 2018.

Meghan thanks Luyanda, aged eight, who has presented her with flowers when she arrives at ActionAid in Johannesburg on the autumn royal tour of South Africa, 2019.

Putting her arm around a surf mentor when she visits the Waves for Change mental health charity at Monwabisi Beach in Cape Town.

Meghan embraces designer Misha Nonoo at the launch of the Smart Works capsule collection on the rooftop of John Lewis, Oxford Street, London, in September 2019.

Making friends easily – Meghan shares a hilarious story with tennis great Serena Williams and swimsuit model Hannah Davis at a charity flag football event in Manhattan, February 2014.

Out and about in New York City with *Suits* pal Abigail Spencer during Meghan's baby shower weekend in February 2019.

Meghan has a giggle with two of her oldest friends, Genevieve Hillis (left) and Lindsay Roth, at Wimbledon in July 2019. They were courtside to cheer on Serena, who won a second-round match.

Meghan has long been an accomplished public speaker: she is composed at the closing ceremony of the Invictus Games in Sydney, October 2018.

Meghan is all smiles speaking in front of a portrait of the Queen at a reception in Government House, Wellington, to celebrate 125 years of women's suffrage in New Zealand.

During her farewell tour of the UK she is committed to empowerment for women while addressing pupils at the Robert Clack School in Dagenham, March 2020.

Meghan cuddles baby son Archie while watching Prince Harry play polo in Wokingham, Berkshire, in July 2019.

Dancing the day away with Harry and the women of the Justice Desk initiative in Nyanga township, Cape Town, before she made her famous speech, addressing her audience as a 'woman of colour'.

Harry and Meghan – the look of love.

Many of the big parties were held at the Soho Beach House and Markus Anderson was heavily involved in sorting out guest lists and making sure everything went smoothly.

At one lunch, Markus had placed Meghan next to another close friend, an up-and-coming fashion designer called Misha Nonoo. The two women became instant best friends. Misha, blonde and very elegant, grew up in London but was born in Bahrain to an English mother and an Iraqi–Jewish father. They were members of a prominent Jewish family in the Gulf kingdom.

Nobody pronounces her second name correctly at first. It's 'Noo-Noo' and roughly translates from the Arabic as 'little one'. After a few pleasantries, Meghan told Misha she had just been to Dublin and chatted about the debate on gender equality. The designer, it was clear, was a kindred spirit, who also had a similar self-deprecating nature. Misha recalled, 'We talked about a shared passion for equality, women's empowerment ... and our love of dogs.'

They met up again at a beach party when Misha was with her then-husband, the old Etonian auctioneer and businessman Alexander Gilkes. At the time, his online auction site, Paddle8, employed Princess Eugenie, who had moved to New York for a couple of years. More intriguingly, he had been a guest at the wedding of Prince William and Kate Middleton, and was an old friend of Prince Harry, despite being a few years' older. It really was a small world at the top of high society.

Meghan, who wrote all of The Tig's posts herself, would often include pieces about her friends, telling the world about their latest projects. Misha was no exception. Meghan revealed how they had sipped cocktails and danced the night away. She was 'the kind of woman you instantly adore,' she said.

In the future, Misha would become a loyal fixture on Team Meghan. Even though she had already been a finalist in the

Council of Fashion Designer of America (CFDA)/Vogue Fashion Fund annual award, it was her association with Meghan that made her world famous. She split abruptly from Alexander in 2016 and they divorced after four years of marriage. He is now the partner of the tennis player Maria Sharapova.

Meghan's social circle may have been a small world but she was about to experience the bigger global picture. The day after leaving Miami she joined a group of US celebrities at a military facility in Maryland to set off on an entirely new adventure – entertaining American troops abroad.

Meghan was one of a magnificent seven who met up at the Joint Base Andrews passenger terminal to fly to five different countries in as many days to put on shows as part of the USO Holiday Tour to cheer up the service personnel who would not be home for Christmas. One of the others was a new friend, the actress Dianna Agron, a star of the TV series *Glee*. They had met over cocktails the previous year in New York and had stayed in touch. Meghan described her as possessing 'equal part charm and salt of the earth kindness' and had featured her in a Tig Talk in the summer.

The other well-known American names on the trip included country singer Kellie Pickler, a past winner of *Dancing with the Stars*; her songwriter husband Kyle Jacobs; comedian Rob Riggle; Washington Nationals baseball pitcher Doug Fister and the former Chicago Bears linebacker Brian Urlacher. They were escorted by the Chairman of the Joint Chiefs of Staff, General Martin E. Dempsey and his wife Deanie. She told the entertainment squad, 'Embrace this experience, you will be so proud of our service members and their families.'

They flew to the US naval base in Rota, northern Spain, on a Boeing plane that's known as Airforce 2 when the US Vice President is on board. They moved on to meet troops in Italy,

Turkey and Afghanistan – where they put on a show in a hangar at Bagram Airfield. While this was not the front line of the conflict in the war-torn country, it was still a military base and the show went on while fighter jets taxied outside.

Meghan's role was one that many TV and film stars had fulfilled over the years – greet the serving men and women with a cheery smile and a sympathetic ear and meet as many of them as possible. She posed for selfies and joined the others for seasonal singalongs. She didn't have to be Hollywood glamorous – jeans and a sweater with a baseball cap or a Santa hat was the dress code, although she had packed some of Rachel Zane's killer heels for the trip. She was good at improving the mood in any situation, observing, 'I have always had such a profound respect for our nation's troops and military families. I cannot thank them enough for everything they do for us.'

The last stop before the flight home was at the Lakenheath air force base in Suffolk and a toast to a job well done in The Anchor pub in Cambridge. Finally, Meghan could return to Toronto, put her feet up and enjoy some quiet time with Cory. She acquired a second dog. She had decided that Bogs might like a companion, especially as she was travelling so much, although 'Uncle' Markus was always available for dog-sitting duties. She saw an advertisement for a sweet-looking beagle in a rescue centre in Kentucky and thought he would be perfect.

When the dog arrived in Canada, she realised that he didn't have a name – the only reference on his paperwork said 'little guy'. He didn't respond to any of the names she tried so, in the end, she just called out to him 'little guy' and his ears pricked up. 'Your name will be Guy,' she told the new addition. Best of all, he and Bogs became 'thick as thieves' and from then on The Tig was full of pictures of her two dogs looking cute together.

She took both of them with her for Christmas when she and Cory went to stay with his mum and dad. His Swedish-born mother, Joanne, was taken aback when Bogs and Guy showed up but the pets were on their best behaviour and the two women got along famously.

2014 had been a year when Meghan had begun to announce herself on a world stage. The following year promised a bigger role.

15

THE LION'S ROAR

On the dusty road back to the Rwandan capital of Kigali, Meghan faced a dilemma. She had seen for herself the hardship in the Gihembe Refugee Camp and now, tired and hot in the back of a van, she read an email from her management company saying she had received an invitation to the 2015 Baftas. Normally, she would have punched the air, but not this time.

Admittedly, it wasn't an acting invite connected to *Suits* but one from a high-end jewellery company. The idea was for Meghan to jet off from Kigali airport to Heathrow, be whisked straight to a fitting for an exclusive designer dress, then hair and makeup before arriving on the red carpet outside the Royal Opera House where that year's British Academy Film Awards were being held. Her jewellery would be waved prominently for the camera.

She had always wanted to attend one of the great nights of cinema but here she was completing a mission to the small East African country. For seven days she had seen for herself the effect female empowerment might have on a struggling nation. She had meetings and long discussions with the leading female members of parliament. Rwanda was the first country in the world where women held a majority in government.

She travelled the fifty miles to Gihembe to meet local leaders battling to improve living conditions for many thousands of Congolese refugees who had fled the dreadful conflicts and genocide that had blighted the region in previous years. It was a sobering experience and a million miles away from the champagne and congratulations of an awards night.

Meghan looked out of the window as they bumped along, gazing at the rolling fields and the farmers diligently tending to their goats. 'It was a bucolic bliss,' she later wrote in *Elle*, one of a number of serious articles she provided for that particular magazine. Meghan realised she had to turn down the polished glamour of the Baftas: '"No", my heart said. And it wasn't a soft whisper; it was a lion's roar.'

Meghan understood that her life was a delicate balance between feminine and feminism. She did not see them as mutually exclusive and knew The Tig would get more clicks if she recommended a lip gloss than when she wrote about the more serious things that mattered to her. She called it a swinging pendulum that moved from Hollywood fantasy to third-world reality.

She was in serious mode when she cemented her association with UN Women by appearing in a short advertisement that the organisation used in social media to emphasise how working women around the world were leaders in waiting. It proclaimed, 'We see potential leaders everywhere.' Meghan appeared at the end scribbling some notes as the anthemic 'Spectrum (Say My Name)' by Florence and The Machine blasted out. 'It's time for more women to see it for themselves; Nominate A Woman in your Life,' was the rallying call.

Meghan had vowed to return to Rwanda, a country that she would reference in one of her famous speeches when she addressed a UN Women conference later in the year. The title of the New York event on 8 March 2015 was the '20th Anniversary of the Fourth World Conference of Women in Beijing', which did not trip off the tongue. Twenty years earlier that event had heard one of the epic speeches of modern times, a tour de force from the First Lady, Hillary Clinton. Her thoughts on freedom speak through the generations: 'Freedom means the right of people to assemble, organise, and debate openly. It means respecting the views of those of their governments. It means not taking citizens away from their loved ones and jailing them, mistreating them, or denying them their freedom or dignity because of the peaceful expression of their ideas and opinions.'

Mrs Clinton argued powerfully for the human rights of women all over the world, ending her address: 'As long as discrimination and inequalities remain so commonplace around the world – as long as girls and women are valued less, fed less, fed last, overworked, underpaid, not schooled and subjected to violence in and out of their homes – the potential of the human family to create a peaceful, prosperous world will not be realised.'

Meghan was a huge Hillary fan and, unsurprisingly, was firmly in her camp during the following year's US Presidential election, which she lost narrowly to Donald Trump. She had included the #ImWithHer hashtag on her Twitter page. Now she had to channel her inner Hillary for her own speech in front of a distinguished audience at the UN Headquarters in New York that included Ban Ki-moon and Phumzile Mlambo-Ngcuka. This was daunting even for an experienced actor.

Her preparation did not go well. She could not find the right outfit – again! All men have to do is to decide on the colour of their tie but Meghan wanted a look that conveyed strength and intelligence, and looked good. Fortunately, her publicist, Elizabeth Tuke, was available to step in as an unofficial stylist. She dashed home and grabbed a Preen-designed black tea-length dress from her own closet. Meghan tried it on and to their delight it fitted perfectly. The portrait neckline was simple and unfussy. As Elizabeth recalled proudly, 'The speech – and my dress that she wore to deliver it – became a defining moment for her.'

Meghan was introduced on stage as an 'American TV and film actress and UN Women's advocate for political participation and leadership'. After a thin, nervous-sounding aside about good evening really sounding better as great evening, Meghan announced, 'I am proud to be a woman and a feminist' and received a round of applause.

She told the guests about writing to Hillary Clinton when she was eleven and persuading Procter & Gamble to change their commercial tagline from 'Women all over America are fighting pots and pans' to 'People over America'. She talked about her trip to the refugee camp in Rwanda and praised that country's President Kagame as a role model for encouraging female leaders in parliament. She also commended her dad for championing her eleven-year-old self and standing up for what is right.

Among these positive words was the grim reality that in the last twenty years – since Hillary's speech – the percentage of female parliamentarians globally had only increased by eleven per cent, still less than twenty-three per cent, a shameful statistic considering that women make up more than half of the world's population. 'Come on,' implored Meghan, adding, 'This has to change.'

She ended her address with a rallying call, 'Women need a seat at the table, they need an invitation to be seated there, and in some cases, where this is not available, then you know what, they need to create their own table.' The words resonated with her schooldays when her father encouraged her to draw her own ethnicity box, in other words: taking action and responsibility yourself.

When she left Immaculate Heart sixteen years before, she looked to Eleanor Roosevelt for her graduation quote in the High School Yearbook. Now she returned to the distinguished former first lady, fashioning her famous sentiments of 1951 on peace into a rousing finale. Meghan substituted the word equality for peace: 'It is said that girls with dreams become women with vision. May we empower each other to carry out such vision – because it isn't enough to simply talk about equality. One must believe it. And it isn't enough to simply believe in it. One must work at it. Let us work at it. Together. Starting now.'

Ban Ki-moon immediately got up out of his chair to lead a standing ovation for Meghan – an amazing achievement for someone who the year before had starred in an inconsequential movie called *When Sparks Fly*. This is what Meghan meant when she declared that she wanted to be an actor and an activist.

Up until this point her activism had centred on the empowerment of women, but in July 2015, she wrote a now famous article for *Elle* magazine entitled 'I'm More than an Other' about finding her voice as a mixed-race woman. As well as relating her personal history of ethnic ambiguity, as she called it, she highlighted the undercurrent of racism that is 'so prevalent, especially within America'. She was saddened by the then-recent racial unrest in Baltimore sparked when a black man, Freddie Gray, had died from a spinal cord injury while in police custody; and in Ferguson, Missouri, where a year before an unarmed black teenager, Michael Brown, was shot dead by a white police officer. Meghan observed that tensions that have 'long been percolating under the surface in the US have boiled over in the most saddening way'.

Five years before the now-infamous killing of George Floyd, she concluded prophetically that America had 'perhaps only placed bandages over the problems that have never healed at the root'.

Perhaps, just as incisively considering the British attitudes she would later have to confront, she drew attention to the casual racism that is so prevalent it almost goes unnoticed by those men and women who do not start each day as people of colour. She called out those that always led with ethnic descriptions such as 'that black guy Tom' rather than just describing someone as a guy who works at 'blah blah' and dates 'fill in the blank' girl.

Meghan didn't spend every waking moment, of course, immersed in good causes. There was still the day job. Without *Suits* and the movie career she was progressing, her public profile would have shrunk dramatically: the bigger the fame, the louder the voice – not that the release of *Anti-Social* did much to increase public interest or critical presence. *Time Out* called it 'another fa-a-h-kin London gangster film'. The magazine did not even mention Meghan by name, which perhaps was a relief, although worryingly it said it was vile about women. The *Radio Times* noted the 'one-note flimsiness of the plastic plot'.

Meghan would not have been paid a fortune for it but she was already a millionaire thanks to *Suits*, which was still ticking along nicely and showed no sign of slowing down. The long-running show had reached Season 5 and Rachel was planning her wedding to Mike. In real life, there was no indication that Meghan was planning a second marriage.

Her life was reasonably settled when she was filming: her morning routine would be to take Bogs and Guy for a walk before heading off to the studio – provided she wasn't being picked up at 4.15am, then it was no walkies. She always found time for yoga two or three times a week, especially now she was running less – the years of pounding pavements had not been beneficial to her knees, which were becoming creaky.

Occasionally her attention would be drawn to a local project that didn't require travelling halfway round the world. She was the guest speaker at a workshop sponsored by the recently launched Dove Self-Esteem Project, a global initiative aimed at improving girls' view of themselves and their worth to society. She told the one hundred or so teachers, community workers and youth counsellors about her own struggles to fit in as a youngster, joining every lunchtime club so that she wouldn't have to eat her school lunch alone.

In particular, she praised the 'amazing' teachers at Immaculate Heart who advised her that she was valuable to each and every one of the clubs she joined. 'They bolstered my self-esteem,' she said, simply. She also warned against believing too much in the smoke and mirrors of celebrity. Rachel Zane, so polished and 'put together', was not real: it took two hours of hair, makeup and Spanx for Meghan to emerge as her *Suits* character. Girls needed to know, she stressed, that 'in real life that is not what it looks like'.

Meghan Markle was quite clear in her view that she did not want to be the kind of actor who went on social media to say 'look at these great shoes I got'. Her dilemma, especially as she loved fashion so much, was balancing that ambition with her celebrity as a TV star who swanned around a fictitious office in *Suits* wearing top-of-the-range designer outfits. She would laugh about it: 'There's a lot of Tom Ford because, as all paralegals do, she wears a Tom Ford skirt to the office.'

She was now so well known in Toronto she faced the everyday fact of life for celebrities – especially those playing a character on TV – that passers-by think they know you. Meghan would be stopped in the street and asked what was that skirt that she wearing in last week's show. Following the mantra of *Baywatch* star Yasmine Bleeth from all those years ago, she would be patient and friendly and reveal it was a Tom Ford design: 'You don't really want to know that it was a $5,000 skirt and I don't get to keep it.'

Meghan's – or more precisely Rachel Zane's style – evolved through the *Suits* years. She was discovering what worked best for her and her hourglass figure. Fashion commentator Alison Jane Reid described her wardrobe as a perfect example of an 'investment dresser' – body-hugging skirts with cropped tops or soft sweaters and tailored white shirts. Alison Jane explained, 'It's also important to look like you haven't tried too hard, but that your clothes are reassuringly and terrifyingly expensive.'

The colours Rachel wore would depend on her mood. When she was stressed, she would turn up to the Pearson Hardman offices in black or dark grey; but if she was feeling happy and in love with Mike Ross, she would slip on a lighter pastel shade. And then there were always the eye-catching sky-high court shoes. 'The killer heels are very important as they are a look-at-me, impractical yet fabulous status symbol of wealth and power – and being able to take cabs everywhere,' observed Alison Jane.

Meghan found a kindred fashion spirit in *Suits* costume designer Jolie Andreatta. They loved Rachel's clothes, declaring they could live in Ms Zane's outfits. Jolie enthused, 'Designing Rachel's look was like being a kid in a candy store.'

Inevitably, considering her fashion exposure on the programme and on The Tig, Meghan was approached to be the face of a new campaign. It wasn't by Tom Ford or any of the other designer labels she wore as Rachel, including Nina Ricci, Le Kasha, The Row, Prada or Burberry. She was asked to be a brand ambassador for Reitmans, one of the best-known clothing chains in Canada.

You might well see a Reitmans store in any Canadian shopping mall you visit. Pronounced *Reetmans*, it has become an institution since being founded in Montreal in 1926. There are hundreds of them – ubiquitous in the way Marks & Spencer is in the UK. And like M&S, the brand is constantly fighting a battle to keep older customers happy while trying to attract younger buyers. Meghan was a young-looking and glamorous thirty-four, who could appeal to any age. She could look a million dollars in clothes that did not cost more than $100.

Meghan said all the right things when she signed up in August 2015. 'Reitmans is perfect for the affordable and chic pieces that I absolutely love.' One attractive element of the new deal was the opportunity in the near future for Meghan to front her own-name brand throughout the stores. She would also star in a television campaign.

The commercials basically followed the same theme. Meghan would enter a trendy bar and restaurant looking fabulous and be recognised: 'It's Meghan Markle', they would whisper while trying to work out what very fashionable label she was wearing. Meghan, overhearing, would turn round and declare: 'Ladies, it's Reitmans … Really', implying that you could look as good as she did if you popped to the mall tomorrow and shopped at the store.

Meghan's ex-husband, Trevor Engelson, had once declared that Meghan was 'a big deal' and she was finally proving the point. Her relationship with Cory was ongoing but he too was branching out from the kitchen and increasing his national presence through television.

He starred as one of four celebrity chefs in a TV series called *Chef in Your Ear*, a laboured idea in which the chefs could only communicate with rookie contestants via an earpiece. Cory and the other professionals had to show off their communication skills more than their culinary ones. While it was good publicity for his restaurants, the show only ran for one season.

Inevitably, the couple were leading more separate lives. During the year, Meghan had travelled solo to the Mediterranean islands of Malta and Gozo, at the invitation of *Elle* to explore some of the European heritage of her father. She discovered that her great-great grandmother Mary Bird was from Valletta. She was able to explore the island by bicycle with Gina Nelthorpe-Cowne, reporting back for The Tig that she loved Gozo's 'bucolic bliss' and posting a photo of a herd of goats.

She also travelled solo to Istanbul to support Markus at the opening of a new Soho House in the city, where fellow guests included the Oscar-winning actor, Eddie Redmayne, who had been a classmate of Prince William at Eton and played rugby with him. Of course, this meant he had been at the famous public school at the same time as Harry, but a couple of years above the younger prince.

Istanbul was just one of many memorable destinations that Meghan had visited around the world – from Marrakech in Morocco, to Iceland to see the Northern Lights and a glorious trip in a camper van around New Zealand where she swam with dolphins and drank Sauvignon blanc. She was so impressed with that particular country that she wrote a 'love letter to all things Kiwi' in The Tig.

Meghan could have bundled up all her travel pieces into a book – *The Tig Guide to the World*. Before the end of the year she was back to Vancouver, this time to shoot her second Hallmark TV movie, *Dater's Handbook*. Again, she had the starring role. She played Cassandra Brand, a successful marketing executive whose private life is going nowhere.

She comes across a self-help book entitled *The Dater's Handbook* by Doctor Susie and decides to follow its advice to sort out her disastrous love life. She has to choose between two men: the dependable, boring one who takes her to a classical concert and corrects her table manners or the fun-loving fan of rock band REO Speedwagon who joins her for ten-pin bowling and a round of crazy golf.

This was a heartwarming, snugly story for Valentine's Day, so no prizes for guessing who she chooses. In her promotional video, Meghan said, 'It makes everyone feel good,' except, presumably, anybody who recognises themselves as being a bit boring. The moral of the story was that it's best to find someone who loves you for the person you really are and not for who you are pretending to be.

One bonus of filming in and around Vancouver was that her *Suits* co-star Sarah Rafferty was making a movie there at the same time, so the two friends were able to keep each other company over dinners in the city, including celebrating Sarah's forty-fourth birthday. She too was making a film for Hallmark, called, unsubtly, *All Things Valentine*.

Both films would be shown on television in the days immediately before 14 February to take advantage of romance in the air. Ironically Meghan didn't spend the special day with Cory. Instead, she was with friends on the lower East Side of New York, 'flying solo', as she put it.

It wouldn't be long, though, before Meghan needed a new love in her life; but she wouldn't turn to *The Dater's Handbook* when she found him.

Cory was still around to give her an enthusiastic shout-out when she was chosen as a global ambassador for the charity World Vision Canada in March 2016. He posted, 'So proud of my lady Meghan Markle being named Ambassador for World Vision.' Her new role meant that she would once again be leaving Toronto, on this occasion keeping a promise to herself and returning to Rwanda. She was part of a learning mission gathering insight and publicity for the organisation's Clean Water Campaign. Meghan warmly hugged the children at a refugee camp and at a school, calling the experience 'as inspiring and affirming as you can imagine'. She was particularly moved by one girl who would, uncomplaining, walk three hours to collect some medicine for her father.

Meghan saw firsthand the impact that clean water has on the lives of children and communities in Africa. She visited the Mbandazi Primary school, a village near the capital, Kigali, where World Vision had built water wells and latrines. She understood that access to clean water was not just about providing the water itself. She observed, 'It's much more than that. Access to clean water in a community keeps young girls in school because they aren't walking hours each day to source water for their families.' She understood that clean water, a basic life source, was the key to a better life for children and adults in this part of Africa.

One visit from a celebrity cannot change the world but it can draw attention to a cause that needs action. Nicaise Ugabinema, a co-ordinator for World Vision Rwanda, said they would always remember Meghan's face 'full of compassion and empathy when she was looking at children fetching unclean water'. Her impact combined with contributions from others raised funds that allowed the charity to support nearly 60,000 people with clean water.

Her experience on a trip such as this brought home to Meghan what was truly important in the world. Away from the superficial and superfluous demands of the entertainment industry, it was a chance to redefine what she called 'my barometer of what is valuable'. She said her friends noticed that in the photographs she showed them she looked genuinely happy. She admitted, 'It's a different smile than the one for the paparazzi.'

While at the school, Meghan had given the children a lesson in how to paint with watercolours, using water from a newly installed pipeline in their community. She encouraged the young students to paint pictures of what they wanted to be when they grew up. Their work was collected and Meghan took it back with her to Toronto, where it would form part of a World Water Day event later in March 2016, called The Watercolour Project. The exhibition hosted by Meghan at the LUMAS Gallery raised $15,000, which allowed World Vision to build a new water source in Rwanda.

The publicity for The Watercolour Project described Meghan Markle as an 'actor and an activist'. It had been a long haul from clambering through the boot of her car so she could make an audition in Hollywood to speaking at a UN conference about female empowerment and making a difference to the lives of children in Rwanda. She had found her voice entirely by herself and not by clinging to the coattails of others. As yet, she had no connection whatsoever to the Royal Family. That was about to change.

PART THREE

TO BE CONTINUED …

16

THE ONE

Traditionally the Royal Family are not expected to voice any political views or opinions. That didn't matter to Meghan, who was still nowhere near The Firm when she was in New York in May 2016 to guest on Comedy Central's satirical *The Nightly Show with Larry Wilmore*. She was one of the panel in a round-table forum discussing Donald Trump, who was running for the presidency against Hillary Clinton.

Meghan didn't hold back, describing the future Potus as 'divisive' and 'misogynistic'. This wasn't exactly a big talk show like those hosted by James Corden or Jimmy Kimmel, but it did give her the chance to make her views on the candidate perfectly plain: 'You are not just voting for Hillary because she is a woman. You are voting because Trump has made it easy to see you don't want the kind of world he is painting.'

Back in Toronto, she was single again. She and Cory had seen little of each other over the past few months and now was the right time to go their separate ways. He was very discrete about Meghan, limiting himself to just a few complimentary remarks, stressing that there was no bitterness and he had a lot of respect for his ex-girlfriend. 'She's a great girl' is the most he has had to say. His mother, Joanne, may have been disappointed that things didn't work out for them but she has spoken warmly about Meghan, describing her as a lovely, very sincere woman.

In the future, Cory would be offered vast sums of money by the UK tabloid newspapers to reveal the complete story of their relationship, but to his credit he has always turned them down. He was still very much part of Toronto's higher social scene and would quickly have been ejected from that sphere if he had blabbed. You won't be invited for a glass of wine in Soho House with Canadian premier Justin Trudeau and his wife, Sophie Grégoire, if you are going to reveal your conversation to the world the following day.

Sophie had only been Canada's first lady for a year. In the small world of Toronto, she was advised on style by Meghan's friend Jessica Mulroney. They had known each other for some years; Jessica's husband Ben had introduced them when Sophie had worked as a presenter for eTalk. With Meghan in tow, the three women would cut a very fashionable trio enjoying cocktails on the roof terrace. They also shared an enthusiasm for yoga. Sophie, like Meghan's mother, was a qualified instructor. Jessica, now a mum of three, preferred to call herself her fashion strategist rather than her stylist.

The important criterion for both ladies was to promote Canadian labels. Sophie wore Sentaler coats at her husband's swearing-in ceremony in November 2015 and again when they met the Queen at Buckingham Palace later that month. The luxury outerwear label would receive even more of a boost when Kate Middleton wore one of the coats during a royal tour of Canada in September 2016.

Meghan had discovered the Serbian-born designer's coats independently in the early days of *Suits* but had struck up a friendship with Bojana Sentaler through Jessica. The unforgettable wide-collar wrap coat in camel she wore for the traditional

Christmas church service at Sandringham in 2017 was a classic. The 'Meghan coat', as it became known, sold out instantly.

She was taking small steps in the fashion world herself with her first Meghan Markle Spring Collection for Reitmans. She was helping to design four distinct pieces that reflected her own personal style. Meghan did not have the sort of personality that allowed her to swan about taking credit while someone else did all the work.

The first design was called The Soiree and was a Rachel Zane-inspired little black dress for an adventurous evening out; the second was The Sunset, a cool long dress for a Hollywood evening – perhaps on Sunset Boulevard; the third was simply Date Night, a 'flirty' and bold red mini that Meghan might wear if she ever had another date – Alison Jane Reid thought it 'divinely feminine, sensuous and sexy and yet demure'. Finally, there was The Terrace, a white version of the LBD, a sleeveless number for those cocktails on the terrace.

Alison Jane observed, 'This is Meghan's go-to wardrobe. It can be hard to make mid-market fashion look seriously covetable, but she pulls it off because the pieces reflect her authentic personal style.' Meghan modelled all the dresses and, as ever, looked ten years younger than a woman approaching her thirty-fifth birthday. The line virtually sold out overnight.

Meghan prepared to fly solo again – this time to London where she would hook up with Gina Nelthorpe-Cowne and take part in some new season promotional work for *Suits* and for the high-end designer label Ralph Lauren, which had a VIP Lounge at Wimbledon. She was planning to watch her friend Serena Williams play. The trip would also be a chance to do some more networking.

One of the strategies Meghan used to boost her profile was putting herself next to a famous person; they could both benefit from the resulting publicity. This approach had worked well, for instance, when she was photographed with the champion Irish golfer, Rory McIlroy. He poured cold water over her as part of the ALS ice bucket challenge that was very fashionable for a while. Rory had nominated Meghan, which meant he was the one throwing the water and she was the one getting drenched.

They were both in New York at the time and chose the roof terrace on top of Misha Nonoo's apartment building as the location. Meghan, wearing shorts and a denim shirt, shrieked as she was soaked but managed a laugh for the cameras. The challenge helped to raise awareness for ALS, a progressive neuro-degenerative disease.

As usual with these celebrity get togethers, there was no romance, even though Meghan and Rory were pictured later having dinner together at a New York restaurant. The friends who had joined them for the evening were not included in the paparazzi snaps: more good publicity.

Meghan never minded cold-messaging someone. She was an old hand at using social media to reach out. She had done so boldly when starting The Tig and making contact with super-model Heidi Klum, who she had never met. Heidi responded positively and Meghan featured her online in one of the first 'Tig Talks', describing the mother of four as a 'megahouse role model who used her beauty to open doors, and stayed in those rooms because of her wit, intelligence and inimitable personality.'

In 2015, she struck up an online conversation with former *X Factor* winner Matt Cardle. They had followed each other on Twitter and he later revealed she sent him a few DMs saying she was a big fan of his, in the hope of getting a response. They exchanged a couple of messages and, reportedly, Meghan suggested they meet up but that never happened.

She used the same gambit on TV personality Piers Morgan, who by coincidence was another speaker on the books of Kruger Cowne. Again, she had been in touch when they followed each other on Twitter. He followed several of the stars of *Suits*, including Rick Hoffman and Gabriel Macht. Meghan sent him a DM, which, he later revealed to the world, said: 'Well hello there – thanks for the follow. Big fan of yours!'

She may or may not have actually been a fan but she obtained the right response and the two exchanged occasional messages over the coming months. According to Piers, Meghan sent him some episodes of *Suits* before they were broadcast and they traded funny messages. He also had some jokey exchanges with Rick and he sent both actors the same message after watching Season 4 of the show. It said: 'Wowza.'

Piers would certainly have been on both Meghan and the show's radar as a person who might be useful for publicity in the UK. In the US, he had been a judge on *America's Got Talent*, appeared alongside Donald Trump on *The Apprentice* and hosted his own nightly talk show on CNN. The latter was axed because of poor ratings in 2014, although the network also had to formally deny his dismissal had anything to do with phone-hacking allegations.

When she arrived in London, Meghan sent Piers, now a presenter of daytime television and a newspaper columnist, a message: 'Hey, I'm in town, do you want to meet up?' Piers said he responded, 'Sure, come to my local pub.'

According to Piers, they spent two hours in the Scarsdale Tavern, a cosy pub near his five-bedroom townhouse in Holland Park, which he bought for a reported £4 million pounds in 2009. Meghan declined the offer of a pint of his favourite London Pride in favour of a couple of dirty vodka martinis. 'We got on brilliantly,' he later recalled.

As she clambered into an Uber and left Piers on the best of terms, she thought it had been a successful evening and could not possibly have known that within three years he would have become one of the leaders of the anti–Meghan chorus, changing his glowing description of her from 'fabulous, warm, funny, intelligent and highly entertaining' to 'a piece of work'.

One of the confidences that Piers later revealed about their conversation was that Meghan told him she was out of practice with the dating scene. She wasn't the only one. Prince Harry could not get a date. Quite simply, he was the most eligible bachelor in the country – probably the world – so popping up on Tinder to swipe right was not an option. Harry really wanted to meet someone special and settle down. His days of being a teenage tearaway were long gone.

He had been a young man traumatised by the tragic death of his mother and who had said and done a few things in the past that had received front-page coverage in the tabloid papers. He was only twelve and asleep in his bedroom at Balmoral when his father and elder brother woke him with the news that his mum was dead. All three could be heard sobbing down the corridors of the Scottish castle.

The world missed a heartbeat when Diana died. She was thirty-six. Her premature death would guarantee her immortality in much the same way it had Marilyn Monroe, James Dean and John Lennon. They never grow old; their youthful images remain forever frozen in the collective mind.

To say that Harry and William were devastated is inadequate. The emotional difficulty for the two boys was made much worse by the absurd if understandable level of public fascination with their private grief. They were never left alone to mourn.

Harry explained what it had been like to NBC's Matt Lauer: 'When she passed away there was never that time, there was never that sort of lull. There was never that peace and quiet for any of us due to the fact that her face was splattered in the paper the whole time.'

The events of that fateful August night in Paris are well known. Diana, her lover Dodi Fayed and her personal bodyguard were in a black Mercedes that was driven at furious speed through a tunnel by a chauffeur, Henri Paul. They were being pursued by a posse of paparazzi when Monsieur Paul, whose blood contained more than the permitted level of alcohol, crashed into a pillar. Only the bodyguard survived.

Nearly a week passed before the Queen eventually addressed the nation and told the world of her family's grief and acknowledged the public despair. She had been urged to do so by the Prime Minister, Tony Blair, who had called Diana the 'People's Princess' when he had spoken on television the day after the tragedy. He described the Royal Family's reluctance to speak publically about her death as 'bizarre'.

In reality, Diana had been cut adrift by the Royal Family and hasty declarations of sadness might have seemed the height of hypocrisy. In any case, they didn't do public tears, preferring a stiff upper lip at all times – as Meghan would discover.

Instead, there was the heartbreaking sight at Diana's funeral of her two young sons, heads bowed, walking solemnly behind the coffin and trying not to cry. Harry was dwarfed by Prince Charles on one side and by Diana's brother, Earl Spencer, on the other. In his eulogy address, the Earl singled out the media: 'Of all the ironies about Diana, perhaps the greatest was this: a girl given the name of the ancient goddess of hunting was, in the end, the most hunted person of the modern age.'

Both Harry and William were consumed by what Tony Blair's press secretary Alastair Campbell described as a 'total hatred of the media' after their mother's death, blaming, as many did, the paparazzi chasing the car for causing it. Harry later put those feelings into words, 'One of the hardest things to come to terms with is the fact that the people that chased her into the tunnel were the same people that were taking photographs of her while she was still dying in the back seat.'

Harry wasn't spared media attention as he grew up, often shamed into apologising for saying or doing something stupid involving drugs, racist insults or badly misjudged fancy dress. Some of the stories may have been fiction, some fact, but they were always front page. Unlike his elder brother, Harry was perceived as being a naughty boy. He was seventeen when he was alleged to have been ejected from a pub in Wiltshire for calling the French bar manager a 'fucking frog'.

He was eighteen when the now-defunct *News of the World* ran a story under the banner 'Harry's Drug Shame' about allegations of teenage parties involving drinking and drug taking. At twenty, he notoriously dressed in a Nazi uniform for a friend's fancy dress party; a picture was taken and sold to the tabloids and, quite rightly, there was public disgust. Harry apologised for the offence.

William was also at the party, but, for some reason, had not taken his younger brother aside and told him the blindingly obvious – 'don't wear it, mate'. And there were other racist incidents. It emerged that on the polo field, he, his brother and his father would affectionately refer to an Indian teammate as 'Sooty'. In the army, he called a fellow Sandhurst military cadet 'our little Paki friend', was filmed calling another soldier a 'raghead' and found himself in hot water for telling the comedian Stephen K. Amos that he 'didn't sound like a black guy.' After the last incident, another apology was made and he was sent on a course in equality and diversity.

It was quite a rap sheet and Meghan, you might have thought, would have had no time for this character. But a boy can grow up to be a better man. Of course, the press or the less forgiving elements of social media will never let him forget his younger indiscretions, using them time and time again to accuse him of hypocrisy or as a man who should keep his now more-enlightened opinions to himself.

He kept the damning and distressing words of his mother with him: in one of her last interviews she told the French news-paper *Le Monde*: 'The press is ferocious. It forgives nothing. It only hunts for mistakes. Every motive is twisted, every gesture criticised. I believe that abroad it is different. I'm welcomed with kindness. I'm taken for what I am, without prior judgement, without looking for blunders. In Britain it's the opposite. And I believe in my position, any sane person would have left long ago. But I cannot. I have my sons.'

In 2004, after he left school, he was involved in a scuffle with a group of paparazzi outside a London nightclub. One photo-grapher was left with a cut lip after the altercation, during which Harry shouted, 'Why don't you just leave me alone?' The late columnist Carol Sarler apparently had no intention of doing so and wrote in the *Daily Express* that Harry 'rarely lifted a finger unless it's to feel up a cheap tart in a nightclub.' His spokesperson at Clarence House said the article was 'grossly inaccurate and ill informed' about the facts of his gap year.

During that year he spent two months in Lesotho, a kingdom in southern Africa that had been ravaged by Aids. The trip was largely organised by Prince Seeiso, who like Harry was a second son – the brother to the present king. Together they travelled around the country visiting Aids orphans and other disabled and disadvantaged children. The two princes became firm friends. They had much in common, despite a nineteen-year age gap.

Prince Seeiso observed, 'Fortunately, we do not have an aggressive media in Lesotho because I am sure if we had there would have been stories about me rather like the ones printed about H.'

Prince Seeiso's mother, Queen 'Mahamato, who had died the previous autumn, had been vigorous in her support of Lesotho's vulnerable children. Together the two princes worked out a plan where they could honour the memory of their mothers and make a difference to the nation's orphans and disadvantaged children. The result was the Sentebale charity, officially founded two years later in 2006, which means 'Forget-me-not' in the local dialect. It has proved to be a startlingly successful project and one very dear to Harry's heart, continuing the legacy of Diana and her work with HIV sufferers.

Harry's acts of kindness or empathy are often left unknown or unreported, such as the time when, as a tank commander in the army, he stood up for an openly gay serviceman and gave a proper military telling-off to a group of ignorant soldiers who were taunting the man. They never insulted their comrade in arms again.

The military had been the making of Harry to a large extent. He had been undistinguished academically at Eton and his A-level grades ruled him out of following his brother to university. Instead he went to Sandhurst, before joining the Blues and Royals regiment in 2006. His 'passing out' parade, as graduating is called in the military, took place in front of the Queen.

Harry stayed in the army for ten years, quietly serving two frontline tours in Helmand Province, Afghanistan. The first, in 2008, ended abruptly when news of his whereabouts appeared in an Australian magazine and he needed to fly home for security reasons – not just for his own safety but also that of his fellow soldiers.

The flight back to the UK changed everything for him. The coffin of a Danish soldier was loaded onto the plane that Harry shared with three injured soldiers, who were all missing limbs. Despite being a serving officer, he hadn't seen close up the devastating effects of such injuries. He knew then that he needed to help these brave servicemen and others like them to overcome the physical and psychological scars of being wounded in action.

His second tour of duty came at the end of 2012 when he was Captain Harry Wales, Apache Attack Helicopter pilot. He probably would have liked to have stayed as a serving officer abroad but again he was recalled to London. He came back to work as a staff officer with responsibility for helping injured soldiers with their recovery.

In that role he founded the now world-famous Invictus Games, a mini Olympics for wounded, sick or injured veterans, which at that point featured nine sports, including wheelchair basketball and tennis and sitting volleyball. Harry's obvious delight while watching his fellow servicemen at the Queen Elizabeth Olympic Park in London demonstrated that he was leaving his twenties behind and had grown into an empathetic and caring man.

He was also a man coming to terms with his own mental health issues. He had kept them hidden, not as result of the grim realities of war, but the long-standing legacy of losing his mother. It would be a further ten years, in more enlightened times perhaps, that he would finally admit losing his mum had led to twenty years of shutting down his emotions. He admitted, 'I thought that thinking of her was only going to make me sad and not going to bring her back.'

Harry was finally ready to settle down. He didn't keep that ambition secret. He had told TV presenter Denise van Outen earlier in the year: 'I'm not dating and for the first time ever I want to find a wife.' At the second Invictus Games in Orlando, Florida, in April 2016 he said in a newspaper interview, 'I am not putting work before the idea of family and marriage. I just haven't had the opportunity to meet many people.' A long-standing friend was about to supply that opportunity.

He had been single for more than a year when his old friend Violet von Westenholz suggested he might like to pop into a private drinks party she was arranging in her role as PR director for Ralph Lauren. There was someone she wanted him to meet who was also unattached and who might be perfect for him.

Violet was one of the best-connected PRs in the business. Her father is Baron Piers von Westenholz, a well-known antiques dealer and interior designer specialising in 'by appointment' bespoke work for large country houses. He had skied for Great Britain at the 1964 winter Olympics in Innsbruck, Austria, but more pertinently had remained a close friend of Prince Charles through the years. Growing up, Violet and her sister Victoria had enjoyed many skiing holidays with Princes William and Harry.

Violet liked Meghan and believed that as a mature, high-achieving woman she might be better suited to the Prince, now thirty-one, than a nineteen-year-old debutante. She would prove to be an inspired matchmaker. It's been hinted that both Misha and Markus were in on things as well, so there was much excitement among Meghan's closest friends.

Meghan would later maintain that she didn't know much about Harry before she met him. She probably knew more about him than he did her – the whole world followed the progress of the son of Princess Diana. Most importantly, though, she didn't have any pre-conceived notions about him through poring over the pages of the British tabloids and filing away any previous bad behaviour in the minus column. Hopefully she had missed his naked hi–jinks in Las Vegas a few years earlier, which he admitted were more 'army than royal'.

It was the first day of July 2016. Meghan had a lunch scheduled during the day with Gina Nelthorpe-Cowne at the fashionable and always busy Delaunay restaurant in Covent Garden. They had to catch up with Meghan's diary, especially as she was due in Ottawa in a few weeks' time for the next One Young World conference.

Meghan was clearly in an excited mood and confided the reason: 'I'm going on a date tonight with Prince Harry.' The restaurant was so noisy Gina wasn't sure she had heard properly and needed her to repeat her amazing news. She couldn't believe what she was hearing and was almost as excited as Meghan.

Although she was a client, Gina was an admirer of Meghan who she thought was warm, personable and hugely charismatic. She also realised that she was so stunning it would be a major surprise if Harry could resist her. The prince genuinely didn't have a clue who Meghan was when Violet suggested they should meet. He admitted, 'I'd never watched *Suits* and I'd never heard of Meghan before.'

Meghan was patiently nursing a glass of wine when Harry arrived at the Dean Street Townhouse in Soho and saw her for the first time. The mutual attraction was instantaneous. Harry recalled sweetly, 'I was beautifully surprised when I walked into that room and saw her. There she was sitting down and I was like, "Ok, well I'm going to have to up my game, sit down and make sure I've got good chat."'

It turned out he did. They didn't talk about New York fashion week, what Elton John was up to or shooting at Sandringham. Instead they slipped easily into a conversation about the most important things in their lives and, as Meghan put it, 'how passionate we were about seeing change.'

Touchingly, Meghan was impressed that Harry was a complete gentleman. He would later confide that he knew the first time they met that Meghan was *the* one. They were both at a time in their lives when they needed a touch of old-fashioned romance. It would turn out to be an epic story.

17

AFRICA CALLING

———

Meghan soon realised how important Africa was to Harry. She could tell him about her two trips to Rwanda but he had treated the continent as a second home, perhaps even wishing it was his first. When he was asked about his ambitions while on his gap year trip to Lesotho, he had replied. 'Professional surfer, wildlife photographer, helicopter pilot and live in Africa.' He wasn't really joking. It was an open secret that he would jump at the chance of changing his life and leaving the Royal Family if he could.

Botswana was his destination of choice if he was really serious about a girl. He had taken his first love, Chelsy Davy, there ten years earlier in 2006, before he reported for duty with the Blues and Royals. They made several romantic trips to the country that became more familiar to Britain as the setting for the phenomenally successful *No. 1 Ladies' Detective Agency* novels of Alexander McCall Smith.

Harry and Chelsy were a couple for seven years and friends thought she might have said yes if he had proposed. She was a force of nature but was far more than just the fun-loving blonde who the media characterised unfairly as some sort of colonial Essex girl. She was described as being 'pneumatic', a sexist insult that suggested she was one step away from being a Page 3 girl.

The press were right that Chelsy enjoyed a party but she had been expensively educated, is very intelligent and has a serious side to her. She was the daughter of wealthy parents in Zimbabwe but her family had moved to South Africa when Mugabe's regime took over her native country.

She went to school in England at Cheltenham College, conveniently close to Highgrove, the home of Prince Charles, and obtained a good degree from Cape Town University in politics, philosophy and economics before studying law at the University of Leeds. Most interestingly, in the light of what would happen to Meghan, she hated the media attention that came with her relationship with Harry.

Chelsy understandably 'freaked out', according to a friend, when she found a mobile phone stuck to the underside of her car in Cape Town: 'This was very scary, thinking someone was monitoring her.' She would later admit that the attention she received was crazy and uncomfortable, admitting, 'I found it very difficult.' She hated being chased down the road by photographers and just wanted a normal life, something that proved to be impossible with Harry. Inevitably they split up for good: 'I just couldn't cope,' she said.

His relationship with another attractive blonde, Cressida Bonas, suffered the same fate after two years together that included a romantic safari holiday in Botswana. Harry did his best to protect her from the spotlight but she hated it, too, not least because she did not want to be defined by a famous man. Also interestingly from Meghan's point of view, she observed, 'People in this country are very quick to put you in a box or put you in a corner.'

Both Chels and Cress, as Harry called them, have achieved much since they left the royal orbit – Chelsy runs her own business AYA, a company that sells ethically sourced designer

African jewellery, while Cressida has a blossoming acting career, playing the ill-fated Sheila Caffell in the 2020 drama series *White House Farm*. She also married a Harry – her long-term boyfriend, property developer Harry Wentworth-Stanley – in a low-key ceremony in July of the same year.

Meghan was different from these young women. In a month's time, she would be thirty-five and had already lived a rich and fulfilling life. That maturity didn't stop her posting a playful image on Instagram on 3 July; it was a peach-coloured Love Heart sweet that bore the words 'Kiss Me' with the caption underneath: Lovehearts in #London.

She had to fly back to Toronto on 5 July, so she and Harry had time for just two more dates before the Atlantic Ocean separated them. They enjoyed a quiet dinner in a private room at the Dean Street Townhouse, part of the Soho House group – something arranged by the dependable and very discrete Markus Anderson. They discovered they liked each other just as much after their second encounter as their first. Their third date was arranged even more discretely for the next evening – this time it was in Harry's mews cottage within the grounds of Kensington Palace. By now it was quite clear to both of them that this was a proper romance.

Meghan managed to catch one more Serena match at Wimbledon before she left, but missed her friend's triumph in the final against Angelique Kerber and her win in the doubles with her sister Venus. Now, Meghan had to fulfil the usual annual commitment to pre-season publicity for what would be the sixth series of *Suits*.

Harry and Meghan kept in daily touch as best they could, trying to work out how they were ever going to see each other again. Very full diaries were consulted before Harry suggested she join him for a holiday in Botswana – as you do. Meghan readily agreed. He was due to be in Africa for a month while she was flying to Italy for a holiday after completing her commitments in North America: perhaps she could go on to Johannesburg after that instead of returning to Toronto?

Before she came back to Europe she took part in an amusing segment with the TV channel Dave, which broadcast *Suits* in the UK, in which she was quizzed on her understanding of all things British. She was hopeless but was good-natured about her lack of knowledge – although, to be fair, not many native Brits would have known many of the answers. She failed to identify Hoptimus Prime as a real ale; or that Sandy Balls, Happy Bottom and Crotch Crescent were real places. She did, however, know that a trashcan was called a bin.

Meghan was staying at the St Regis New York in Manhattan when she turned thirty-five, preparing to be maid of honour at Lindsay Roth's grand wedding ceremony two days later in the five-star hotel. Linds was marrying Gavin Jordan, a risk manager from London. She had remained one of Meghan's most loyal friends and one of the very few she trusted with the news that she was dating Harry.

Lindsay posted on Instagram to wish Happy Birthday to the 'most kind, generous and wickedly smart and gorgeous (inside and out) #maidofhonor a girl could have.' Meghan herself marked the day on The Tig: 'I am feeling so incredibly joyful just now, so grateful and content that all I could wish for is more of the same.'

She also revealed that the following week she was heading off grid to spend time with some friends, some cocktails and the sound of the lapping sea. That was Ibiza, where she sipped tequila sodas with Misha Nonoo, Priyanka Chopra and Benita Litt. Priyanka was a new fast friend. They had met in January at the *Elle* magazine's annual Women in Television Dinner at the Sunset Tower Hotel in West Hollywood.

Priyanka, a former Miss World, was the bigger name. She is a superstar in her native India, a veteran of countless Bollywood films and subsequently a big name in the US, where she starred as FBI recruit Alex Parrish in the TV series *Quantico*. Meghan observed that 'they just clicked'.

Benita had been a friend since LA days and had slipped under the radar, keeping a low profile and never speaking to the media about Meghan. She was formerly an entertainment lawyer but more recently co-founded Legend of Lido, a fashion enterprise that sells eye-catching carry-all bags. Meghan could often be seen heading off to a yoga class with one of their exclusive designs. They were also perfect for days on the beach. Part of the proceeds from every sale was set aside for a nominated charity. Moving on to Italy, Jessica Mulroney joined her for some lazy luxury at Le Sirenuse hotel in Positano on the beautiful Amalfi Coast. Lovely and relaxing as this break was, it could not have been more different for what lay in store for Meghan the following week – the spectacular vistas of southern Africa. Harry was there to meet her in Johannesburg. He had been working on an elephant conservation project in Malawi and had taken time off to attend the adults-only wedding in KwaZulu-Natal of his cousin, Princess Diana's nephew George McCorquodale, to South African Bianca Moore.

Meghan was in the habit of posting numerous images on Instagram or The Tig on her travels: not this time. Her five-day trip to Botswana was a taste of paradise that she was not willing to share. They flew from Jo'burg to Maun International airport in Northern Botswana, then boarded a light plane that landed on a remote landing strip before scrambling into a 4x4 to brave the scrubland and dirt tracks, eventually finishing their journey at the Meno a Kwena tented camp on the edge of the Makgadikgadi Pans National Park.

This was no ordinary campsite, boasting nine luxurious tents with ensuite bathrooms and wonderful views over the Boteti River, where the elephants, wildebeest and zebra would splash around to drink and cool off. During the day there were safari trips into the national park to watch lions and cheetah, deer and antelope and the ever-popular meerkats. At night they sipped sundowner cocktails and ate chicken and game stew cooked over open grills.

Harry recalled that they had an 'absolutely fantastic' time, 'We camped out with each other under the stars.' Meghan had been all over the world but she had never been to anywhere like this. It was the perfect place to fall in love; and they did.

From idyllic days and nights in the middle of nowhere, both Harry and Meghan now had to face reality. They needed to work out how to manage a blossoming relationship when they were so busy. They decided before they left Africa that they would make a proper commitment and try their hardest to make things work: that meant not going longer than two weeks before they saw each other in person, although it would take a while to get their diaries in sync.

Meghan's most important immediate concern was the One Young World conference in the Canadian capital, Ottawa. Some familiar faces from two years' earlier in Dublin were there, including Mary Robinson and Bob Geldof, who described himself as the 'grumpy uncle of One Young World'. As before, there were an eclectic mix of names who were on the books of Kruger Cowne: superstar singers Cher, who was launching a campaign to protect wild animals in captivity; Bruce Dickinson of Iron Maiden, as well as the former secretary of the United Nations, Kofi Annan.

Meghan walked into the opening ceremony on Parliament Hill on the arm of fellow counsellor James Chau, the well-known London-born broadcaster and former news anchor on China Central Television where his nightly audience was eighty-five million viewers. She had also met him in Dublin; the two enjoyed a good rapport, kept in touch and she featured him in the pages of The Tig. He was a fellow UN ambassador, in his case for UNAIDS, who she described as 'savvy and charming'. His wish, he said, was to make Aids history.

Another Tig veteran from Dublin was Fatima Bhutto, the Pakistani writer and activist for gender equality. Meghan strongly empathised with the misogynistic racism that Fatima faced as she travelled the world. Fatima, the niece of the assassinated Pakistani premier Benazir Bhutto, explained, 'When I travel around I regularly get lots of really racist comments. A common one is "you're a Muslim, how nice that you are allowed to travel."'

Meghan told Fatima that she would be travelling to India in 2017 as a global ambassador with World Vision as part of her ongoing campaigning for gender equality: 'It's about women knowing their worth,' she said.

A third familiar face with whom Meghan could spend time catching up was Justin Trudeau, the Canadian premier. He addressed the 1,300 delegates from 196 countries around the world at the opening ceremony, declaring, 'Your generation is politically engaged, educated, innovative, inclusive and progressive.' Justin, casually dressed in a white shirt with his sleeves rolled up, urged, 'You need to harness that potential to make the world a better place.'

Those sentiments, aimed specifically at young people, resonated strongly with Meghan, who always sought to reach out to a younger generation. She and Justin had much to discuss as they chatted easily on a sofa and posed for pictures after the ceremony.

One Young World is an example of how big-name celebrities can give an event oxygen, providing publicity and a voice to issues that matter: at this summit the counsellors and delegates discussed key issues affecting young people: human rights, the victimisation of the LGBT (as it was then) community; mental health; the effects of terrorism and gender equality.

Meghan was able to fly to London after the conference to stay with Harry at his home, Nottingham Cottage, for the first time. Nott Cott, as it's known in royal circles, is one of the cosiest royal properties, with just two bedrooms and low ceilings that Harry had to be careful not to hit his head on. That was even more of a hazard for his brother William, the tallest of the Royal Family at 6 foot 3 inches to Harry's 6 foot 1 inch.

The house had been the grace and favour home of the Queen and Princess Margaret's renowned governess, Marion Crawford, known as Crawfie, who had to leave the property in 1950 when it was revealed she was the source of stories in the newspapers about the Royal Family.

William and Kate lived there for more than two years after returning to London from Anglesey, where the prince had been a serving helicopter pilot. They left a few months after the birth of their eldest son George and moved round the corner to the palatial Apartment 1A. The 2014 Sovereign Grant report revealed that £4.5 million was spent on renovations for the couple, including major roof repairs. They paid separately for a family kitchen, something more homely for their growing family.

Harry moved into Nottingham Cottage when they left and it was, more or less, a bachelor pad when Meghan first stayed there. She would have been disappointed if she had been expecting something grander – it was even smaller than her home in

Toronto. One advantage of its size, however, was that there was no room for any live-in security, so she didn't have to share her breakfast muesli with a protection officer.

At this stage, Meghan could slip in and out of the Kensington Palace gates without anyone realising who she was. She could even take herself into the lion's den by shopping for their supper unrecognised in the trendy Whole Foods supermarket in the Barkers Shopping Arcade on Kensington High Street, next to the offices of the *Daily Mail*. They were still in the early days of their relationship and were happy to spend romantic nights in with Meghan cooking dinner.

Her visit was too short, although she did meet some of Harry's friends as well as pop round to see Princess Eugenie in her apartment in St James's Palace. They arranged to meet up again in Toronto at the end of the month when Eugenie would be there with her future husband, Jack Brooksbank.

In the meantime, Meghan needed to fly home to continue filming *Suits* as well as prepare for the launch of the winter capsule collection for Reitmans. First, though, she headed to Atlanta, Georgia, for the Create and Cultivate conference, a powerhouse forum for women looking to succeed in the modern world.

The organisation had been founded by millionaire entrepreneur and businesswoman Jaclyn Johnson, reaching out to women online and through conferences around the country aimed at inspiring the next generation. Jaclyn's slogan encapsulated its message: 'Behind every great woman, are great women.'

Meghan explained she had flown in from London when she was interviewed by Jaclyn on stage at the Mason Fine Art Gallery. She gave her audience six pieces of advice: her favourite – don't give it five minutes if you are not going to give it five years; don't be afraid to cold email; proofread your messages and add a personal touch if you can (Meghan still handwrote thank-you notes); be grateful for the little things that happen on your journey; and be aware of the bigger picture – you can't win every part but you can win the room.

Her most memorable comment came in response to a question from the audience: she was asked how she balanced being a feminist with being feminine. She replied with her philosophy that they were not mutually exclusive: 'You can be a woman who wants to look good and still stand up for the equality of women.'

She didn't mention Harry, of course, although she was wearing a beaded bracelet that was the same as one that he would be seen sporting a while later – it was a private, romantic gesture.

The Meghan Markle Collection for Fall at Reitmans adopted much of the same thinking as before – five outfits costing no more than $100 that would take you from work to the weekend – a faux-leather pencil skirt that Rachel Zane might have worn; a boyfriend-style blouse that was obviously inspired by Meghan herself; faux-leather leggings, a turtleneck bodysuit and a super-soft cashmere blend poncho that would be ideal for the Canadian winters.

She had posed for all the photographs for the launch at the beginning of November, shot three episodes of *Suits* and was ready for Harry to visit her home in Toronto for the first time. The top-of-the-range black SUV with the blackout windows and the two slightly out-of-place bodyguards in dark suits looking nonchalant were the only clue that he was in Seaton Village.

They were keeping everything as low key as possible, popping out every so often to have drinks at Jessica and Ben Mulroney's house or catching up with Markus at Soho House.

Harry met Bogart and Guy and, as ever, enjoyed Meghan's cooking – just a couple enjoying precious time together. Bogart and Harry were not fast friends. Meghan explained that her 'sweet Bogart' was 'more protective of me than any person I've ever known.'

Harry and Meghan were tucked away in Toronto when their romance was revealed to the world. The *Royal World Exclusive* announcing 'Harry's Secret Romance with a TV Star' was the front-page story of the *Sunday Express* on 30 October 2016. They were unaware of the publicity storm brewing at home and were able to slip out unnoticed to Soho House on Halloween to have a quiet dinner with Princess Eugenie and Jack Brooksbank before wandering around the home neighbourhood to check out the decorations.

Meghan's life had changed forever when she met Harry at the beginning of July. Then it was love and romance, excitement and shared memories. Now, her life would change forever for a second time – but not in a way that anyone would describe as good.

18

A WEEK IN HELL

————

Meghan's friends had told her that she would be a target for the British tabloid press. She didn't want to hear any negativity. She was a woman in love intent on being positive about her new relationship. Harry had done his best to warn her but he too was taken aback by what followed in the days after their relationship became public: 'You can have as many conversations as you want and try and prepare as much as possible, but we were totally unprepared for what happened after that.'

The scoop by the *Sunday Express* royal reporter Camilla Tominey was pleasant enough about Meghan, describing her in the opening paragraph as a 'stunning TV actress, model and human rights campaigner'. In one ghastly week, however, Meghan went from being that to a saucy divorcee porn star who was not a suitable candidate for a princess because of the colour of her skin.

The minute the story broke, reporters were despatched, chequebooks at the ready, across the Atlantic to find out anything and everything juicy about Meghan Markle. They were in Los Angeles, Toronto, Chicago – everywhere there might be a possible Meghan footprint. They even went to Florida to seek out her half-sister Samantha, who she hadn't seen for years.

Meghan, perhaps not quite capturing the gravity of what was going on, posted a frivolous image on Instagram, where she had built nearly a million followers, of two bananas apparently spooning; the caption read, 'Sleep tight xx'. The light-hearted picture received some good-natured comments on social media and some less enthusiastic ones in the papers.

There were many reasons to write something about Meghan on the front page of a popular newspaper. Imagine the positive headlines: Meghan in UN Women triumph; Meghan Volunteers at Soup Kitchen; Meghan campaigns for Fresh Water in Africa; Meghan Markle is a self-made millionaire.

Wow, lucky Harry, you might have thought on reading any of these – this is a woman of substance, but *The Sun* had other ideas: 'Harry's Girl on Pornhub', it declared on Friday 4 November. An exclusive by Lucy Jones revealed, 'Prince Harry's new girl Meghan Markle features on adult site Pornhub. She can be seen stripping off and groaning in …' The implication on the front page was clear – Meghan Markle was a porn star. And, despite being a high achiever, this 35-year-old woman was relegated to being described as 'Harry's Girl' as if she were a teenage starlet.

Turning to page five, readers were informed that she was 'groaning in a host of steamy sex scenes from *Suits* – one raunchy clip sees Meghan take off her clothes and straddle co-star Patrick J. Adams in a filing area. It also includes close-ups of her crotch and her lacy bra …'

The journalist Tamara Khandaker, writing for the Toronto-based *Vice News*, put the revelation into nice perspective when she observed, 'The clips on the website are of Markle's appearances on *Suits* and wouldn't even fit into your religious grandmother's idea of pornography.'

On the front page there was a flattering picture of Kate Middleton on the red carpet showing some shapely pins, inevitably inviting comparison between our home-grown princess and this American woman of dubious moral character. But the main splash on the front page was a story putting the boot into self-made millionaire and Brexit opponent Gina Miller. She was helpfully described as a Guyanan-born fund manager and a foreign-born multi-millionaire, in case we didn't get the point. And there was an accompanying picture revealing her ethnicity – again, just to make the point absolutely clear.

Almost every story about Meghan in the first few days seemed intent on showing her complete lack of suitability for Harry. The royal reporter for the *Daily Express*, Richard Palmer, set the tone. No longer was Meghan described as a 'human rights campaigner'. Instead she was an 'American actress'. In the story he wrote, 'As a Roman Catholic and the daughter of a white father and black mother, she is hardly out of central casting for princesses.'

His observation set a narrative for much worse to come. The writer and broadcaster, Afua Hirsch, neatly identified the state of play in an article for the *Guardian*. She drew attention to descriptions in the *Daily Mail* that Meghan was a 'glamorous brunette', a 'departure from Prince Harry's usual type' and 'not in the society blonde style of previous girlfriends'. Afua observed, 'I think what they are trying to say is that Markle, actor, global development ambassador and lifestyle blogger is black.'

The *Daily Mail* wasted no time in focusing on the colour of Meghan's skin. They went with both barrels on 2 November, displaying the now notorious headline: 'Harry's girl is (almost) straight outta Compton: Gang-scarred home of her mother – so will he be dropping in for tea.' The 'straight outta Compton' referenced a notorious rap song by N.W.A. Doria, however, lived in View Park–Windsor Hills, the so-called 'black Beverly Hills' where an average property might cost $750,000. Her house was in the hills well above the Crenshaw district that had been plagued by gangs in the past.

The American radio station Majic-123 immediately called out the coverage as racist: 'Meghan Markle is experiencing clear racism from the media.' It declared that the story by Ruth Stiles attempted to 'fasten Markle to a "crime and street gang"-riddled area of LA by pointing out that her mom still lives in the old neighbourhood, adding, "Crenshaw has endured 47 crimes in the past week." What that has to do with Toronto-based Markle – unless she somehow committed any or all of those crimes – we have no idea.'

The BET.com (Black Entertainment Television) put the coverage into perspective. Entertainment editor Smriti Mundhra said it was ridiculous to suggest Harry would be in any danger. He observed, 'There's been a lot of loaded language and race-baiting language about Meghan.'

In another article the *Mail* compared her family history with that of Harry and highlighted the 'stark contrast' in class between the two: 'his includes kings, queen and earls; hers a tailor, teacher and a cleaning shop worker.'

The *Mail* group hadn't finished, however. In the following weekend's *Mail on Sunday*, their star columnist Rachel Johnson considered the woman she described as 'Harry's Hottie' and a 'showgirl'. Her gross assessment: 'If there is issue from her alleged union with Prince Harry, the Windsors will thicken their watery, thin blue blood and Spencer pale skin and ginger hair with some rich and exotic DNA.'

The Johnson family had form where racism is concerned. Her elder brother Boris, the then Foreign Secretary and future Prime Minister, labelled black Africans in the *Daily Telegraph* in 2002 as 'flag-waving picaninnies' with 'watermelon smiles', an opinion he claimed was taken out of context. It was not a view that would have found favour with Meghan or Harry – and nor would his view on colonialism in Africa in *The Spectator* the same year: 'The problem is not that we were once in charge but that we are not in charge anymore.' His opinion of Harry's mother and gender equality would not have impressed the couple either. He blustered, 'The Princess is a symbol for every woman who ever felt wronged by a man.'

His sister wasn't as blatantly insulting towards black people in her column but she made the observation that 'Miss Markle's mother is a dreadlocked African–American lady from the wrong side of the tracks.'

Rachel suggested that Meghan had 'played' the playboy Prince and that she was unsuitable because she was divorced, then repeated an unfounded allegation that she had dropped Cory like a hot brick when she had reeled in Harry: 'As far as the Royal Family is concerned, a bolter is far worse than a black sheep' – throwing in yet another timely and thinly disguised reminder that Meghan was a woman of colour.

Afua Hirsch again summed up the tabloid coverage to date: 'They have made it clear that her relationship with Harry is scandalous, for a number of reasons: she is divorced; she is older (Markle is 35, Harry 32); she's played raunchy scenes in the US TV series *Suits* – and her mother is visibly black, with dreadlocks.' The 'scandalous list' it seemed was growing by the day.

Not everything in the papers was completely negative. The *Sunday Mirror* ran a far more positive piece in which former royal butler Grant Harrold said, 'Harry loves her and she loves him. And that will be what matters in the eyes of the Queen and

Prince Charles. I don't see any reason why Meghan couldn't be The One.' He did caution, however, 'Meghan's got to be aware that she will be in the firing line.'

She already was. Sister paper, the *Daily Mirror*, didn't get the memo. Meghan was now described tackily as 'the actress, who once stripped to her knickers in the legal drama *Suits* for a sex scene with her screen lover.'

By and large, the negativity was relentless. One of the most striking was a story in *The Sun* – followed up by one and all – under the headline: Princess Pushy: 'Prince Harry's new flame Meghan Markle is a social climber' who 'is not fit to be royal' – according to her own SISTER.

Samantha, who now lived in Florida, was sixteen years older than her half-sister and was not in contact with her, but that didn't stop her sharing some gems, including the observation that Meghan had a 'soft spot for gingers'. The implication in the story was that Meghan had ditched her after she had been diag-nosed with multiple sclerosis in 2008 – 'I didn't feel a separation from her until I was in a wheelchair.'

The Sun arguably topped everything with its headline on 7 November: 'Fancy a Quick Puck?', a seedy story suggesting with no proof whatsoever that her first marriage ended because of an affair with ice hockey player Michael Del Zotto. The headline implying that they had enjoyed a quick fuck might have seemed amusing in the pub at lunchtime but was deeply upsetting to Meghan and Harry.

The usual tabloid tricks were employed in the story. Pals, a pal and a friend were all quoted anonymously. The headline continued, Prince Harry's girl Meghan Markle 'split from hubby after getting close to Canadian ice hockey star Michael Del Zotto'. It was in quotation marks but nobody had actually said that in the text.

The old picture of Michael, Meghan and Rick Hoffman was dragged out as proof – but the article simply referred to Rick as an 'unknown man', not even bothering to identify a television star and Michael's buddy.

Harry had seen, heard and read enough. His communications secretary, Jason Knauf, issued a statement on his behalf on 8 November which said unequivocally that a line had been crossed during the past week: 'His girlfriend, Meghan Markle, has been subject to a wave of abuse and harassment. Some of this has been very public – the smear on the front page of a national news-paper; the racial undertones of comment pieces; and the outright sexism and racism of social media trolls and web article comments.

'Some of it has been hidden from the public – the nightly legal battles to keep defamatory stories out of papers; her mother having to struggle past photographers in order to get to her front door; the attempts of reporters and photographers to gain illegal entry to her home and the calls to the police that followed; the substantial bribes offered to her ex-boyfriend; the bombardment of nearly every friend, co-worker, and loved one in her life.

'Prince Harry is worried about Ms Markle's safety and is deeply disappointed that he has not been able to protect her. It is not right that a few months into a relationship with him that Ms Markle should be subjected to such a storm. He knows commentators will say this is "the price she has to pay" and that "this is all part of the game." He strongly disagrees. This is not a game – this is her life and his.'

The statement was a defining moment in that it set the tone for much of what was to follow. To anyone outside looking in, it was a strong and human declaration, clearly from both of them and not – as the newspapers would suggest the next day – a rant from a 'hot-headed prince'. It clearly stated his issues, trying to develop a thick skin against media interest – with her concerns – sexist and racist smears.

The statement was phrased with careful politeness, hoping but not demanding that 'those in the press who have been driving this story can "pause and reflect" before any further damage is done.' It concluded with Harry's hope that 'fair-minded people will understand why he has felt it necessary to speak publicly.'

He was telling the media, politely, to back off. They ignored it. In fact, it was seized upon happily by the tabloid press to generate more front-page headlines about Meghan. Their relationship made page one of *The Sun*, *Daily Star*, *Daily Express*, *Metro*, *Daily Mirror* and *Daily Mail*, which continued coverage of the story on pages three, five, six and seven.

The leader writers and royal correspondents were at their most sanctimonious, playing the victim, as if 'strait outta Compton' or 'Harry Girl's on Pornhub' were entirely reasonable and respectful headlines. *The Sun* said Harry 'needs to get real'.

Their royal reporter, Emily Andrews, observed, 'Legitimate press interest in who's dating the fifth in line to the throne is exactly that. Entirely legitimate. Sure, the British press have contacted her friends and family to see if they want to comment. Some did, some didn't and that was respected. Harry, we're on your side.' She did not say we are on your *and Meghan's* side. Nor did she reveal how much the 'legitimate' press interest was costing. She didn't, for instance, reveal how much – if anything – Samantha was paid to diss Meghan. Nor did she mention the 'substantial bribes' – clearly 'entirely legitimate' – that had been offered to Cory Vitiello. Nor did she mention that it was her byline on the entirely legitimate 'Fancy a Quick Puck?' story.

The *Daily Mail* called Harry a 'hot-headed prince'. On the front page it plugged a comment piece by Sarah Vine, the wife of politician Michael Gove: 'Harry's an admirable chap. But to claim the publicity-hungry Meghan is a hapless victim is crazy.'

Sarah warmed to her theme in her article: 'the idea that Ms Markle is some media ingénue, some hapless victim of unfair and unwarranted scrutiny, is simply preposterous.' Sarah decided not to mention Doria and the scrutiny she was enduring.

Sarah's weapon of choice with which to beat Meghan was The Tig, which she belittled, describing it as similar to Gwyneth Paltrow's Goop so that she could get in the gag about Meghan being a mini-Gwynnie. She said of the website, 'we learn that her nickname is Flower, she has two rescue dogs, she likes to give money to charity and her favourite thing is … hot sauce. Ooh-la-la.' It was classic case of sarcastic put-down by an experienced columnist.

For probably the first but definitely not the last time Meghan and Harry were compared unfavourably with William and Kate. Sarah said, 'the Duke and Duchess of Cambridge are today the exemplar, consummate professionals who present a Barbie and Ken-like image of married life. Reliably dull, diligently dutiful, they are the perfect model of the modern Royal Family, the healing balm for the jagged scars left behind by Diana.'

Perhaps Sarah, unwittingly, had hit on something that she thought a compliment, namely William and Kate were 'dull'. Her mention of Diana was interesting. A creeping narrative in recent years has sought to absolve the media for any blame in the death of Harry's mother in favour of the argument that it was a 'drunk driver who ultimately caused Diana's death'. Sarah chose not to mention the paparazzi in pursuit of their prey.

The *Guardian* reminded its readers of some of the details mentioned in the statement, including that journalists had tried to enter Meghan's home, her ex-boyfriend had been offered bribes and her mother had been harassed by photographers. The tabloids, it said, were employing an old game, 'deliberately confusing what is in the public interest with what is interesting to the public.'

The headline in a piece in the paper neatly summed up the reaction: 'Tabloids on Prince Harry and Meghan Markle: don't blame us, guv.' One of the more interesting assumptions in the media reaction was that Meghan, a mere woman, played no part in it, when it transparently was something that they worked out together.

So, did Harry's plea for a pause have any effect? Apparently not: unless two days counts as a pause. The tabloids all ran a still of Meghan from *Knight Rider* in a black bra for her role as a cage fighter. The *Daily Mail* showed just how seriously they took Harry's request: 'Prince Harry told this week how he was keen to protect his new girlfriend Meghan Markle, but evidence has emerged to show she's more than a match for anyone.' Apparently she showed off her 'toned body in a sports bra'.

Meghan had slipped unnoticed into London for a stay at Nottingham Cottage. She was seen shopping in Kensington High Street close to the offices of the *Mail* where another Rachel Johnson column was about to ridicule the heartfelt statement as reading like the script of the Julia Roberts' film, *Notting Hill*: 'I'm just a Prince standing in front of an actress I love, asking for us to be left alone.'

She recalled that she had described Meghan as a 'drop dead gorgeous campaigner and actress' when in fact she described her as 'Harry's hottie' and an 'accomplished actress', which is not exactly the same thing. Rachel continued, 'And yes I also said it would be lovely if you and she had offspring as Royal stock would be improved by "rich and exotic DNA".' – except, she didn't say 'lovely' at all. Nor did she say 'improved'. The word she had used a week earlier was 'thicken'.

Surprisingly perhaps, one of the few positive commentaries about Meghan came from Piers Morgan, who wrote glowingly about her in his column in the *Mail on Sunday*. In the days long before he described the couple as a 'pair of tools', he wrote 'Harry, ignore all the poisonous rubbish you're reading or hearing about her. Meghan Markle is perfect princess material. Just put any proposal in writing.'

Yet another female *Daily Mail* columnist, Jan Moir, thought of the jolly idea of pretending to be Harry's agony aunt. She had exactly the opposite view to Piers. 'Have fun by all means – but marriage? Do you really expect Meghan to give up her career and move to the UK? Or are you going to do a Duke of Windsor and live in exile with her?' She concluded: 'So whatever you do, please make sure the next piece of jewellery you buy her is not, repeat not, a ring.'

Meghan was completely astonished by the unwelcome attention or 'scrutiny' as the press likes to call intrusive and abusive commentary. She explained, 'There's a misconception that because I work in the entertainment industry that this would be something I was familiar with. But even though I had been on my show for six years, and working before that, I have never been part of tabloid culture.'

She would later reveal how 'disheartening' it was that so much of the 'scrutiny' was centred on her ethnicity: she thought it a shame that there was so much 'discriminatory focus on that'.

Nobody else within the royal orbit sought to pass comment on her treatment, although eventually Prince William came out in support of his brother's statement. It took three weeks. He shared the same spokesman, Jason Knauf, who said, 'The Duke of Cambridge absolutely understands the situation concerning privacy and supports the need for Prince Harry to support those closest to him.'

It was the very opposite of a powerful endorsement. The sentence was such a pompous tongue twister that it tied itself up in knots to ensure that it didn't mention Meghan by name or her ongoing ordeal. Its effect was to ensure that nobody got the message. All he had to say was: 'Come on guys, leave them alone.' Instead it was the first indication that all was not rosy behind closed doors.

19

TIME FOR INDIA

———

Meghan listened to the girls' stories, deeply concerned that they felt too embarrassed to go to school during their periods. The actress, deemed by some media commentators not suitable to be a princess, had travelled to India to see for herself the plight of teenage girls whose education was being sorely affected by the stigma surrounding menstrual health and the lack of access to proper sanitation.

The paparazzi were not invited and nor were the pack of royal reporters still scrabbling for Markle information. Instead, in January 2017, she slipped quietly into Delhi and Mumbai in her role as a Global Ambassador for World Vision Canada. It was a world away from her New Year treat when Harry had surprised her with a trip to remote Tromsø in Norway to see the Northern Lights.

Three weeks later she was shadowing women living and working in the slums of Govandi, one of the poorest areas of Mumbai. She was seeing for herself the hardship they and their daughters faced every day.

Meghan spent two days with the Myna Mahila Foundation. In Hindi, Myna means talkative and Mahila, woman. She had first heard of the organisation in April the previous year when she attended *Glamour* magazine's College Women of the Year Awards in New York, and one of the winners was a graduate of Duke University, Suhani Jalota.

Suhani was a young woman of twenty-one, who had grown up in a privileged household in India. Her life changed in tenth grade when she visited the slums for a research project on sanitation. She was inspired by Dr Jockin Arputham, the founder of Slum Dwellers International, who spent forty years working in the poverty-stricken areas of Mumbai and who, according to Suhani, 'singlehandedly improved the lives of millions of women.' Suhani co-founded Myna Mahila with a kindred spirit, Meena Jagdish Ramani, and it has become her life's work.

Suhani hadn't watched *Suits* when she met Meghan, but she was happy to take a selfie with a TV star. She hadn't realised then that Meghan had taken on board the work that Myna Mahila was doing with women in the poorest communities to de-stigmatise periods by providing their own-brand sanitary products directly to them on the doorstep and conducting workshops on the importance of menstrual hygiene. Myna Mahila was more than just an education facility, though – it sought to help women earn an income through meaningful work. The organisation itself employed more than twenty local women.

After their first meeting, Meghan went away and did her research, following up by personally contacting Suhani to ask if she could visit her in Mumbai to see for herself the problems they were facing and help if she could. She had not realised how grave the menstrual hygiene problems were. The only proviso was that this was to be a visit under the radar and she asked that no one took photographs – although a brief film clip did make its way onto YouTube a couple of years later.

Suhani was impressed that her guest understood the challenges they faced in India, absorbed some of the culture and spoke of 'actionable steps' that might be taken to improve things. She observed, 'She didn't pretend to be what she was not. When she was here, this place didn't even have electricity, but that didn't seem to bother her.'

Meghan visited local women and girls in their homes, shared a meal with Suhani and some of their female employees at a local school. She explained, 'Enrolment at this school went up by three times once the latrines were built so that girls had access to clean hygiene and bathroom facilities.' She spoke with Dr Arputham, who was nominated for the Nobel Peace Prize in 2014. He told her that it was vital that the employees of Myna Mahila lived and worked in the slums, as that was the key to breaking the cycle of poverty and allowing access to education.

Suhani was impressed that Meghan didn't seek to glamorise her visit or turn it into a shallow celebrity jaunt. Overnight they made her a sari and helped her to put it on; they presented her with bangles and she wore a bindi as a mark of respect to her hosts. 'She is one of the most humble people we've met,' said Suhani, appreciatively. Meghan left India assuring Suhani that she would support Myna Mahila in any way she could. She kept her word.

The first wave of 'media scrutiny' had died down, although Jan Moir in the *Daily Mail* continued the theme of belittling Meghan, referring to her as 'the American actress', 'Prince Harry's love interest' and, for some reason, a 'saucebox', which is another way of describing a cheeky or impudent person. She also noted that, 'like many of her generation, 35-year-old Meghan shares much of her life on her social media account.'

On her return home, the 'saucebox' wrote a powerful article for *Time* magazine entitled 'How Periods Affect Potential'. The figures she quoted were depressing: only fifty per cent of secondary schools in India have toilets; twenty-three per cent of girls in India drop out of school because menstrual hygiene management (MHM), access to toilets and sanitary pads were not part of the conversation, neither in government nor in homes.

She made the point that the female leaders of tomorrow needed a full and proper education, something that is taken for granted in the West but is a luxury in India, Iran, sub-Saharan Africa and other poverty-stricken regions. Why, she argued, should a girl's education and potential to succeed be sacrificed because of shame surrounding her period? 'We need to rise above our puritanical bashfulness when it comes to talking about menstruation.'

Meghan's passion for this cause was clear and undeniable: 'When we empower girls hungry for education, we cultivate women who are emboldened to effect change within their communities and globally. If that is our dream for them, then the promise of it must begin with us. Period.'

Suhani was the youngest name on Meghan's list of the ten women who had changed her life, published in *Glamour* magazine in August 2017. Perhaps more importantly, she did not forget Myna Mahila and included it among the charities she wanted to benefit from the Royal Wedding the following year.

Before then there would continue to be enormous change in Meghan's life as she tried to integrate into the Royal Family and become better acquainted with its antiquated protocols. It soon became apparent that she would need to start with a clean slate.

One of the first casualties was her commercial contract with Kruger Cowne. She sent a message to Gina Nelthorpe-Cowne explaining the situation – it was a disappointment because there were some big deals in the pipeline for her, but one of the taboos for the Royal Family is endorsement. You can wear a designer's dress and look sensational but you can't say how much you love it because it would give an unfair commercial advantage. It will sell out anyway, of course.

Inevitably, therefore, she didn't renew her contract with Reitmans after honouring her commitments to her winter collection. There would be no more 'It's Reitmans ... Really'. They parted on good terms and the company was gracious about it, declaring, 'She was a great partner.'

A much bigger wrench was the closure of The Tig in April 2017. She had already stopped posting on Twitter and Instagram and now she said goodbye to her much-loved online site. She wrote a final message: 'After close to three beautiful years on this adventure with you, it's time to say goodbye to The Tig. What began as a passion project (my little engine that could) evolved into an amazing community of inspiration, support, fun and frivolity. You've made my days brighter and filled this experience with so much joy. Keep finding those Tig moments of discovery, keep laughing and taking risks, and keep being "the change you wish to see in the world".'

She ended with her familiar rallying call to women everywhere – one that could become a campaign slogan if she ever decided to fulfil her childhood ambition to run for the Presidency: 'Above all don't ever forget your worth – as I've told you time and time again: you, my sweet friend, you are enough.'

Ironically, just as she seemed to be winding down her current commitments, she was pictured in *Vanity Fair* at the previous year's One Young World summit. Meghan, it suggested, was a strong believer that different aspects of her life could co-exist: 'My life shifts from refugee camps to red carpets. I choose them both because these worlds can in fact co-exist. I've never wanted to be a lady who lunches – I've always wanted to be a woman who works.'

Each change in Meghan's life, some more major than others, seemed a significant preparation for moving full-time to the UK. She still had a commitment to *Suits* but the programme's producers did their best to accommodate her new, exhausting transatlantic lifestyle. Behind the scenes, Aaron Korsch made the decision to write Rachel Zane out of the series.

He didn't want his writers to be caught by surprise, discovering that Meghan's character would have to be excluded abruptly and end up being hit by a bus or some other randomly shocking departure. Aaron could see that the relationship with Harry was blossoming into something life-changing for Meghan. He explained, 'I didn't want to intrude and ask her, "hey what's going on and what are you going to do?" So, collectively with the writers, we decided to take a gamble that these two people were in love and it was going to work out.'

He couldn't be sure at this stage if art was going to imitate life but a storyline was put in motion that would lead to Rachel Zane and Mike Ross getting married and leaving Toronto for Seattle at the end of Season 7. It remained to be seen whether her fictional character would be the first to the altar. Harry and Meghan were pictured sharing a kiss at a polo match at Coworth Park, Ascot, in early May, which suggested everything was progressing nicely in the real world.

Meghan continued to talk about the things that mattered in her life – perhaps before the royal shutters were pulled down firmly. She gave an interview to *Pride*, the UK lifestyle magazine for 'the aspirational woman of colour'. This was a publication that had styled itself as 'the face of black Britain' since it was first published in 1991.

Pride put a picture of Meghan in a white shirt on the front cover with the headline 'Princess in Waiting' and the line 'Most people could not tell I was half black.' In the article Meghan spoke of the jokes she had endured throughout her life because those making them did not realise that she was half black. She said, 'I think I feel an obligation now to talk about discrimination.' Her hope for the world, she explained, is to 'get to a place where it's colour blind'.

That clearly had not happened during the week from hell she had endured when her romance with Harry became public, but she was expressing the hope that it might improve in the future.

Meghan was back in Africa for her thirty-sixth birthday, with Harry taking her to his beloved Botswana for the second time. Again, they stayed at the Meno a Kwena camp, the perfect place to celebrate what was, give or take a few days, their first anniversary. As well as embracing the African landscape – his 'second home', as Harry called it – they spent a day helping Elephants Without Borders.

The couple joined the charity's founder Dr Mike Chase to fix a satellite collar to a magnificent bull elephant. The device would allow the animal to be tracked by conservationists striving to protect him and other members of the herd from the deadly threat of poachers. More romantically, they drove eight hours to stay at a luxury lodge on the Zambesi River close to the breathtaking Victoria Falls.

The *Daily Mail*'s royal reporter, Rebecca English, included a phrase in an article about the Botswana trip that would become a focus of negativity towards them in the years ahead: 'The couple are accompanied by a small team of *taxpayer-funded* police bodyguards …' If all else failed then the cost to the British public of keeping Meghan and Harry safe was a stick with which to beat the couple in the future.

Protection was a tricky subject right from the outset. When Meghan travelled to Mumbai, for instance, the professional bodyguard with her was actually part of Priyanka Chopra's security team. It was part of daily life for A-list film and pop stars and big-name celebrities. Politicians past and present had them and so, of course, did all the Royal Family.

Gone were the days when Meghan could slip out unnoticed. Ken Wharfe, who at one time was responsible for Princess Diana's security, explained his philosophy towards the safety of a royal charge: 'You cannot absent yourself to a nearby hotel.' As far as Ken was concerned, guaranteeing safety was always the priority; respecting her privacy came second.

As Ken shrewdly observed, the negative impact of some social media meant that Meghan would have to be careful in the future – and if that involved proper personal protection, then so be it. Meghan had initially turned down Harry's offer to pay for a bodyguard for her. She would soon have no choice in the matter – especially if she and the prince embarked on a more formal, permanent relationship.

Harry was used to it – this had been a part of his life since he was in short trousers. But the necessity of having full-time security because you were never absolutely safe was not a privilege at all. It was a heavy burden.

Before she left for Botswana, Meghan provided a delicious lunch at her house in Toronto for the renowned *Vanity Fair* writer Sam Kushner. The subsequent interview was upbeat, describing her 'genuine warmth' and putting in the bin the 'tabloid nonsense' written about her. 'Criticism of Markle,' he wrote, 'has been snob-ridden, racist and uninformed. The trolls have really gone after her.' He singled out the *Daily Star* online for announcing that 'Prince Harry could marry into gangster royalty – his new love is from a crime-ridden Los Angeles neighbourhood.'

Meghan was disarmingly straightforward about her relationship with Harry, declaring, 'We're two people who are really happy and in love.' Her simple truth was a refreshing change from the usual buttoned-up starchiness of the Royal Family. She hoped that people would understand that this was their time. Arguably the most interesting of her remarks was the one reflecting her status as woman of achievement who had not changed just because she was dating a prince: 'I've never been defined by my relationship.'

The interview in the September issue of the magazine seemed to pave the way for an official announcement and certainly the media assumed it would be a formality. The third Invictus Games, held conveniently in the middle of the month in Toronto, showed the whole world they were a couple. It was much more than a quick kiss at the polo.

Telephoto lenses were trained on Meghan when she arrived for the opening ceremony to see if she was wearing a ring. She wasn't. Her presence in the VIP box immediately alongside Harry, Justin Trudeau and US First Lady Melania Trump would have been an unwelcome distraction. The event was all about a cause close to Harry's heart and not about his love life.

Instead, Meghan sat next to Markus Anderson, three rows away. The *Daily Mail* continued its narrative about protection, noting that a security man was a few feet away in a stairwell. Meghan, as a commoner, was not actually entitled to a 'taxpayer-funded', armed SO14 police officer, said the newspaper.

The other observation that the paper made was that Meghan's burgundy dress and leather jacket was very different from the demure outfit that Kate Middleton wore when she was first seen in public with William.

Harry and Meghan were much more a couple when they arrived holding hands to watch a game of wheelchair tennis. Meghan wore what would soon become a famous outfit – a loose-fitting white blouse, designed by Misha Nonoo and called the 'Husband Shirt'. It was low-key and natural, with Meghan chatting easily to members of the crowd. At the closing ceremony, Harry joined Meghan and her mother, who had flown in from Los Angeles, the first time the three of them had been seen together, although the prince had met Doria several times.

A couple of weeks later Meghan had tea with the Queen at Buckingham Palace. It was kept top secret. Harry and Meghan drove around from Nottingham Cottage in a Ford Galaxy SUV with blacked-out windows and managed to make their way unnoticed to his grandmother's private sitting rooms.

Tea was very English and very traditional. Earlier in the year Meghan had popped to a traditional tea room in Pasadena while visiting her mum in LA, so she had some idea of what to expect – tiny cucumber sandwiches with no crust that were barely a mouthful and Twinings Earl Grey tea with milk served in a bone china cup.

The Queen, a 91-year-old great-grandmother, needed to warm to Meghan because, officially at least, the sovereign needed to approve should they want to marry. The Royal Family had a poor record when it came to marriage, with divorce far more common than golden weddings: Harry's mother and father of course, Princess Anne, Prince Andrew and the late Princess Margaret did not set the bar very high.

Fortunately, Meghan did well, not least because the Queen's bad-tempered corgis loved her, just laying on her feet as she battled to stop her tea from spilling. 'It was very sweet,' she said.

Harry proposed during a quiet evening at Nottingham Cottage when, for once, he was doing the cooking – roast chicken. He got down on one knee to ask for her hand, holding out a beautiful trilogy ring, which had a central diamond from Botswana flanked by two smaller diamonds from his mother's personal jewellery collection. Meghan had said yes before he had finished.

The official announcement everyone was expecting came on Twitter early in the morning of 27 November 2017. Harry and Meghan were engaged. They handpicked the broadcaster Mishal Husain to conduct their engagement interview. It's easy to see how she would appeal to Meghan: Mishal is a vigorous voice on behalf of gender equality and the desire for women to reach their full potential. As well as being a familiar face on television, she was an ambassador and mentor for the charity, Mosaic, that pledged to help young people shine in their chosen career. She was also writing a soon-to-be published book called *The Skills* that offered women valuable advice on how to succeed.

The interview itself was a relaxed and informal affair, so different from the notorious train wreck of Charles and Diana when the Prince of Wales offered the most unromantic reply when asked about being in love: 'Whatever in love means,' he observed, coldly.

Meghan said all the right things, including that the Queen was an 'incredible woman'. And how she appreciated meeting her through Harry's lens, 'not just with his honour and respect for her as the monarch, but the love he has for her as his grand-mother.' Harry returned the compliment by saying that Doria was 'amazing', but one piece of information was glossed over – he hadn't actually met Tom Markle.

The *Spectator*'s Melanie McDonagh was not enthusiastic about Harry and Meghan's news. She wrote, 'It may be churlish to be unkind about a young couple who have just announced their engagement but needs must,' before observing that 'seventy years ago, Meghan Markle would have been the kind of woman the Prince would have had for a mistress, not a wife.'

The *Daily Mail*, as ever, was negative, declaring in a headline: 'From Raunchy Poems and Anti-Brexit Poster ... to the Unashamed Princess of Plugs.'

Tom Bradby, the presenter of ITN News and bestselling novelist, was more positive in *The Standard*, noting that a 'nod towards an increasingly diverse country wouldn't hurt. A mixed-race campaigner for women's rights in an age when these are the issues at the heart of the national debate? In terms of timing and ability to capture the mood, no screenwriter could have improved on Harry's decision to marry Meghan. It's bang on.'

Tom, perhaps the only commentator who was actually a friend of William and Harry, enthused, 'She is one of the most likeable people you are bound to meet.' He did, however, caution that there would be challenges ahead, not least within the family firm where inevitable tensions over money, status, position and fame stalked the Palace corridors.

He was right.

20

THE CLEAN SLATE

Meghan had already given up so much for love. She had waved goodbye to her career as an actress, her home and friends in Toronto, the familiar streets of Los Angeles, her online accounts and The Tig, her commercial endeavours and even her much-loved dog Bogart.

He didn't get on with Harry so it was for the best that he didn't travel over with her to London, instead staying behind with 'Uncle' Markus. Guy, her beloved beagle – the 'little guy' as she still called him – made the trip so at least she had some part of her past life with her as she settled full-time into Nottingham Cottage.

And of course she had Harry, but it all seemed a very one-sided sacrifice. That was even more apparent when an announcement was made that she was stepping away from her own charitable roles. She would no longer work with World Vision Canada or as a UN Women's advocate.

A statement from Jason Knauf in November 2017 said that she was giving up her work with both organisations and was careful to stress that she had made the decision herself. He explained, 'She wants to start with a clean slate and focus on the UK, and getting to know this country, and travelling around the

Commonwealth. So the only role that she will begin with is as patron of the Royal Foundation.'

He added: 'This is the country that's going to be her home now and that means travelling around, getting to know the towns and cities and smaller communities.'

This all sounded very plausible but, in reality, Meghan would have had no choice. As a member of the Royal Family, she would need to focus solely on being a representative of the Queen at home and abroad. That was the tradition and only Princess Diana had been able to break it.

The Royal Foundation had been set up in 2009 to promote the charitable work of William and Harry. They were later joined by Kate and now Meghan would make it a gang of four. Initiatives had included the Heads Together mental health campaign and the Stop Speak Support crusade against cyber bullying.

Meghan's first venture as one half of a new royal couple was a walkabout in Nottingham. She instinctively had a rapport with the crowds of well-wishers, introducing herself with, 'Hi, I'm Meghan'. One of the onlookers, Zoe Scott, told reporters presciently, 'She doesn't need the Royal Family. She had made it on her own and she has obviously fallen in love.' A young woman from Australia couldn't shake hands properly because it was such a cold day so Meghan gave her a warming heat pack. It was all about being approachable.

The official reason for the trip to the Midlands city was to visit the Terrence Higgins Trust World Aids Day Fair as well as meeting mentors and counsellors working for Full Effect, a new organisation that helped children vulnerable to gang and other criminal influences.

From the very beginning, it was self-evident that Meghan had a natural empathy. You could touch her arm and not feel as if you had done something wrong. As a biracial woman Meghan immediately made the Royal Family more representative of diversity. That was clear when she and Harry visited the Brixton-based community radio station Reprezent 107.3 FM in the New Year. The station entirely staffed by under-25s had been the first to interview the soon-to-be superstar Stormzy in 2014, which went so well that he returned to host a monthly advice phone in-show, full of bad advice, good humour and great music.

Onlookers were impressed that Meghan had obviously read up and memorised her briefing notes about the day ahead. The station was supporting a Youth Music programme of radio training, volunteering and artist development for young people – just Meghan's sort of thing.

She chatted easily with everyone, praising DJ YV Shells for his enlightened views about gender equality.

The cameras were not with her a few days later. Quietly, without fuss, Meghan arrived at Al-Manaar, a mosque and cultural centre in Acklam Road about a mile from Grenfell Tower in West London. Like the rest of the world, she had watched in horror as fire engulfed the social housing block in June 2017, causing seventy-two people to lose their lives and countless more to lose their homes and possessions.

Meghan had been in Toronto when the appalling tragedy unfolded but now she was in London full-time, she had the chance to become involved for the good of a local community so devastated by what had happened. She had come to visit the Hubb Community Kitchen, a group of women who had gathered there the day after the tragedy to cook fresh food for their own families and others who had been displaced, were hungry and no longer had their own kitchens.

Meghan bonded with these wonderful women because that's what she can do. They greeted her with hugs and kisses which she returned with warmth. Then she rolled up her sleeves and started washing the rice for lunch. It was the first of many unpublicised visits. Zahira Ghaswala, who runs the Hubb, observed, 'She is like a friend; she comes, we get together, we cook.'

Throughout her life it seemed Meghan had appreciated the importance of good food to a community in need, whether it was as a Californian schoolgirl serving meals at the Hippie Kitchen to the Skid Row homeless; or as an actress volunteering at the St Felix project in Downtown Toronto.

She embraced the stoicism and spirit of the women at the Hubb, which means 'love' in Arabic. She observed, 'The kitchen buzzes with women of all ages; women who have lived and seen life; laughing, chatting, sharing a cup of tea and a story.'

Meghan asked why the Hubb was only open two days a week and was told bluntly that the problem was funding or, more precisely, lack of it. Meghan immediately suggested a cookbook. A plan was hatched to compile a book of fifty recipes, each a favourite of one of the women at the kitchen. The proceeds could bring much-needed funds that might enable the Hubb to open every day.

Meghan promised to support it, thereby ensuring it would receive the oxygen of publicity. She agreed to write a foreword, emphasising how impressed she was that so many different cultures and personalities could come together harmoniously, a 'melting pot' with roots in Morocco, India, Iraq, Uganda, Russia and at least ten other countries.

By the time it was published nine months later, Meghan would be married, Her Royal Highness and a Duchess.

Blatant racism, however, was on her doorstep. Her neighbour in Kensington Palace, Princess Michael of Kent, who lived with her husband Prince Michael in apartment number ten, had worn a clear and obvious symbol of racism to the Queen's Christmas lunch at Buckingham Palace: pinned to her coat was a blackamoor brooch.

This was not a discreet lapel pin but an ostentatious and invidious piece of jewellery. They weren't always controversial; in the eighteenth century they were a popular genre of decorative art, but in modern times such brooches are deeply offensive, linked to colonialism and slavery – to call someone a blackamoor would be considered racist abuse.

At best, as far as Princess Michael was concerned, it was an example of not living in the real world. She did, however, have form in such matters: in 2004 she reportedly told black customers in a New York restaurant to 'go back to the colonies' in an argument about noise.

She denied the incident in an interview with ITV. Instead she recalled, 'I even pretended years ago to be an African, a half-caste African, but because of my light eyes I did not get away with it, but I dyed my hair black. I had this adventure with these absolutely adorable, special people and to call me racist: it's a knife through the heart because I really love these people.'

Meghan may or may not have seen the brooch. She made no comment when social media users condemned pictures of the Princess wearing it, prompting an apology from a spokesman: 'The brooch was a gift and has been worn many times before.' The fact that the piece had been worn often was not necessarily a good excuse.

The brooch was just one of the examples of racism within the Royal Family that the award-winning journalist Yasmin Alibhai-Brown cited when she robustly advised Meghan not to marry into it. She had witnessed firsthand the flippant racism of The Firm. When Yasmin, a Ugandan Asian, met Prince Philip at an event to celebrate a William Shakespeare anniversary, he turned to her English husband and inquired, 'Is she yours?' For too long, the Queen's husband's many racist comments have been dismissed as gaffes, on a par, you might say, with using the wrong knife at dinner. There is a world of difference between a gaffe and an insult.

And just the previous month Prince Charles had asked brown-skinned journalist Anita Sethi where she came from. 'Manchester', she replied, only for Charles to respond, 'You don't look like it.'

Yasmin pointed out that the Royal Family was nothing of the kind. It's a firm whose 'values and expectations can crush those who join it.' Yasmin's less than optimistic view did not find favour with Piers Morgan, who continued to support Meghan enthusiastically. In a conversation on *Good Morning Britain* (*GMB*) he made his view clear to Yasmin: 'I think he (Harry) has found himself a very good bride here and I think your cynicism should be condemned to the dustbin of old Royal history.'

That would prove not to be the case.

One other point made by Yasmin was easy to overlook amid the debate about the Royal Family's innate racism. She had been told confidentially by a tabloid reporter assigned to monitor Harry's fiancée's every move that Meghan 'feels isolated and alone'.

That was not a promising sign looking to the future; at all. The news agenda in the run up to the wedding was dominated not by racism past and present, however, but by the antics of Tom Markle.

From the outset, Meghan's family were weaponised against her by the media. At first, perhaps, the newspapers might have thought it more fruitful to explore and exploit her black relatives but Doria has never said a word to the press about her daughter; not one. Others, including Uncle Joseph and Ava Burrow, have occasionally spoken but in a complimentary way and nothing earth-shattering. There are only so many 'gang-scarred' headlines you can get away with.

Tom Markle's side of the family, however, proved to be the soap opera gift that keeps giving. Clearly the newspapers thought they would embarrass Meghan and, therefore, were worth pursuing time and time again. Samantha had been fast out of the blocks, reportedly calling Meghan a social climber. She had started referring to herself as Samantha Markle instead of Samantha Grant, the name she had gone by for years. Tom Jr, we learned, had been arrested for brandishing a gun at his fiancée during a drunken incident in January 2017.

And then there was Dad, who had retired to Rosario, a small seaside town in Mexico that became overrun by reporters who took over every spare hotel room and Airbnb to relentlessly pursue Tom, who was now aged seventy-three. The wedding was approaching and still he had not met Harry, although he said he had spoken to him on the phone and the prince had asked for his youngest daughter's hand in marriage. Tom told him, 'You're a gentleman, promise me you will never raise your hand against my daughter and of course I will grant you my permission.'

Tom, who had been declared bankrupt in 2017, was completely out of his depth. For the time being at least, he could forget about a quiet and peaceful retirement. He was hounded by the media. 'They're always here,' he said, ruefully. He found the attention stressful. He foolishly agreed to a series of photographs staged by Los Angeles paparazzo, Jeff Rayner – it may have seemed a good strategy to Tom, to perhaps lessen the daily interest in him. The deal was thirty per cent of all proceeds from sales to Tom, which didn't seem a very fair cut for him. The *Daily Mail* revealed the pictures that had sold around the world for a six-figure sum to be 'fake'. They included set-up shots of him being fitted for a suit, exercising to get in shape and in a Starbucks café.

It was desperate stuff. When it was revealed he was cashing in on Meghan's wedding, his elder daughter Samantha came to his defence, claiming it was her idea to pose for some positive pictures and not ones that made him look bad. The timing was dreadful – just days after Harry's spokesman had asked publishers to respect Mr Markle's privacy, stating that he had been 'harassed' by paparazzi. This completely undermined that request.

Understandably, the negative coverage the staged pictures brought cast doubt on whether Tom would attend the wedding in Windsor. He was clearly stressed and unhappy at what was going on and needed treatment for heart problems at a local hospital. Kensington Palace again tried to persuade the press to back off: 'This is a deeply personal moment for Ms Markle in the day before her wedding. She and Prince Harry ask again for understanding and respect to be extended to Mr Markle in this difficult situation.'

Samantha continued to farm some attention – appearing on *GMB* where Piers Morgan again defended Meghan, accusing her half-sister of being a media vulture: he told her, 'You have treated your sister in a very shabby way.' Tom Jr also got in on the act by writing an embarrassing open letter urging Harry not to wed his half-sister.

The attendance seemed to be a 'will he, won't he' saga. It appeared Tom hadn't learned any lessons where the media were concerned and was now talking to *TMZ*, the Los Angeles-based tabloid news website. He said his heart was 'seriously damaged' after the heart attack but he still wanted to make the wedding.

Guests started to fly in, including her co-stars from *Suits*. Her fictional wedding had finally aired the previous month. Her mother Doria arrived too; it turned out she was the only member of Meghan's family who would be there. The royal experts, who really didn't have a clue what was going on, tipped Doria as the most likely stand-in to walk Meghan down the aisle. It was even suggested that Markus Anderson might step in.

Eventually Kensington Palace issued a statement on Meghan's behalf: 'Sadly my father will not be attending our wedding. I have always cared for my father and hope he can be given the space to focus on his health.' The final decision had been so last minute that his name was still on the order of service.

The saga was just desperately sad. Meghan had even ordered a selection of clothes for her father's trip, including a smart morning suit for the big day. He had no need to be fitted for one in Mexico, with or without a photographer staging the whole thing. She was still trying to reach out to him from her hotel suite at Cliveden the day before the wedding – but with no luck.

With the benefit of hindsight, palace courtiers, as the staff are politely and anonymously referred to, played an absolute stinker where Tom Markle is concerned. Perhaps they were lulled into a false sense of security by the behaviour of Kate Middleton's dad Michael, who didn't care for any attention and wanted to keep as low a profile as possible. When the media turned up on his doorstep in Berkshire, he told them firmly but politely, 'We never talk to the press.'

Richard Kay, in the *Daily Mail*, was bang on when he observed, 'Old royal hands were left wondering why more effort hadn't been taken to ensure Meghan's father was properly brought into his daughter's new world.' It's a legitimate question that remains unanswered.

Ironically, Kate's mother and father were actually at the wedding, fully accepted into royal circles where their discretion is appreciated.

Finally, the day arrived, 19 May 2018. Meghan woke up to the news that she would be Her Royal Highness, the Duchess of Sussex. Previously, there had only been one Duke of Sussex: Prince Augustus Frederick, the ninth child of King George III. The first Duke, who died in 1843 without a legitimate heir, had a liberal attitude for his time, including supporting the abolition of the slave trade. He never married, so Meghan is, in fact, the first Duchess of Sussex. Her wedding was not a big state occasion full of pomp and ceremony and cluttered with world leaders who neither Harry nor Meghan knew. They would have liked to ask the Obamas but were advised that it would be too political; especially as it would mean inviting President Trump as well and he was the last person they wanted to see on their big day.

Inevitably, much of the interest centred on which celebrities were invited. After all, this was Meghan and Harry's world. Later the number of A-listers in attendance would be sneered at, as if that in some way detracted from a grand occasion, but at the time it was fun to spot famous names as if it were the biggest red-carpet event of the year. Oprah was there, George and Amal Clooney, Idris Elba, the Beckhams, James Corden and many more.

As well as the stars of *Suits*, Meghan's closest friends were looking their best, too – Misha Nonoo, Priyanka Chopra, Jessica Mulroney, Markus Anderson, Serena Williams, Benita Litt, Genevieve Hillis and Lindsay Roth all smiled encouragingly as she made her way into St George's Chapel, attended by ten young page boys and bridesmaids. In the end, Prince Charles stepped up to accompany her down the aisle. He enjoyed Meghan's company, finding her cultured, well read and receptive to new ideas; he was happy to do this for her.

Prince William was best man.

The two brothers adopted a united front on the day, although it would later be rumoured that they had fallen out some months earlier when William counselled his brother not to rush into marriage. He had advised Harry to take as much time as he needed to 'get to know this girl.' Harry apparently took umbrage at this, although neither brother has spoken of it publicly. The conversation as reported was a very one-sided exchange. It seems unlikely, though, that Harry would have taken this lying down and may well have aimed a few home truths of his own at the future king.

Nobody would have guessed that they weren't on the very best of terms as Meghan approached the altar with their father. Inevitably, much of the interest was on the bridal gown, which had been designed by Clare Waight Keller, the first female artistic director at the French fashion house, Givenchy. The dress was a triumph of unfussy haute couture that took seasoned fashion observers back to the golden Hollywood age of Audrey Hepburn. Alison Jane Reid thought it sublime: 'It's not about being overly ostentatious, it's about ravishing craftsmanship and extraordinary attention to detail.' The five-metre veil was more dramatic, including an exquisite floral detail representing all fifty-three countries of the Commonwealth.

The ceremony itself combined tradition with what *Forbes* magazine described as 'some modern uplifting and forceful American touches.' The day was also one of joy for the 100,000 people lining the streets of Windsor – including, incidentally, Gigi Perreau, who had flown in from Los Angeles; and for the millions watching on television around the world.

But when the couple had kissed and driven off into the sunset in an E-Type Jaguar, it was time to reflect on whether this really was a game changer for the Royal Family: or was it just an example of what they do best – meaningless pomp and pageantry?

The novelist Jasmine Guillory observed that many people would try to ignore the fact that Meghan was a woman of colour. She observed, 'Because Meghan has light skin, I think a lot of people will try to pretend like, "Oh, she's not really black", but I think she's made it clear to the world that she is a black woman.'

Jasmine cited the example of Doria, a woman with dreadlocks, standing next to Harry and Meghan at the Invictus Games: she was saying proudly to the public, 'this is my mother'.

And, putting race aside for a moment, what was the world to make of what author Diana Evans in *Time Magazine* called 'the partial erasure of a whole person', one who had made so many changes to a successful life for love – including being baptised by the Archbishop of Canterbury using water from the River Jordan.

The wedding was a fairy tale but what would the future hold for Meghan? Would she, the determined advocate for women, be diminished? As Diana Evans wrote, 'Is there a chance that she will simply become another royal waif, swallowed whole into luxury and impartiality, her dresses more important than her voice?'

21

A LABOUR OF LOVE

———

Doria gave the women a hug, just as her daughter did. It was so natural for them both. They were at the lunch in the gardens at Kensington Palace launching the Hubb Community cookbook. The women from the kitchen had made the short journey from the Al-Manaar centre on a cloudy September afternoon to celebrate the publication of *Together*.

Meghan and her mother chatted easily with the assembled cooks, proudly showing off the recipes they had volunteered for the book. Doria made a beeline for Ahlam Saeid's bowl of green rice, announcing 'I love this', and watched approvingly as Meghan added a little olive oil and fresh mint.

'Hi, I'm Meg's mum,' said Doria, as she joined another group of women. She was as excited as they were. 'It's amazing. I'm going to tell everyone I met each of you. I'm going to make everything. I'm serious.'

Each of the fifty recipes had someone's name on it. They were given proper acknowledgement – they weren't just lumped together as the Duchess of Sussex's tastiest recipes or some such nonsense – so it was Halima Al-Hudafi's kofta kebabs with onion and sumac pickle that Meghan turned so expertly as they sizzled on the grill; it was Lillian Olwa's carrot and onion chapatis that she flipped.

Harry was there too, making sure not to steal any of his wife's limelight: this was her day and he was content to stay a step behind. Meghan gave a three-minute speech without notes. Being an experienced actress had some advantages in Meghan's new life. She could learn her lines in advance and not have to stumble around with bits of paper or card. It was twenty years since she had learned the art of speaking in the drama classes at Immaculate Heart. The skill never left her.

She told her audience that working on the project for nine months had been a 'tremendous labour of love'. She praised the women for their warmth and kindness, stressing that *Together* was more than just a cookbook. She explained, 'The power of food is more than just the meal itself. It is the story behind it. And when you get to know the story of the recipe, you get to know the person behind it.

'And that's what we're talking about in terms of coming together, to really engage and talk and to be able to celebrate what connects us rather than what divides us. That, I believe, is the ethos of *Together*.'

Doria had the last word as she said goodbye to a small group of new friends: 'The power of women,' she mused. 'We make things happen. We're curious; we say yes, we show up. I'm inspired.' Within six months, the cookbook had sold more than 130,000 copies worldwide and raised more than half a million pounds for the community kitchen and for other Grenfell Tower support projects.

Her mum was one of few people who knew that Meghan was already pregnant at the launch. The world would have to wait for an official announcement the following month, after she had undergone her twelve-week scan.

The news was released as Meghan and Harry flew into Sydney for their first overseas tour to Australia, New Zealand, Fiji and

Tonga. The so-called royal experts on the press jaunt had the ignominy of being told Meghan was pregnant by their London offices as they waited to collect their luggage.

What a difference a year had made. In Toronto in 2017 Meghan had sat three rows behind Harry at the opening ceremony of the Invictus Games. Now she was at his side at the Sydney Opera House when he spoke of the service made in the past by Australian soldiers and how the Invictus generation had 'reminded us all what selfless duty is made of'.

Meghan had been offered plenty of 'helpful' media advice in the preceding months on how to behave like a royal – as if being noticed for your womb and your wardrobe was the height of feminine aspiration. Claudia Joseph, author of *How to Dress Like a Princess: The Secrets of Kate's Wardrobe*, observed, 'She will have to curb what she says, she's not going to be able to be as political as she was beforehand – and that might be trouble in the future.'

Meghan ignored that, although to some extent it depends on how the listener interprets one of her speeches: is a rallying call to support gender equality a political matter or a human rights issue? Meghan gave two inspiring addresses on her first official tour: first, in Suva, the capital of Fiji, she announced the award of two new grants to the Fiji National University and the University of the South Pacific, where she was speaking to students; the money would fund workshops to empower female staff.

Grants such as these provided women with the skills and training they needed to 'operate effectively in their roles', as well as recognising potential for leadership and ensuring that more women became part of the decision-making process in academic institutions.

The speech was more than just ribbon-cutting announcement, though. Meghan cared passionately about the importance of education: 'Everyone should be afforded the opportunity to receive the education they want, but more importantly the education they have the right to receive. And for women and girls in developing countries, this is vital. When girls are given the right tools to succeed, they can create incredible futures, not only for themselves, but also for those around them.'

Meghan's words were so impressive that everyone forgot that Harry was going to speak as well. The MC even failed to introduce him: 'I thought I got away with it,' he laughed as he made his way to the microphone, 'No way that I could follow my wife after that.' He composed himself to talk seriously about the challenge presented by climate change: 'All of you here are confronted by this threat in your daily lives,' he said.

Meghan's second speech was just as powerful as her first, perhaps even more so. She spoke at a reception at Government House in Wellington, New Zealand, marking 125 years of women's suffrage in the Commonwealth country. Women won the right to vote in parliamentary elections there in 1893. Thirty-five years would pass before women had the same voting rights as men in the UK.

She didn't deal exclusively in sound bites, explaining her view that women's suffrage was not simply about the right to vote but about what that represents: 'The basic and fundamental right of all people – including members of society who have been marginalised – whether for reasons of race, gender, ethnicity or orientation – to be able to participate in the choices for their future and their community.'

A common thread running through many of Meghan's views through the years – from her early steps questioning the use of female stereotypes in advertising dishwashing liquid to standing in front of an august audience celebrating suffrage, was her desire for gender equality – 'feminism is about fairness,' she said.

Meghan ended her address by acknowledging the words of the great New Zealand campaigner, Kate Sheppard: 'All that separates, whether of race, class, creed or sex is inhuman, and must be overcome.'

And then she sat down, fittingly next to the premier Jacinda Ardern, who leaned over and whispered 'Perfect'. The two women, just a year apart in age, were kindred spirits. Jacinda had already openly declared herself to be a feminist and a believer in equality: 'If you believe that women and men performing the same job should get the same pay, you should be a feminist.'

Jacinda, who had just returned from a three-month maternity leave, also echoed Meghan's view that feminism and femininity were compatible: 'You can wear a bra, makeup, have never read Germaine Greer and still be a feminist.'

Meghan was thirty-seven and expecting her first child with the eyes of the world upon her. After making such a success of her first official tour and dealing with important and serious issues, you might have expected the media to be a little respectful or at least kind to her during the final few months of her pregnancy.

Instead, she was greeted by a flurry of negative articles about the cradling of her baby bump. Jo Elvin, the editor of *You Magazine* – the supplement of the *Mail on Sunday* – caught the tone: 'This is the Duchess of Showbiz we have here. It smacks to me of a focus that's contrived and relentlessly photo-op ready. Meghan would be well advised to take the "world's only pregnant woman" vibe down a notch or two.'

The *Daily Mail* had more to say on the matter. Liz Jones wrote, 'Personally, I find the cradling a bit like those signs in the back of cars: Baby on Board. Virtue signalling, as though the rest of us barren harridans deserve to burn alive in our cars.'

Such rants about a pregnant woman stroking or holding her baby bump only encouraged far worse online responses from the so-called trolls on Twitter and other social media. Trolls is a curious word that makes these abusers sound as if they are in an enjoyable Tolkien fantasy film when, in fact, their aggressive insults are very much a joyless reality.

The problem for Meghan was that she couldn't give the metaphorical finger to the columnists or internet aggressors. Khloe Kardashian, of the much-derided but highly successful American clan, was a good example of how to combat that bullying. She tweeted while pregnant earlier in the year: 'People are very opinionated about my bump. I choose to cradle my bump because it's mine. I've waited for this very short moment for years. I have only months to enjoy this phase in my life, so I will touch my bump and love my bump as often as I choose.'

Aside from the obvious bullying of a pregnant woman, it began to dawn on people that Meghan was being treated entirely differently to Kate Middleton. When Kate was expecting and pictured with her hand on her stomach in early 2018, the *Daily Mail* exclaimed, 'Bumping along nicely!' as the Duchess of Cambridge 'tenderly cradled' her bump.

The Sun helpfully provided Meghan with a resumé of the rules she had to follow as a royal. She had to wear a pair of nude tights whatever the weather; no dark or colourful nail polish; no hats after 6pm unless it's a tiara; always pack a black dress in case a member of the Royal Family dies when you are on your travels.

She was not allowed to behave normally because of protocol – one of the most overused words when talking about the Royal Family. It is a nonsense term that is trotted out to give some footling story gravitas. The American author Marlene Koenig put it into perspective: 'Protocol applies to official state events or who sits next to who ... It does not apply to off-the-shoulder dresses or nail polish.'

Apparently Meghan had already breached protocol countless times. She had, for instance, worn a dress with an off-the-shoulder neckline to the Trooping of the Colour ceremony in June. Then she wore a dark nail polish on her toes to the British Fashion Awards at the Royal Albert Hall in December. Photographers were actually taking pictures of her feet. Most heinous of all, she had shut her own car door when arriving for an event at the Royal Academy of Arts, in Piccadilly. One day she was celebrating female suffrage – the next she was being criticized for shutting her own car door.

The CNN Royal Commentator Victoria Arbiter was scathing about the stories: 'Nail polish has NOTHING to do with protocol. Nor do tights, car doors or messy buns. This is WRONG. Enough with this nonsense.'

The *Daily Mail* was not finished with pregnant Meghan. She had committed yet another faux pas by serving avocado on toast to a friend, makeup artist Daniel Martin, visiting from LA. The headline set the tone: 'Is Meghan's favourite snack fuelling drought and murder?' The hard-hitting story from Tom Leonard in New York said that the production of Meghan's tasty treat was linked to water shortages, human rights abuses and general environmental devastation – and was even filling the coffers of brutal drug cartels.

The best satirists in the land would have been hard-pressed to come up with a storyline of using avocados to bash Meghan. She also had to contend with a steady drip of information from Palace circles – all of it seemed to be positive about Kate while negative about Meghan. One was a safe, sporty and slim Home Counties' woman and the other, an upstart, biracial, American divorcee. The former embraced royal protocol while the latter broke the rules.

Kate had a very brief CV before she became a Royal bride. That was not entirely her fault. She had been William's girlfriend for very nearly ten years before they married in a ceremony full of pomp and tradition in 2011. That was practically a full-time job in itself.

She had stuck it out, even when the press mocked her as 'Waity Katy'. She worked for a year as a junior buyer for Jigsaw, the high-street fashion chain, but struggled with the attention. On her twenty-fifth birthday she was surrounded by paparazzi as she left her Chelsea flat to go to work. Clarence House issued a statement that William was very unhappy about the 'intolerable' harassment of his girlfriend. His tone was remarkably similar to the one adopted by Harry when he defended Meghan against media intrusion.

Kate had always got on famously well with Harry. When she and William were finally engaged, he announced, 'It means I get a sister, which I have always wanted.' She did have, however, previous form where the significant others of her brother-in-law were concerned. Her relationship with Chelsy Davy had been at best cordial and at worst frosty. One of Chelsy's friends from South Africa had observed, 'She is a force of nature and doesn't have time for Kate. She finds her boring.' It was also reported that Kate was not that keen on Cressida Bonas either.

That was all in the past, but it appeared that in the present she was not welcoming Meghan with open arms and helping her sister-in-law to negotiate her new world. From the very beginning, the stories were very one-sided – this was not necessarily Kate's fault, but someone from the Royal Household was leaking negative stories about Meghan.

When Meghan asked for scent to be sprayed around the chapel before her wedding, the *Daily Mail* weighed in: 'Kicking Up a Stink:"Dictatorial" bride Meghan wanted air fresheners for musty 15th-century St George's Chapel … but the Palace said no!'

How did the newspaper know this? An unnamed member of the Royal Household staff explained helpfully: 'I don't believe a request of that nature had been made before.' It had though. The *Daily Mail* had reported just before Kate's wedding that she had requested her 'favourite scented candles and toiletries from luxury fragrance brand Jo Malone to be delivered to Westminster Abbey.'

It was just one of many stories unfavourably comparing the two duchesses. Online research revealed twenty such headlines. And then there was the totally uncorroborated story that Meghan had made Kate cry over the issue of bridesmaids' tights on her wedding day. Again, how did we hear about this unless various unnamed people were briefing against Meghan?

Apparently Meghan was nicknamed Duchess Difficult by staff upset at being woken at 5.30am by an enthusiastic employer wanting to get on with things. This was a woman well used to getting up at 4.30am for a day's filming. She had a Californian work ethic that the 'men in grey suits', as Diana called them, disliked as it upset their routines.

The leaks, it seemed, were endless. A royal source is never named, nor is a courtier, a member of the Palace staff or an aide. If a particular strong point is being made, stick the word senior in front of the 'source', then quote what you like to back up the story. We, the readers, are never informed if a deal has been struck, financial or otherwise, in return for the information.

And Meghan could not respond. Suzanne Moore in the *Guardian* described the way in which Meghan was being scrutinised as 'shameful'. She observed, 'All the tabloid fixation with her pregnancy reminds us that she has entered an abusive relationship – in which misogyny is so ramped up that whatever she does is somehow suspect.'

At least Meghan's baby shower was a happy event, held away from prying eyes in the Grand Penthouse suite of The Mark Hotel on the Upper East Side of Manhattan, where the views of New York are breathtaking. The party had been organised by Serena Williams and Meghan's old friend from Northwestern, Genevieve Hillis.

No more than twenty of her closest friends were pictured arriving at the hotel, each carrying a smart carrier bag that undoubtedly contained an expensive gift. Old pals including Lindsay Roth and Markus Anderson were there, alongside newer ones including Amal Clooney and the US television host, Gayle King. Tellingly, she had made no new friends since becoming a member of the Royal Family.

The negative coverage this time focused on the extravagance and the cost of the weekend, rumoured ludicrously to be $300,000, and the fact that she had been treated to a flight on a private jet by the Clooneys. They were all Meghan's friends and what they chose to do for her is neither here nor there. There was absolutely no concrete evidence whatsoever as to the cost of the shower.

From the moment Harry made his speech in Fiji about climate change, stating that there 'cannot be any more excuses' when it comes to protecting the planet, both he and Meghan were sitting targets for cries of hypocrisy every time they parked the pushbike and took a plane. It was another stick with which to beat them; continually shooting the messenger does not mean the message is wrong.

Piers Morgan, previously such a supporter of Meghan, was certainly one columnist who would be shouting hypocrisy in the future to justify his endless negativity about Meghan. He exclusively told the *Sunday People* that he had been friendly with her but she had 'ghosted' him: 'She is someone I thought I was pretty matey with and "bang", she met somebody more important and that was it.' Piers was in LA to drum up some publicity for *Good Morning Britain*'s live show from the Oscars – and Meghan guaranteed that.

Meghan and Piers were not friends or remotely matey. They exchanged a few emails and she met him once in a pub. He was a useful contact but it was nothing more than networking in a business where that was commonplace and important if you wanted to get ahead.

The problem for Meghan was that a negative story about her was going to gather more attention than a positive one. It was a simple fact of life in the modern online world. Her 'inner circle' did their best to help stem the tide against her. Five of them gave a positive interview to *People Magazine* in the US, a course of action that would prove controversial in the future. One, described as a co-star, observed, 'Meg has sat silently back and endured all the lies and untruths. We worry about what this is doing to her and the baby. It's wrong to put anyone under this level of emotional trauma, let alone when they're pregnant.

George Clooney added his support. He compared Meghan's treatment to previous dark times: 'She's a woman who is seven months pregnant and she has been pursued and vilified and chased in the same way that Diana was and it's history repeating itself. We've seen how that ends.'

Meghan couldn't defend herself because the Royal Family never did that sort of thing. Only Harry tried to defend his wife, as he had done right from the start. Kate and William were never going to come to her defence – the gang of four had, we were about to discover, been an idealistic newspaper headline. The reality was very much two separate gangs of two.

The two households officially split in March, with Meghan and Harry coming under the umbrella of Buckingham Palace. They left the Royal Foundation that the two brothers had set up in 2009. It seemed further proof of a rift between them. At least they were no longer living just across the way from one another. At the end of March, Meghan and Harry moved into Frogmore Cottage, Windsor, part of the Crown Estate in the grounds of Frogmore House, where they had held their wedding reception.

Their new home was originally built in 1685 during the reign of Charles II, but it had been converted into five separate flats for workers on the Windsor Castle estate. By the time it caught the eye of Meghan and Harry, it had been allowed to fall into a rundown state and was in need of extensive restoration that had taken six months.

The house would have been renovated regardless of Harry and Meghan's involvement, although re-converting it back into one family home obviously required more extensive and more expensive work. The cost was £2.4 million, paid out of the Sovereign Grant, according to public accounts. Sir Michael Stevens, the keeper of the Privy Purse, explained that the property had already been earmarked for renovation: 'Outdated infrastructure was replaced to guarantee the long-term future of the property.' He added that Harry and Meghan had paid for new fittings.

They barely had time to unpack before *The Sun* had a front-page story bearing the headline 'Not In Meg Back Yard' with the sub text 'Parking Ban for Staff Near Home'. As usual, the story was made all about Meghan with a very large, full-length picture of her clearly pregnant and, yes, cradling her baby bump.

A 'source' was quoted on the second paragraph: 'Everyone's calling them NIMBYs – not in Meghan's Back Yard,' a very tortuous joke. As always, the benefit of using an unnamed source was that you can attribute anything you like to him or her with no comebacks. And, of course, a quote can be adjusted to fit the headline.

That's not to say that was the case with this story. The quote may have been word for word but the story was not true. Harry and Meghan had nothing to do with any car parking changes. The Sun dropped the story online the following day and the stock apology was eventually printed on page two of the newspaper: 'We now accept that the parking charges were not requested by the Duke and Duchess. We are happy to correct the record and apologise for any distress caused.' A page-one story that is talked about in every pub in the land becomes an apology that nobody reads. The same thing had happened when the newspaper apologised for the 'Harry's Girl on Pornhub' story. There are still probably many people who believe Meghan was a porn star.

Both stories, and in particular the headlines, were examples of making everything about Meghan. She was justifiably the story when she gave birth to a son at 5.26am on 6 May 2019, the Spring Bank Holiday Monday, at the Portland Hospital near Regent's Park, London. It had been a long night. She was already back home before an announcement was made, thereby avoiding posing with freshly blow-dried hair, looking shattered and smiling weakly for photographers and TV cameras on the hospital steps.

Doria was already at Frogmore Cottage to help and a beaming Harry, who had been present at the birth, spoke to Alan Jones of PA briefly: 'How any woman does what they do is beyond comprehension,' he said sweetly.

Two days later, Meghan and Harry presented their son to the world in the draughty old St George's Hall at Windsor Castle. Meghan looked radiantly happy in a white tuxedo dress, designed by the award-winning London designer Grace Wales Bonner, whose declared ambition was 'to build a brand that comes from a black cultural perspective and has the same authority, presence and impact as any esteemed European house.' Again, Alan, the only black court reporter, was chosen to conduct the brief interview. Meghan said, 'I have the two best guys in the world', which was perfect.

They didn't announce their son's name then. That would be a couple of hours later on the Sussex Royal Instagram, which had close to eleven million followers. They posted a picture of their baby being introduced to the Queen and the Duke of Edinburgh. Meghan held him in her arms while Harry and Doria looked on. The delight on the Queen's face as she met her eighth great-grandchild painted a thousand words.

His name: Archie Harrison Mountbatten-Windsor. Harry and Meghan decided not to give him an official royal title. Harrison obviously signified Harry's son. But Archie was a change from the more traditional old-fashioned royal choices. It meant genuine and bold. His arrival would prove to be a turning point for his parents.

22

VOGUE

———

Meghan had a code name. This wasn't for some top-level security clearance only known to the Royal Protection Squad and MI5. It was to whisper in the hallowed corridors of *Vogue* magazine in Mayfair where only a few – a very few – knew that she was in daily discussion with the enterprising and charismatic editor, Edward Enninful.

She had sent him an email in January 2019, when she was sat at home, five months pregnant, and trying to connect with Edward to help promote the Smart Works Charity, of which she was now patron. She was hoping to win the magazine's support for the project; perhaps a cover story might be of interest?

She signed it with a simple M. Edward, who was having a New Year's break in the Austrian mountains, wondered at first who M was; it sounded more James Bond than Kensington Palace. The note was a classic cold call from Meghan. She suggested that they would have much in common and would he like to meet up?

A week later they met for tea in secret. 'Hi, I'm Meghan,' said the now Duchess of Sussex, giving her guest a hug. This is the Meghan Markle way, putting people at ease, never patronising, always intelligent, committed and empathetic. She has a gift for making a fast connection. Edward would later stress her 'remarkable immediacy'.

Edward has an impressive CV. He had moved with his parents and six siblings to England from Ghana as a young teenager and enjoyed a meteoric rise in the world of fashion. He was discovered on the Tube in London by a well-known stylist who suggested he should be a model: 'I'll have to ask my mum,' said Edward.

By eighteen, he was the fashion editor of *i-D Magazine*. Over the years he had worked for Italian *Vogue*, American *Vogue* and as fashion and style director at *W* magazine. In 2017 he was appointed the first black editor-in-chief of British *Vogue*.

After his initial meeting with Meghan, Edward was filled with enthusiasm for Smart Works and determined to help if he could. Then he had a text message from the Duchess, as he calls her respectfully, asking if he might consider her guest-editing a special issue to highlight some of the women who were making a difference in the world.

He didn't hesitate and suggested that they call it 'Forces for Change', a title Meghan loved. Edward decided it should be the September issue, traditionally the most important edition of the year for *Vogue*, in which they preview the new season and the fashion changes expected in the autumn.

As ever, Meghan threw herself into learning about the editorial process; she and Edward were in daily contact through the five months it took to put together the issue. Edward told only one or two trusted lieutenants and they were under strict instructions not to tell their partners. Those not in the know were working diligently on an entirely fictitious edition.

The most important task was finding the right candidates to feature. Some, such as climate change activist Greta Thunberg, Jane Fonda, and Jacinda Ardern were already household names.

Others, such as model and former Sudanese refugee Adut Akech and Sinéad Burke, an advocate for disabled women, deserved to be.

This was an issue about women of substance intent on empowering others. There were actors, of course – as that was, after all, Meghan's world. As well as Jane Fonda, they included transgender star Laverne Cox and Yara Shahidi, founder of the online platform for the younger generation, Eighteen x 18. And then there was Salma Hayek Pinault, the acclaimed actress who had spoken out so eloquently against Harvey Weinstein; while the often controversial Jameela Jamil wrote an article urging women to be positive about their bodies.

It was, as Meghan said, about the 'power of the collective'. One of the first on board was the New Zealand premier, who met secretly with Meghan at Kensington Palace and promised not to breathe a word about the plan.

In the end, Meghan and Edward chose fifteen women, all with something inspiring to share. They were photographed by the renowned fashion photographer Peter Lindbergh, who took a series of images in black and white, his preferred medium. The front cover was a masterpiece – sixteen squares featuring each of the women and one square left over, not filled by Meghan herself, but by a simple silver mirror inviting the readers to picture themselves on the page.

Perhaps the most memorable of the portraits was of the model Adwoa Aboah, who had been on the cover for Edward's first edition in charge in December 2017. Then, she looked flawless in a printed headscarf and diamond earrings. In the Forces for Change issue she wasn't a 'model' but a beautiful biracial woman with a mass of freckles – just like Meghan, in fact. She had founded Gurls Talk in 2016, an online forum where girls could discuss mental health, sexuality and education.

Harry was included in the *Vogue* project, too. He had a sit-down conversation with Dr Jane Goodall, the legendary expert on animal behaviour and a long-time friend. They obviously discussed issues of conservation but Harry also referenced racism and how it reflected 'unconscious bias' in so many people – the perennial argument about referring to the colour of someone's skin as your first description of them: 'Despite the fact that if you go up to someone and say, "What you just said, or the way you behaved is racist", they'll turn around and say "I'm not a racist."'

Camilla Tominey, now with the *Daily Telegraph*, said in the opening lines of her reaction to the issue: 'May I make the following remarks without being accused of racism (either consciously or unconsciously).' Camilla had counted the number of white women featuring in the fifteen forces for change and noted that only five were white.

She wrote, 'I wonder if Meghan was conscious of the bias she showed in choosing 15 forces for change for the *Vogue* cover, all of whom were women, of which only five were white. If I was pale, male and stale I'd be feeling pretty discriminated against right now.'

Melanie Phillips in *The Times* tied herself up in knots trying to avoid being called racist: 'The list, however, is beyond parody as reflecting the shallow aspirations of a social justice warrior. The only achievement of several of them is being famous, being the right non-white skin colour or, like the Duchess, aspiring to making the world a kinder and gentler place. Oh, some just happen to have connections with *Vogue* itself.'

Meghan did not feature herself in the magazine but she did interview Michelle Obama, the former First Lady, who Melanie Phillips might have noted had the 'right non-white skin colour.' Michelle elegantly enforced one of Meghan's principal causes in life – the need for female education around the world. She declared, 'Every little girl, no matter her circumstances, deserves the opportunity to learn, grow and act on her knowledge.'

Sarah Vine in the *Daily Mail* put the boot in again, drawing attention deprecatingly to her nationality: 'As you Americans are fond of saying, "We need to talk," referring to 'dear Meghan' on two instances and 'my dear' on a third. Bizarrely, she criticised Meghan for her failure to recognise the Queen as a force for change: 'You fail to nominate the one truly inspirational woman in your life, the Queen, whose years of selfless devotion to this country knock all the others into a cocked hat.' (Whether the Queen is a force for change or a force for no change would be an interesting discussion point.)

Tellingly, Sarah's article was under the banner: 'My memo to Meghan Markle following her *Vogue* editorial – we Brits prefer true royalty to fashion royalty.' Just one month earlier she had written one that boasted: 'How Kate went from drab to fab! From eyebrows and Pilates to a new style guru, our experts reveal the Duchess of Cambridge's secrets to looking sizzling.'

An article by Piers Morgan for the same publication declared in its headline: 'Me-Me-Meghan Markle's shamelessly hypocritical super-woke *Vogue* stunt proves she cares more about promoting herself than the Royal Family or Britain.' Was this really the same Piers Morgan who fourteen months before had described Meghan as a 'very good bride'?

Whereas Camilla had been affronted that there were only five white women on the cover, Piers was outraged that only five of them were British. Incidentally, in an article about 'Me-Me Meghan', he referred to himself nine times and failed to spell Edward Enninful's name correctly.

Dan Wootton, in his role as a showbusiness correspondent for the *Lorraine* show on daytime television, complained, a little self-importantly: 'The Queen will think this is an absolutely idiotic, ridiculous decision, as do I.'

He added, 'Remember, Meghan doesn't want to be a celebrity, she says she wants to be a royal. Royals don't guest-edit magazines, celebrities guest-edit magazines. Do you get me? Do you see the point that I'm making?'

The senior reporter for BuzzFeed News in Washington, Ellie Hall, disputed that, pointing out that Charles, William and Kate had all collaborated with different media organisations in this way during the past six years.

Charles had guest-edited *Country Life* magazine twice – in November 2013 and again in November 2018 – the latter time being so recent that it could hardly be described as a distant memory. On the more recent occasion, he stressed the importance of the British countryside, William spoke of his plans to preserve the natural world and the Duchess of Cornwall featured her charity for medical detective dogs.

Kate took the helm of the *Huffington Post* for a day in February 2016 and worked with the editors and commissioned columns – one of them, ironically, by Michelle Obama, who wrote movingly about removing the stigma that surrounded mental health. Rather like Meghan's Letter from the Editor, Kate too wrote of the 'privilege to have the opportunity to be Guest Editor of the *Huffington Post* today'. It was part of the initiative for her Young Minds Matter campaign: 'Together, we have the chance to make a real difference for an entire generation of young people.'

And then there was Harry himself, who had guest-edited the BBC Radio 4 flagship programme *Today* in December 2017, five months before his wedding. The show was a tour de force, including interviews with Barack Obama and Prince Charles. *The Guardian* was impressed, describing Harry as 'the official interpreter of an ancient, archaic institution to the generations that are already distant both in time and culture from the world that sustains his grandmother.' Harry spoke of the need to shine a spotlight on issues that need it.

In *Vogue*, Harry had shone that light on 'unconscious bias', and a classic example of that occurred when the morning television presenter Eamonn Holmes described Meghan as being 'uppity'. The word is completely unacceptable in modern-day culture. The Canadian writer Elaine Lui, who was on the show at the time, wrote on her website Lainey Gossip: 'The implication here is that when a black person is being "uppity" it means they don't know their place, that there is a limit to how high their place should be.'

Eamonn, who clearly shares the morning doughnut tray with Piers Morgan, did not apologise, but ITV said the word would not be used again.

The reaction to *Vogue* perfectly encapsulated all four bullets with which the media sought to shoot the messenger: Meghan Markle. There were not enough white women (race); no men (gender); too few Brits (nationality) and too many actors (profession). There was also the implication that Meghan was not royal enough – that she was not part of the 'we' conversation.

Edward Enninful, while acknowledging that some of the coverage was racist was more insightful than just focusing on that concern. He observed, 'It was more than racism. I thought it was personal – attacking someone you don't know, attacking *her*.'

The September 2019 issue of *Vogue* was the fastest-selling in the magazine's 104-year history, selling out in ten days; it also had the biggest overall sale of the decade, so perhaps Meghan and Edward had the last laugh. A sad postscript, however, was the death the same month of Peter Lindbergh.

In July 2020, the issue was awarded the Diversity Initiative of the Year at the PPA (Professional Publishers Association) Awards. Meghan and Edward had definitely had the last laugh. Edward was also named magazine editor of the year. On Instagram, he said, 'Like so many of my black colleagues working in media and fashion, there is often something bittersweet about these moments of recognition. It would be disingenuous of me not to point out that I am the first black person to ever win this award – the first black person in forty years!'

Edward questioned diversity in workplaces, asking just who was allowed to get to the top. He could have referenced the royal correspondents of tabloid newspapers. There are no black reporters or people of colour among them.

Meghan said she was honoured to receive the award: 'Creating Forces for Change with Edward was an opportunity to reflect the world as we see it – beautiful and strong in its diversity.'

23

THE END OF
THE FAIRY TALE

Meghan had not forgotten Smart Works. While *Vogue* was still hot on the news stands she launched a new fashion line to specifically benefit the charity that had been founded in North London in 2013.

Smart Works provided good-quality interview clothes and coaching to boost the confidence of women struggling to find a job. They would often be referred to the organisation from job centres, care homes, prisons, homeless shelters and mental health charities. What the women had in common was a need to regain their self-worth and belief in their abilities.

The idea was a simple one, and in some ways mirrored the Glass Slipper Project in Chicago that Meghan had volunteered for at Northwestern University. Women would be fitted and styled at the charity's dressing rooms that were brimming with mostly-donated clothes and would see the new version of themselves before having a one-to-one session on interview technique. They would then be able to keep their final outfit.

The capsule collection, called The Smart Set, was launched on the roof terrace of John Lewis in Oxford Street, who, along with Marks & Spencer and Jigsaw, had backed the venture. Misha Nonoo had helped Meghan come up with designs for a dress, blazer, shirt, trousers and a bag. Misha had also provided one of her signature shirts for the collection, more tailored than usual and costing £125.

Proceeds from the sale of the clothing would go to the charity, so Meghan was thrilled to announce the leather tote bag costing £100 had sold out before she had finished her speech. This time speaking for seven minutes without notes, she emphasised the importance of feeling that you were looking your best. She made everyone laugh by recalling forty or fifty lilac blazers hanging up at Smart Works. She said, 'You want to feel confident, you want to be wearing the pieces of clothing that make you feel that way and not the leftovers that didn't sell from the end of the season.'

She urged women not just to donate clothes that they didn't want anymore but to find something in the wardrobe that might make a difference – perhaps the blazer they themselves had worn when they were chosen for the job they wanted.

Ten days later she was on her way to Cape Town. Not quite so top secret as the *Vogue* project was the news that broadcaster Tom Bradby was making a documentary for ITV about Meghan and Harry's official royal tour to Africa, which began on 23 September. The original idea was for a straightforward film about their official visit to the continent Harry loved so much.

Tom had heard that things were not brilliant behind the scenes for the couple, but he had no idea how their situation would develop as the days went by. Tom had chatted at length with the prince before they set off, but it was only after arriving in South Africa that he sensed more acutely how Harry and Meghan were feeling. He told *Good Morning America*, 'I found a couple that seemed a bit bruised and vulnerable.' He did his best to tell the story as 'empathetically as I could'.

His subsequent interview with Meghan confirmed how she herself, on the verge of tears, was 'existing rather than living' thanks to her treatment by the media. Harry, meanwhile, confirmed he was on a 'different path' to William, suggesting strongly that it was not just the press who were to blame for their sorry state.

When Tom had first met Meghan, before she and Harry married, he had tried to explain to her the unique relationship the British public had with the Royal Family. He wasn't warning her exactly – he was trying to offer her some insight and he left the conversation thinking, 'Good luck with that one.'

Meghan really hadn't understood. America has a rose-tinted view of the monarchy but, now, since her pregnancy and the first year of her child's life, she got it. She admitted, 'I did not have any understanding of what it would be like.'

Brenda Powell in the *Daily Mail* reinforced the reality of what it was like, in case she needed reminding: 'Meghan Markle is probably one of the most privileged human beings on the face of the planet. And as of last week, I reckon, she is definitely one of the most irritating.'

Certain members of the press were sympathetic. Jane Martinson of *The Guardian* was supportive: 'All Meghan wants is to be treated fairly by the press and I don't blame her.' The argument was that a wealthy woman shouldn't complain, especially while touring such poverty and deprivation in Africa, but Jane concluded, 'Do we really want to live in a world in which pain is a competition and the Royal Family is just a TV drama, not a group of real people?'

Nobody quite believed it at the time, but when Harry and Meghan returned home, their days as working members of the Royal Family were numbered. Harry, certainly, had become more focused on what he wanted in the future for his wife and son. He wanted no part of a TV drama. While his wife had embarked on a legal case against the *Mail on Sunday*, Harry's lawyers had just issued proceedings against *The Sun* and the *Daily Mirror* for allegedly hacking his phone.

Meghan was still getting support from celebrity friends. They included Elton John, who had jumped to her defence earlier in the summer when she and Harry were criticised for using his private jet to fly to the South of France for a holiday with Archie at his home near Nice. Elton said he had made sure the flight was carbon neutral by making the 'appropriate contribution' to a carbon footprint fund.

Elton said he and husband David Furnish had provided the flight to 'maintain a high level of much-needed protection'. Elton added, 'I am calling on the press to cease these relentless and untrue assassinations of their character that are spuriously crafted on an almost daily basis.'

Finally, someone who was not a celebrity, a journalist or a close friend came out in strong support of Meghan. And it wasn't just a single someone. Seventy-two female MPs had seen and heard enough of the press coverage of Meghan. They spoke up, signing a powerful open letter to the Duchess of Sussex from Holly Lynch, the MP for Halifax.

The women from across all parties expressed their 'solidarity' with Meghan against the 'often distasteful and misleading nature of the stories printed in a number of our national newspapers concerning you, your character and your family.'

The letter stated, 'On occasions, stories and headlines have represented an invasion of your privacy and have sought to cast aspersions about your character, without any good reason as far as we can see. Even more concerning still, we are calling out what can only be described as outdated, colonial undertones of some of these stories.'

Some of the signatories were the younger generation in Westminster, moving up the ladder of political prominence, including Angela Rayner, Lisa Nandy and Anneliese Dodds, as well as Tracey Crouch, who had already served in Theresa May's Government as the Minister for Sport and Civil Society. But the older generation were also well represented, figures such as Yvette Cooper, Margaret Hodge and Diane Abbott, the first elected black woman MP, who continues to suffer the most online abuse of anyone in Parliament and that's before she opens hundreds of abusive letters, literally every day.

Colonial undertones refers to the long-established racism in the UK, but Holly Lynch also highlighted the sexist and xeno-phobic inferences in the press, implying, 'You're different, you're not from this country, you're an outsider, we don't trust you.' Holly observed, 'It's been unpleasant to watch.'

Meghan phoned Holly to personally thank her for the women's gesture – an example of connection. On the positive side, Meghan made the point – a favourite – that they could work together to be a real force for good to bring about the changes they wanted to see: Forces for Change.

Holly's final word on the matter: 'It doesn't matter who you are, whether you're a princess or a million miles from that, you shouldn't be subject to bullying or racism.'

The tabloids were not about to think again, however, but Harry had made up his mind.

He did not want things to remain the same; practically living in exile with his wife and child within the walls of Frogmore Cottage. He wanted to change things, and thereby he set in motion an explosive chain of events by asking his father if he and Meghan might adapt their role.

After the African trip, they travelled to Los Angeles to spend Thanksgiving with Doria before moving on to Vancouver for a private Christmas. They were, it was confirmed, taking a break from royal duties and would not be celebrating with the Queen and the rest of the family at Sandringham.

As Christmas approached, Harry was hoping to arrange a private conversation with both the Queen and his father but instead was told by officials to put his thoughts in an email. As Tom Bradby would later observe, Harry didn't want to do that because he was worried it would leak. But he was still told to do it.

It leaked.

On 7 January 2020, Dan Wootton ran the story in *The Sun*, stating that Harry and Meghan were considering a move to Canada and that they would be discussing their options with the Queen and Prince Charles in the coming days.

Before those conversations took place, however, Harry and Meghan, stung into action by the leak, released a statement. It began by pointing out that they had been thinking about a new role for many months. They didn't say so directly, but the birth of their son had been the most influential factor in their future decisions.

Confirming that they intended to balance their time between North America and the UK, they continued, 'We intend to step back as "senior" members of the Royal Family and work to become financially independent, while continuing to fully support Her Majesty the Queen.'

One of the tricks the media plays on the public is to deliberately confuse the Queen as a figurehead, the chairman of a successful business, with her image as a sweet granny in her nineties. So it was 'a cruel snub' to the Queen and a 'grave insult to her Maj'. Dan Wootton observed, 'What on earth has the Queen done to deserve this type of shoddy treatment?'

Behind the scenes, flustered officials moved quickly to try to shut down too much speculation. A statement from the Queen herself expressed support for Harry and Meghan, confirming there would be a period of transition: 'Although we would have preferred them to remain full-time working Members of the Royal Family, we respect and understand their wish to live a more independent life as a family while remaining a valued part of my family.'

She did not ask the press to leave them alone, which might have set a welcome precedent for the future. Yasmin Alibhai-Brown observed, 'If the Queen had once said, in her way, "Hey, guys, this is my grandson and his wife. They just got married. Back off and let them build a life for themselves." The hounds would have backed off. But she never did.'

Instead, the daily updates about Meghan and Harry's life would prove to be a welcome diversion from the serious allegations surrounding Prince Andrew and his links to convicted paedophile, the late Jeffrey Epstein. Harry and Meghan had already decided to opt out of the royal rota, although to be fair, it would have been better for them if there was an off switch for the anti-Meghan commentators.

Much of the speculation about their move centred on them cashing in on their royal status alongside faux outrage that we the taxpayer paid for Frogmore House and their security. The taxpayer indeed pays for many things in the UK, including MPs' salaries, their expenses and their security. Much of the household costs for the Duke and Duchess of Sussex, however – an estimated 95 per cent – are paid for by Prince Charles, not the taxpayer.

Not all the coverage was hysterical. Oliver Duff, the editor of I newspaper, was more thoughtful, noting that they could still expect scrutiny, which was 'the price of life in the public eye'. He added, 'A royal existence must be tiresome, though, despite the luxury, and one suspects that several of Harry's relatives are green with envy.'

Rachael Bletchly in the *Daily Mirror* blamed Meghan for changing Harry, ignoring the fact that he was in his thirties and determined to continue his mother's legacy and promote his charities around the world. The press had called him the 'Prince of Woke', as if to care about the issues that matter in the modern world was the ultimate folly. For many, particularly of the older generation, 'woke' has become a word with which to abuse others.

Rachel was clear, 'I'm fed up with her bleating about how hard it is for her being a new mom when everyone is picking on her: And especially, the outrageous suggestions that any criticism of her is racist. They can bugger off to Canada.'

The double Booker Prize-winning author Hilary Mantel did not agree: 'I do think abominable racism has been involved. People who say that's got nothing to do with it – well, they need to check their privilege.'

Piers Morgan, unsurprisingly, did not agree that race – or gender – was a factor in the media's treatment of Meghan. The Labour leadership contender Lisa Nandy, daughter of the Indian academic, Dipak Nandy, countered on *Good Morning Britain*: 'If you don't mind me saying, how on earth would you know?' She continued to address the position of the white privileged class: 'As someone who's never had to deal with ingrained prejudice, you're not in a position to understand people who have.'

In the *New York Times*, Afua Hirsch explained the link between privilege and race in Britain's rigid class society – represented most clearly by the Royal Family, of course. The relatively few people of colour who rise to prominence are often told they should be 'grateful'.

She described Meghan and Harry's act of leaving as 'two fingers up at the racism of the British establishment'. She observed, almost sadly: 'No matter how beautiful you are, whom you marry, what palaces you occupy, charities you support, how faithful you are, how much money you accumulate or what good deeds you perform, in this society racism will still follow you.'

24

THE DEFT GOODBYE

———

It was a rare moment of rapture. Aker Okoye, the handsome head boy of Robert Clack Upper School, in Dagenham, composed himself, looked at Meghan and then told the cheering students, 'She really is beautiful, innit. I had to speak the truth there.' Meghan didn't mind a bit and playfully wagged her finger at Aker.

He had answered her call for a male volunteer to join her on stage at the school where she was speaking about the importance of International Women's Day the following weekend. She was expanding on the theme she had introduced at the One Young World conference in Dublin in 2014 during the Bridging the Gender Gap discussions. Now she was addressing seniors at a school that, fittingly, was in the town that had witnessed the strike of sewing machinists at the Ford Plant in 1968.

Two years after that unprecedented action Parliament had passed the Equal Pay Act. The story of the strike had been the subject of *Made in Dagenham*, the acclaimed 2010 film starring Sally Hawkins. Disappointingly, the controversy over a gender pay gap is still ongoing.

Meghan seized her chance to explain to the school's boys the importance of the girls they were sat beside and their role in society. She urged them to 'continue to value and appreciate the women in your lives and also set the example for some men who are not seeing it the same way. You have your mothers, sisters, girlfriends, friends in your life. Protect them. Make sure they are feeling valued and safe.'

Aker, at sixteen, matched Meghan's words, telling his fellow students: 'International Women's Day is a reminder that women can do it all and do do it all. He then addressed the boys directly: 'This is a message to all you guys: maybe this Sunday could be the one day we don't look at women as objects.'

After he had finished speaking, Meghan gave him the biggest hug and concluded her own remarks that this was not solely about women but about all of us. She was given a standing ovation.

The visit was a one-woman tour de force, not only for promoting her views on gender equality but also the encourage-ment she gave black girls just by being there – being a presence; a role model. She accepted a customary posy from Fiona Addai, aged eleven, who said, 'She is black and you don't normally get that in the Royal Family and so I hope when I'm older she's taught me that no matter what colour you are, I am able to do what any other person can do. She has helped me believe in myself.'

Fiona added, 'I was so happy, I thought I was going to faint.' Meghan joined in a classroom discussion on gender equality and the role of women and spoke of her regard for the inspirational black poet and civil rights activist, Maya Angelou. She praised the students' eloquence and then posed with them, making the equals sign with her hands that represented the EachforEqual campaign, the theme of the 2020 IWD.

It wasn't all about message, however. Meghan was happy to talk about Archie, who had stayed at home in Vancouver while they made this last royal trip. She told wellwishers simply, 'He's changed my life.'

The trip to Dagenham was the first event of Meghan's four-day farewell tour – a whistlestop mission in March 2020 that resembled the military precision of the overseas tour to entertain the troops that she had undertaken six years before. Harry, meanwhile, was having a boys' day out with Lewis Hamilton, opening The Silverstone Experience, a museum at the famous Northamptonshire grand prix circuit. In *New Yorker* magazine Rebecca Mead summed up the last hurrah of the couple: 'It was hard not to appreciate how deftly the couple bid Britain goodbye.'

Her last solo engagement was a low-key affair at Buckingham Palace where she hosted an informal lunchtime reception for twenty-two scholars from across the Commonwealth in her role as patron of the charity, the Association of Commonwealth Universities. As was her custom, Meghan had read and absorbed her brief and talked easily with the students about micro-plastic pollution, climate change and sustainable travel, pointing out how much tourism money was leaving countries instead of helping communities within them. 'There has to be a symbiotic relationship,' she declared.

She had one more obligation to fulfil, a stuffy and formal affair but an important one. They were part of a strong royal presence, including the Queen, at Westminster Abbey honouring Commonwealth Day.

This last time we would see Meghan officially she wore a bright green, long-sleeved cape dress by British designer Emilia Wickstead with a matching fascinator. The photograph of her arriving with Harry at the Abbey, in a suit and tie, would be published time and again over the coming weeks.

Meghan's love of fashion and the care she takes with each outfit is obvious. She has always had it, being the centre of attention for pictures as a child; at the mother and daughter's fashion show at Immaculate Heart or posing in a carefully chosen outfit for the school's photographer, John Dlugolecki. She wanted to dress the part, as if her wardrobe was the costume department of her personal TV show. As she has made clear, fashion was very much part of her persona as a strong woman: 'There's no uniform for feminism.'

Walking purposefully into the Abbey with her husband she was a gorgeous emerald peacock. Bethan Holt, the fashion writer for the *Daily Telegraph* observed, referencing Dylan Thomas: 'There was no going gently into that good Canadian night for Meghan.'

By this time, though, it was apparent that the relationship between the Cambridges and the Sussexes was fractured, probably beyond repair. Harry and Meghan had arrived first and took their seats just before William and Kate, who were seated in the row in front. Meghan did her best to say hello with a smile. Clearly the gang of four hadn't set eyes on one another during this visit. Mark Landler of the *New York Times* wrote, 'The brothers scarcely spoke – their icy formality a metaphor for a once-close relationship that has all but unravelled.'

We could see it with our own eyes on the television coverage. Harry had turned to Meghan and whispered, 'He just said Hi.' William and Kate literally turned their backs on Harry and Meghan in front of an entire nation. They blanked them. As the *Observer* noted wryly, 'Kate reveals she is up to carrying out that vital royal duty … bearing a grudge against relatives. Catherine Bennett noted, 'She couldn't manage to grin and bear it for one more hour with Meghan and Harry.' Meanwhile, said Catherine, 'Meghan radiates artless goodwill.'

It seemed such a sad parting.

The photographs of Meghan and Harry at the Abbey was not the most enduring image of her farewell tour, however. That was the glorious picture of the couple arriving at Mansion House, London, for the Endeavour Fund Awards, celebrating the achievements of wounded, sick and injured Armed Forces personnel.

The photographer Samir Hussein feared it wasn't going to be his night to get a great picture of the couple because it was pouring with rain. Fortuitously, though, a flash from a camera in the crowd lit the couple just as they walked the short distance from their car into the building, illuminating them under their umbrella just as Samir clicked. The result was instantly iconic. 'All the elements you could wish for as a photographer came together – perfect timing, great lighting, strong symbolism and amazing subjects,' he said, modestly.

The strongest ingredient that gives the photograph its timeless quality was the undeniable look of love between the couple. They are just two people, walking closely together in the rain, smiling widely and looking into each other's eyes. Nobody else was in their world, even though they were surrounded by a noisy crowd.

This was the point that the millions of words written about Megxit failed to grasp; Harry and Meghan were in love and that mattered more to them than so-called duty, the Royal Family, or the views of tabloid newspapers and their cynical white columnists.

After the final hurrah in Westminster Abbey, Meghan said goodbye to the staff at Frogmore House and caught the last flight out of Heathrow to return to Canada and her beloved Archie. She had, as they say, checked out. Her dogs were waiting for her, too. They had been shipped across the Atlantic. Guy the beagle had been joined by a new addition to the household, a rescued black Labrador called Pula. He was a reminder of their love for Botswana – Pula is the official currency and also means rain in the local language of Setswana. Rain is such a precious commodity in this part of Africa that *pula* would be considered a blessing.

As boltholes go, the waterfront mansion in North Saanich, Vancouver Island, was as good as it gets. The sprawling eight-bedroom property with two private beaches was far roomier and more private than Frogmore Cottage. The neighbours were mindful of her privacy as well.

The house had been arranged for them by an old friend of Harry's, the millionaire composer and producer David Foster. Harry had a few final engagements to fulfil in the UK after Meghan's departure, but he flew out to join her just before the Covid-19 lockdown came into effect in the UK.

Their absence did not stop them being considered newsworthy when the pandemic took hold.

The big story on Saturday, 28 March 2020 was that the Prime Minister, Boris Johnson, the Health Secretary Matt Hancock and the Chief Medical Officer Professor Chris Whitty had all been struck down by coronavirus. However, that national emergency was only part of the day's major events for the *Daily Mail*.

According to the newspaper's front page, there were 'Two Corona Bombshells'. Sharing equal billing was a picture of Harry and Meghan leaving an aircraft with the headline 'Harry and Meghan's corona dash to LA'. The photograph used was actually of the couple arriving at Fua'amotu airport in Tonga during their first royal tour in October 2018.

The couple were strongly criticised over four pages of speculation. On a day when the rest of the country was reeling from the news that 181 people had died, Meghan and Harry were considered so important that the coverage came under the banner in red 'CORONAVIRUS CRISIS'.

Readers didn't actually learn much more than had been revealed the day before in *The Sun* by Dan Wootton – namely that the couple had left Canada before flights between the two North American nations had been suspended. Covid-19 had clearly brought forward a move that made sense – whether permanent or temporary. Los Angeles was the place where Meghan had an established support system that would benefit both of them – but most importantly they would be close to Doria, Archie's grandmother; Meghan was her only child.

The provocative columnist Jan Moir gave Meghan a right going over as usual. It was clearly all her fault. The narrative, as ever, was that Meghan called the shots and Harry was not capable of making any decisions for himself and would end up holding her handbag. She wrote: 'This week, in the middle of the biggest public health crisis this country has ever seen, the Sussexes already seem self-absorbed, detached and utterly irrelevant.'

Their crime was a simple tweet supporting the NHS that said: 'Thank you for all you continue to do! Applauding you from across the pond.' Ms Moir was in fine form: 'Honestly, Harry and Meghan, if that's the best you can do, don't bloody bother.'

Unsurprisingly, she praised the very sweet pictures of William and Kate's young children clapping the NHS staff. This was undeniably a lovely video but it was also blatantly devised to tug at the heartstrings of a beleaguered nation.

She made no mention of William's potentially catastrophic blunder earlier in the month when he had made light of the virus on a visit to Dublin. He joked to a first responder: 'I bet everyone's like, "I've got coronavirus, I'm dying." And you're like, "No, you've just got a cough."' He added, 'It does seem quite dramatic about coronavirus at the moment. Is it being a little hyped up, by the media?' That misjudgement by the future king is perhaps one that could rightly be listed under coronavirus crisis – just imagine if Meghan had made the comment.

Over the page of the *Daily Mail*, Rebecca English, the paper's Royal Editor, repeated an old story about Harry dumping The Firm by email. She dusted off a fourteen-year-old picture of Harry posing in a Sentebale polo shirt with his arm around her during a visit to Lesotho to promote the charity. Ever since, this has been the excuse for the sub headline that she was the royal editor who knew Harry so well.

In the first paragraph she asked the question, would Harry begin to experience 'niggling' regrets? Niggling – that word again – the one that had stirred up so many concerned comments about subtle racism when the *Daily Mail* used it back in December 2017. Now it seemed like two fingers stuck up at those who found it offensive back then.

Meghan's biggest crime in this two-page story was that she had not worn a hat when she should have done. Apparently, you have to wear a hat if the Queen wears one. According to Rebecca, 'She didn't understand how bad it was to get something as simple as that so wrong.'

To finish, Rebecca bundled everything together as 'sources'. Strangely they shared one quote as if they had all said the same thing at the same time. It was the usual: 'The Queen doesn't deserve to be treated in this way.'

By the end of the article, Rebecca had quoted three insiders, six sources and one courtier – sounds like a Christmas carol for the unnamed. Coverage of this 'Corona Bombshell' was not quite done with, however. The waspish columnist Amanda Platell in her *Platell's People* column couldn't resist her weekly dig at the Sussexes 'being supportive of themselves'.

The newspaper's gossip columnist Richard Eden carried an interesting story for society watchers about Misha Nonoo, who had given birth to her first child, a son named Leo. Harry and Meghan had attended her wedding to billionaire businessman Mikey Hess in Rome in 2019.

And so as the death toll for coronavirus spiralled towards a thousand, Meghan Markle featured on six pages of the UK's biggest-selling daily newspaper, which once again failed to say she was suing the Mail group. On Monday, 30 March, two days after the 'Corona Bombshell', the front page of the *Daily Mail* declared that President Trump had said the US would not pay for Harry and Meghan's security. The headline screamed: 'Trump: We Won't Pay For Megxit.' He didn't actually say that and, in any case, the US had not been asked to contribute. Harry and Meghan had made arrangements to pay for their own security. This was actually a proper story. A statement on their behalf said, 'The Duke and Duchess of Sussex have no plans to ask the US government for security resources. Privately-funded security arrangements have been made.'

President Trump found the time to tweet about Harry and Meghan even though the US now had the most cases of coronavirus in the world. In his tweet, which was claimed to be 'highly embarrassing for the pair', the President had stated that he was a great friend of the Queen. He has met her twice. According to the *Guardian*, he has, however, met Prince Andrew, currently a highly toxic figure, numerous times, despite claiming not to know him.

The historian and broadcaster, Professor Kate Williams, put everything into perspective: 'The US rates of infection are soaring, ventilators and equipment desperately needed, thousands of deaths projected, docs and nurses struggling to cope … and the President is tweeting about #Harry and Meghan.'

That day it was also reported that the first frontline doctor, Dr Amged El-Hawrani, a dedicated consultant, had died aged fifty-five – a story relegated to page six and evidently not as important as Harry and Meghan's security arrangements.

So, at this point, Harry and Meghan had agreed not to use their HRH titles, had agreed to pay for all the renovations at Frogmore House and now agreed to fund their own security. Harry, in addition, had relinquished his military roles.

They weren't exactly rushing into new projects, although Meghan did narrate a compelling documentary for Disneynature called *Elephant*, about a herd of the endangered beasts making their way across the Kalahari Desert from the Okavango delta in Botswana to the Zambezi River and back again. Much of the publicity surrounded the fact that it was Meghan's first job since stepping away from royal duties. *Variety* thought she did 'an inviting version of the wholesome but amused Disney narrator.' *Indiewire* said Meghan 'bridged the gap between entertainment and education.'

The *LA Times* amusingly observed that the film was about a majestic family whose way of life, though rooted in centuries-old traditions, has never felt more imperilled. Meghan wasn't boosting her own bank account – all the money made by the documentary was earmarked for Elephants Without Borders, the charity that had close links with Harry's conservation work in Africa.

While coronavirus continued to grip Los Angeles in lockdown, Meghan asked her mum if she could do anything to help in the West Hollywood area. Doria told her about Project Angel Food, which delivered food to the sick and vulnerable in the area. The project had begun in 1989 with the aim of giving love and nourishment to those living with HIV.

Today the charity has 2,000 clients, many living in poor housing and suffering not just from HIV but heart disease, cancer, diabetes and other critical conditions. Meghan and Harry decided that Easter Sunday would be a good and symbolic day to join in and made six deliveries in the Burbank and Glendale neighbourhoods.

Richard Ayoub, the project's director, was with them for one visit to a client called Frank who had cancer. Richard was impressed that Harry posed a poignant question that he had never thought of asking: 'Do your neighbours check up on you?'. Frank told him they didn't. 'We all need to look out for each other,' said Harry.

Meghan and Harry found the day so worthwhile that they got back in touch with Richard and ended up spending another two days delivering the food that, during lockdown, was cooked by ten professional chefs who were all temporarily out of work. The couple dropped off food to thirty-five clients, always making sure they made time for an all-important chat.

One of the clients rang up Richard to tell him that he had lived with HIV for thirty years and that Harry and Meghan had 'brightened up my day'. Apparently he had told Harry that he liked hamburger and fries. Harry told him, 'That's not good for you.' As Richard observed, he would never forget the visit.

The couple were caught on CCTV and stills from that footage made their way into the press.

One constructive benefit of the involvement of Harry and Meghan was that donations rose sharply. Without being too sentimental about things, this was just the sort of project Diana would have approved of and also showed that Harry could take the lead. It wasn't all about Meghan. They were a partnership.

Any pictures of Harry and Meghan were obviously going to be highly prized. They were living in some splendour at a mansion owned by the media mogul Tyler Perry, a friend of

Oprah Winfrey's. The property in the Hollywood Hills was reported to be worth $18 million and was practically a palace.

Eventually, on 18 April, both *The Sun* and the *Daily Mail* carried the same 'exclusive' photograph on their front pages of Meghan wearing a scarf over her face, complete with sunglasses and baseball hat. She was carrying Guy the beagle. They were on a hiking trail in the Hollywood Hills.

Nobody would have recognised it was Meghan unless they had been following her or stalking her. The story went that she had been 'spotted' but a quick glance at the picture credit revealed that it was copyright Coleman-Rayner/Jeff Rayner, the same paparazzo who had faked the pictures of Tom Markle in Mexico – presumably not Meghan's favourite.

The *Daily Mail* was actually using Meghan and Harry as unpaid front-page advertising. Above the picture of the Duchess wearing that mask was an ad for a £5 shopping voucher if you signed up to the Mail + digital edition. The ad that was repeated inside included a large image of two stories with a picture – 'Megxit's £4m a year security bill' and 'Trump's Revenge After All Their Insults'.

It seemed that negative stories about Meghan were a very positive money-spinner for the newspaper. So perhaps not so 'utterly irrelevant' after all.

25

REBUILDING

———

Meghan knew that anything she said in the aftermath of the killing of George Floyd would be examined word for word. She hesitated. The old Meghan would have plunged in, speaking up defiantly about what was right. But the relentless and ongoing negativity from the British media combined with the way the Royal Family ground down any hint that one of the Firm might put their head above the parapet had inevitably had its effect.

She was like a prisoner who had escaped down a dark tunnel and, surfacing, needed time to adjust to the light outside. Originally she said yes when approached by the filmmaker Patrick Creadon to contribute a graduation address to Immaculate Heart. The class of 2020 had been denied their big day at the Hollywood Bowl because of the Covid-19 pandemic so the school was trying to make the best of it. Patrick, whose daughter Fiona was a senior, had filmed a ceremony in the school grounds which included a commencement speech from Meghan's theology teacher Christine Knudsen, now recently retired, as well as a prayer from Maria Pollia and the collection of diplomas by more than one hundred students. Proceedings took two days because of coronavirus precautions.

The idea was that the whole school could view a video of the occasion on Wednesday 3 June, the date on which they would have held the ceremony at the Bowl. As an added bonus, there were some more surprise messages: first up was Congressman Adam Schiff, whose district included Immaculate Heart; he had been a supporter of the school for a long time. Then it was the turn of Tyra Banks, who continued to keep in touch with her alma mater; she was very popular with the students who she referred to as 'her sisters', much to their delight.

And finally Meghan – at least that was the plan. That weekend, the civil unrest and public disquiet following the killing of George Floyd exploded across the country and the world. It was really the only topic of conversation in town. Younger students were busy organising Black Lives Matter protests off campus and volunteering to help clean up any businesses vandalised in LA.

Callie Webb, the school's director of communications, explained, 'Over the weekend, Meghan felt she could not ignore the news because it was so personally upsetting to her, so she had incorporated her thoughts into her message to the graduates. Upon reviewing the message, she grew reluctant about releasing it for fear that if it became public, she would get picked apart. We respected her decision. Well, twenty-four hours later, she had a change of heart and sent it to Patrick. We were so pleased she did!'

Meghan, wearing a simple white top and matching cardigan with her hair swept back from her face, made sure the focus was on her words and not on the way she looked. She spoke purpose-fully and directly to camera. It was the old Meghan, powerful Meghan: 'I wanted to say the right thing and I was really nervous that I wouldn't, or that it would get picked apart, and I realised that the only wrong thing to say is to say nothing – because George Floyd's life mattered and Breonna Taylor's life mattered and Philando Castile's life mattered and Tamir Rice's life mattered. And so did so many other people whose names we know and whose names we do not know. Stephon Clark, his life mattered.'

George Floyd was killed in Minneapolis by a policeman who notoriously knelt on his neck for nearly nine minutes. The other four named by Meghan were all black victims of police shootings.

Meghan referenced some of the key moments in her life – the LA riots of 1992, twenty-eight years ago. She spoke of volunteering while a teenager at school and the words of Maria Pollia to 'put others' needs above your own fears'. And here she was making a circle, re-connecting with Immaculate Heart, one of the most important stops on her quest to find her own identity in the world. She once told Gigi Perreau, her drama teacher, that she wouldn't go back to the school 'until she'd made it'. Now she had a voice and she was using it to encourage a new generation not to see what was happening as the end but 'to see this as a beginning of you harnessing all of the work, all the values, all the skills that you have.'

Meghan wanted the graduates to be part of rebuilding: 'I know sometimes people say, "How many times do we need to rebuild?" Well, you know, we're going to rebuild and rebuild and rebuild until it is rebuilt.'

Afterwards, Callie observed, 'Her message was embraced by everyone as powerful, moving and inspiring. Her strong delivery and personal memories just left the students speechless. It was really all they could talk about later.'

Callie was also amazed at the 'pretty harsh and unfair' comments on Twitter and elsewhere following Meghan's address. Some wrote directly to her and questioned how on earth Immaculate Heart could associate with Meghan Markle. The school was bombarded by emails from individuals 'clearly consumed by hate, who wrote lengthy tirades against her that also revealed a lot of ignorance'.

Inevitably, the anti-Meghan media had their say. Amanda Platell, in her weekly snipe at her, said that her 'performance' was 'like watching a 15-year-old Joan of Arc in her first school play'.

That was not the view of the graduating seniors of Immaculate Heart. Maya Al-Mansour Matthews observed, 'I cannot fully express the joy of hearing her wholeheartedly state that Black Lives Matter; that we as young people in this world are already on our way to make change.' Another, Audrey 'Andy' Valcourt, said, 'In a time of extreme pain, righteous indignations and chaos, Meghan's words brought me a moment of clarity and peace. As she said, "The only wrong thing to say is to say nothing".'

And Keana Rose Hilario added, 'Watching her speech, I did tear up a bit, because of how empowering her words were. I understood that her comments about Black Lives Matter were very close to her heart, especially as a black woman who has been fighting against injustice at a young age. I hope she aids us, the youth, in our struggle against racism.' The thoughts of Maya, Audrey and Keana were the positive ones that Meghan would have wanted to hear: young women finding their voice.

Meghan was not speaking to them as a member of the Royal Family. She is a biracial American woman addressing young people in her home country, her home state – her hometown. Perhaps we never properly grasped her identity – this supremely accomplished woman who the United Kingdom has now lost: we didn't own her body; we didn't own her mind; we didn't own her spirit … we didn't own her.

LAST THOUGHTS

Meghan was the interviewer but, unsurprisingly, it was her own remarks at the virtual summit that engaged most with the online audience. She was speaking with Emily Ramshaw, the journalist and co-founder of The 19th, when she said, 'It's good to be home.'

It was the final proof that we, the British public, had lost Meghan in just four years. In my opinion we lost her right at the start – within one week.

In context, Meghan was not at a coffee morning telling the ladies that lunch that it was good to be home after a tiring and tiresome trip to Europe. The 19th describes itself as 'a non profit, non partisan newsroom reporting at the intersection of gender, politics and policy'. It declares, 'Join us in our mission to empower all women', a rallying call that would always find favour with Meghan Markle.

The 19th Amendment, after which this new organisation is named, enshrines the right of women to vote in the US. Meghan was asked to close 'The 19th Represents Summit', a week of interviews with well-known women in the world of politics and public affairs. They included the newly announced Democratic vice-presidential candidate Kamala Harris, the first black woman on a major party's presidential ticket.

Kamala is also the only black woman serving on the US Senate, representing California, her home state – as it is Meghan's. Kamala pointed out, 'Joe Biden has the audacity to choose a black woman to be his running mate – how incredible is that?'

In her remarks a few days later, Meghan stressed the need to vote. She also referenced racism, commenting on the aftermath of the George Floyd murder. She confessed to being devastated when she returned to the US, where she hadn't lived for ten years: 'It was just sad to see where our country was at that moment.'

But if there was any silver lining to be had from the dreadful turn of events, she believed it was in 'the peaceful protests that we're seeing, in the voices that were coming out, in the way that people were actually owning their role and acknowledging their role that they played actively or passively in the discrimination of other people specifically of the black community – it shifted from sadness to a feeling of absolute inspiration because I can see the tide is turning'.

Meghan also drew attention to the negativity, particularly where the media was concerned. She could have been addressing the opinionated columnists when she declared, 'The loudest voices are often the negative ones, sadly.'

She added, 'What's so fascinating, at least from my standpoint and my personal experience the past couple of years, is that the headline alone, the clickbait alone, makes an imprint. That is part of how we start to view the world, how we interact with other people.' She highlighted the toxicity that both she and Harry had faced: 'If you're just trying to grab someone's attention, you're going for something salacious versus what is truthful.'

'From my standpoint,' she continued, 'it's not new to see this undercurrent of racism and certainly unconscious bias [in the media], but I think to see the changes that are made right now is really something I look forward to being part of – and being part of using my voice in a way that I haven't been able to of late.'

It was vintage Meghan. She looked very different, as if casting off once and for all the stilted formality of royal protocol that dictates the colour of your nail varnish. Her hair hung loose in gentle waves, almost to her waist. The fashion magazines helpfully pointed out that she wore a peach-coloured silk top by Hugo Boss, accessorised by some favourite bangles, including her Cartier love bracelet.

Meghan wouldn't have minded the acknowledgement of her look – as I have discovered in this book, she strongly believes that feminism and femininity are compatible. The problem for the royal women left behind in the grand homes of Britain is that the media and the men in grey suits who lurk in palace corridors treat them as little more than Stepford Wives.

For the conversation with Emily, Meghan seemed very much at ease in her own home. The media had once again become hysterical over her and Harry's mansion in upscale Montecito. Helped by Doria, they had managed to move ninety miles north of Los Angeles with Archie without anyone in the press or on social media knowing.

They had the chance to settle in for six weeks before everything kicked off with the usual preoccupation about the cost (rumoured to be $14.65 million), their uber-rich neighbours (Oprah and Ellen apparently) and the number of acres (seven), bedrooms (nine) and bathrooms (sixteen). It wasn't clear whether the last figure included showers, rooms with actual baths or simply toilets. This is really important stuff because the future of the world might depend on it.

The *Daily Mail* helpfully pointed out their property boasted a two-bedroom, two-bath guest house that was perfect for Doria, who, the paper said, is acting as one-year-old Archie's 'nanny'. Oh dear: nearly forty years ago, Doria was assumed to be Meghan's nanny when she walked around the streets in a predominantly white neighbourhood.

Let's be clear. Doria, a black woman, is not Archie's nanny. She is his grandmother. I don't think the newspaper was being deliberately racist on this occasion, but just offer it as an example of the unconscious bias that Meghan highlighted. Doria is a well-educated woman with a degree – she is not a domestic.

This year, 2020, marks the centenary of the passage of the 19th Amendment, so it's the perfect time for Meghan to speak out about one of the causes closest to her heart – urging women in her home country of the USA to vote in time for the presidential elections. But – and it's a big but – the centenary celebrates the anniversary of when *white* women were allowed to vote. Black women were not eligible until 1965.

A week after The 19th interview, Meghan continued to be part of a drive to encourage the vote when she teamed up with Michelle Obama's non-profit organisation When We All Vote. She took part in the Voter Registration Couch Party. Michelle wasn't part of the online panel. She had recorded a video keynote speech to the Democratic Convention that *The New Yorker* described as an 'unmatched call to action'. The magazine called her a 'cultural celebrity'; it made me think that was also a good description of Meghan Markle.

Meghan even mentioned her 'friend' Michelle Obama when she spoke and subsequently delivered pitch-perfect sentiments about the need to vote. She began by drawing attention to the 19th Amendment not applying to women of colour when it was first introduced: 'It had taken decades longer for women of colour to get the right to vote, even today we are watching so many women in different communities who are marginalised, still struggling to see that right come to fruition – it's just simply not ok.'

It was a metaphorical call to arms – get out and vote if you want your voice to be heard about the rights of women, the rights of children and healthcare. Courting controversy, she announced that there was much work to be done before the presidential election: 'We all know what's at stake this year. I know it. I think all of you certainly know it and if you're here on this fun event with us, then you're just as mobilised and energised to see the change that we all need and deserve.'

Let's state the absolute obvious here. Both of these online events were part of a push by the Democratic Party to kick Donald Trump to the kerb. Michelle Obama and Kamala Harris are two of the highest-profile women in the US. They are black and they are Democrats, and so is Meghan.

Her remarks sparked faux outrage among the 'opinionators', which is a real word but sounds more like enemies at the gates of Hogwarts. Both Piers Morgan and Dan Wootton called for the Queen to strip Meghan of her title of the Duchess of Sussex because royal protocol – that horrid little word again – dictates that members of the Royal Family do not interfere in politics.

Predictably these sentiments generated a reaction among other media, including the social kind. It always amuses me that columnists bridle at being lectured by celebrities and then proceed to lecture us, the reader or listener. In this case, both Dan and Piers were also lecturing the Queen and telling her what she should do.

What is more important to such columnists in 2020 – upholding the right of women to vote, especially those disadvantaged by their colour, or continuing to bore on about royal protocol? Professor Kate Williams, summed it up: 'So, just to recap for everyone, Meghan's horrendous crimes against the monarchy while in the UK include eating avocados, a one-shoulder dress, closing a car door and touching her bump.'

Opinionators have a simple job. They shout the odds from the top of the tallest building and hope that someone looks up. With a bit of luck that person will nudge the person next to them. It doesn't matter in the slightest what that opinion is – just so long as it gets a reaction. Sometimes it's a good call; who could begrudge the support given to the wonderful Captain Sir Tom Moore and his fundraising efforts for the NHS?

Sometimes it's a bad call. Piers referred to Lady Gaga as a 'bloody singer' when she was announced as a special guest at a World Health Organization COVID-19 press conference in April 2020. He hastily apologised when her One World: Together at Home concert raised $127 million for coronavirus relief.

It doesn't really matter one way or the other. One of the more amusing things about Piers's continued criticism of Meghan is that he is a Sussex boy. Though born in Ireland, he was brought up in Newark, East Sussex, and now owns a splendid mansion in the area, complete with swimming pool. So Meghan is his duchess. In bygone times, she would have ordered him to be placed in the stocks.

More seriously, the former editor of the *Guardian*, Alan Rusbridger, now principal of Lady Margaret Hall, Oxford University, advised everyone to 'keep their wits about them' when considering the media coverage of Meghan – and indeed Harry. He pointed out that none of the major newspaper players that filter stories about Meghan and Harry is a disinterested bystander. They were being sued by the couple for assorted breaches of privacy and copyright. 'There is, to any reasonable eyes, a glaring conflict of interest that, for the most part, goes undeclared.'

He highlighted Meghan's action against Associated Newspapers (now DMG Media) regarding the publication in the *Mail on Sunday* of extracts from a private letter to her father. It was a fascinating ongoing legal saga. Alan observed that while it played out, 'There's no harm in portraying her as a ruthless hypocrite and gold-digger. If Morgan's on hand with the vitriol, everyone's happy.'

And he continued, 'In the background, there are quite a lot of worried newspaper executives and former editors, who have absolutely zero interest in treating the couple kindly or even-handedly.'

It would be ridiculous to prevent newspapers discussing public figures just by starting legal proceedings – the curse of the super-injunction. In my opinion, however, the fact that a case is being pursued should be mentioned, perhaps with an asterisk at the end of the story. That should be a minimum requirement.

The newspapers do seem to report Meghan's relationship with her father in a very one-sided fashion – how Meghan has treated her dad rather than how her father has behaved towards her. Caitlin Flanagan, writing for *The Atlantic*, memorably described him as the King Lear of Rosario County.

I asked Gigi Perreau, who liked and appreciated Tom Markle while Meghan was at Immaculate Heart High School, what she thought about him now after they met up again for the first time in years in 2019. She observed, 'He was very nice, obviously, and I found him rather sad.

'I found him missing Meghan and I found him questioning why it wasn't believed that he had been in the hospital and had a mild heart attack. He said that there was some article or some speculation that it wasn't true and that he had made it up. And he said that he had all his papers from the doctors. He said, "There is really not much more I can do."'

Gigi has little time for those who appear to have manipulated Tom: 'He was definitely misguided and mishandled by whoever was doing those pictures and so on. It was just ridiculous.' She recalled that he was intrinsically a shy man – 'a behind the camera guy'. For someone so reserved, the thought of appearing in front of billions of people could, Gigi thought, be 'paralysing'.

Tom may or may not see his daughter again, or meet her husband or his grandson. Meghan's fictional father, Wendell Pierce, offered some simple advice to her real dad: 'If you love your daughter, just love your daughter. It's not for public consumption.'

At least Gigi and Wendell are on the record. You are always going to speak to people who don't want to be named. It happens to me researching my biographies. But, as we have seen in this book, nothing can compare to the cast of 'sources', 'well-placed sources', 'courtiers', 'senior courtiers', 'aides', 'senior aides', 'palace insiders', 'friends'. Did I mention 'senior sources'? They all seem to have royal reporters on speed dial or belong to the same WhatsApp group. We don't know at all the *veracity* of the tittle-tattle being peddled, but this sort of story is easily knocked up over a morning cuppa.

I do think there are real sources, however, spreading gossip about Meghan behind the scenes, perhaps for money or perhaps with an agenda to keep juicier stories about other members of the Royal Family well away from the spotlight. These stories are easily found on Google or Twitter. And they're by no means all about Prince Andrew – although the columnists might be more justified demanding the Queen strip Andrew of his title unless he speaks frankly to the FBI about Jeffrey Epstein.

But they won't. The columnists and reporters are happy to go along with the assassination of the character of Meghan Markle, knowing there is far more going on behind palace doors than the simplistic inanity they trot out. They take the public for fools to be manipulated at will. I've been both a national newspaper reporter and tabloid diary columnist, so I know exactly what goes on in this unkind, thoughtless world.

Meghan is an easy target. Unless I've missed something, she hasn't actually done anything wrong: no sex, no drugs, and no rock and roll. In the introduction to *Meghan Misunderstood*, I wondered whether Meghan was a 'victim of rampant racism, sexism and xenophobia because she's American, or was it just old-fashioned British snobbery at her being actress?'

The answer is all of these things. The headline on her famous essay for *Elle* is: 'I am more than an Other.' She was talking about being biracial but the problem has been that in the UK she has always been treated as an 'other' – as a woman, as a woman of colour, as an American and as an actress/celebrity.

The racism she encountered in the UK is crystal clear and obvious – as seen in the very first week of her outing as Harry's new love. The racist deniers – columnists and broadcasters – are white, the tabloid royal reporters are white and their editors are white. People – white people – generally ask for examples regarding Meghan: they are in Chapter 18 of this book – 'A Week in Hell'. The cries of derision that greeted Harry's call for a pause were, for me, the beginning of the end for Meghan in the UK. That feeling grew tenfold when Archie was born.

Let's not forget *seventy-two* female MPs expressed their solidarity with Meghan and basically called out the racists. Britain is a racist country that pretends it isn't. Although she was writing about the US, I particularly liked the observation about privilege by Melissa Wright in the online student magazine *The Red & Black*: 'Look at your life and think about how the colour of your skin opens so many doors for you that are shut to people of colour.'

The debate opened up in 2020 with the killing of George Floyd, and the subsequent large-scale protest of Black Lives Matter has brought to the public attention some of the shocking instances of racism in the UK. The black BBC newsreader Clive Myrie believes the abuse he receives is more prevalent now than at any time since he began his career in 1988. It is getting much worse and is obscene, quite frankly. He also acknowledges the unfairness of stop and search: 'You can't just stop people on the street because they're black, and that is what is happening.'

Clive's observations are informative, but a point of view I have read several times recently is that it is not up to black people to educate white people about racism – especially when it is perpetuated by the white majority. I am a white author and it is up to me to reflect on the privileges I have enjoyed throughout my life; I don't recall, for instance, there being any black person in any newsroom in which I have worked. I also should not be asking people of colour to make me aware of what has gone on and what is going on: the unconscious bias that seeps into so many aspects of modern society.

One of the saddest postscripts to Meghan's exit from the UK is that she could have been someone for *all* of this country to accept and someone within the Royal Family to whom we could feel a connection. In the modern world, standing up for the empowerment of women and articulating that concern, achieving self-made success and wealth, and actually looking like a million and more girls and women around the country should have led to a warm embrace, not the death of a dream by a thousand cuts.

The Royal Family has missed its chance. Those pesky court-iers will be pleased. The newspapers and Twitterati will continue to be obsessed with Meghan because what we are left with representing The Firm is an entitled, dull bunch. I am intrigued to see how Archie will be viewed in the future. Unlike Meghan, he is actually in line to the throne – seventh at present – and is mixed race.

For the moment, the Queen is the glue that binds the institution together. She is a fine and excellent symbol for good nostalgia, the fortitude and bulldog spirit that carried the nation through the Second World War – even though in reality the conflict brought misery and death to so many. Goodness knows what will happen to the Royal Family when she passes.

Meghan will be in the US, hopefully still using a strong voice for a better world. Perhaps she will be mentioned in the same breath as Michelle Obama and Kamala Harris. She might make the jump from cultural celebrity to serious politician. Let's hope so. And if she's no longer called the Duchess of Sussex – well, so what? Senator Markle sounds much better anyway.

MEGHAN'S STARS

Slender, graceful, glowing, the epitome of good health, Meghan is beautiful and beauty is power. Meghan's responsive Moon – ruler of the chart area associated with appearance – is in Venus-ruled Libra, suggesting someone whose sense of security is tied up with being attractive. Meghan will have grown up knowing instinctively that good looks and gracious behaviour confer protection and advancement. With ambitious Saturn joined to her Moon, she would have the discipline and determination to maximise and refine her appeal and, once gained, this justifiable pride in looks would be the bedrock for the attainment of other important ambitions.

The confidence and assurance may not have come quickly – a Moon and Saturn link suggests some early lack of self-esteem and a sensitivity to rejection, which can result in building defences against possible hurts. Meghan may well have developed a pragmatic approach to relationships, a rational, business-like approach to emotional issues. Expansive, optimistic Jupiter is part of the Saturn–Moon mix, too, providing Meghan with that exhilarating instinct that few aspirations would be too far-fetched, and hinting at a hunger for social acceptance, status and authority.

This urgency both to be gracious and be part of a polished sociable world will have been learned early on: Libra, the sign of diplomacy and bridge-building, rules the chart area associated with home and roots and gives an important indication of family life. Certainly, early life events would prompt within her the questions, 'What is right?' and 'What is fair?' alongside awareness of social issues. Meghan will have also honed excellent mediator and communication skills, which will be of much importance in later life.

But that strong initial need for approval will have come at a cost. The pile-up of planets in conciliatory, harmony-loving Libra sits at odds with a moody, wilful Mars. The planet of fight and action, Mars is placed in an area associated traditionally in the chart, with 'hidden enemies'. Whilst in life one may indeed have hidden enemies, more often we are the authors of our own mishaps if we refuse to be self-aware. Our hidden enemies are our blind spots, which can undermine us. Meghan may have learned to disown her legitimate aggression, anger and compet-itiveness if being compliant and pleasant seemed the better or safer option. Disowning or projecting this would mean that in confrontational situations it might seem to her that she is some-times unfairly the victim.

Further, impatient Mars is in the sign of sensitive, easily offended Cancer, suggesting a touchiness in her temperament – perceived slights may provoke a gut reaction that leads her to act impulsively. Because Meghan has a genuine desire to be charming, kind and fair, this will create much inner tension. Tension or not, goal-driven, angry Mars can be very explosive and will often win the tussle.

Finally, there is the issue presented by the placement of Meghan's feisty, independence-loving Mars in family-focused, clannish Cancer. This can be problematic because the emphasis

294

on fiery and cardinal elements in her chart indicates how important it is for her to be spontaneous, vital and embracing of change and challenge. She is highly motivated, restless, a leader – her Mars in Cancer may simply feel too suffocated by traditional families and will fight to break free. With this smothered Mars in the area of her chart associated with hidden enemies, problems may be compounded here by a lack of self-awareness or a reluctance to acknowledge aspects of her behaviour which to her would be uncomfortably unattractive and to some may look like self-sabotage.

Meghan's Mars can deliver many positives. In Cancer, it often creates loyalty and interest in ancestry. With Meghan's heritage embracing differing cultures and her desire for fairness, she is likely to be an informed and stimulating communicator on the issues of identity.

Additionally, she has very strong nurturing and protective instincts and will be a warm, determined mother, fighting hard to establish her children and create every advantage she possibly can to make their lives secure. With this trait linked to a further Martian proficiency – that of initiating projects and energetically getting things off the ground – it is possible to see the public roles that fit very nicely with the symbolism of her Martian Midheaven. Meghan can be an outstanding ambassador for the disadvantaged and those who need their message articulated with flair and passion.

Few will be surprised that Meghan's Sun, planet of creative energy and potential, is in the determined, strong-willed, theatrical, fun-loving sign of Leo. Meghan has much spirit and a liking for being centrestage. It is important for her to be recognised and respected for herself and she will work hard to be worthy of that respect. Above all, Meghan wants to lead and shine brightly in her leadership role, which means, if she can, she

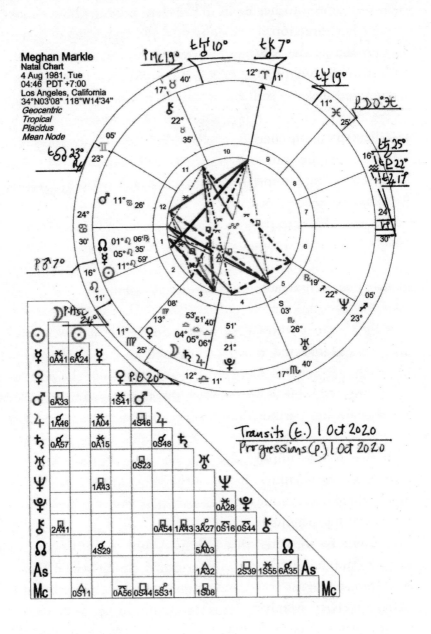

Meghan Markle
Natal Chart
4 Aug 1981, Tue
04:46 PDT +7:00
Los Angeles, California
34°N03'08" 118°W14'34"
Geocentric
Tropical
Placidus
Mean Node

Transits (t.) 1 Oct 2020
Progressions (p.) 1 Oct 2020

will welcome into her life those who can be appreciative and accept her direction. The Sun forms supportive links to wise Jupiter and serious Saturn, hinting at her strong sense of fairness and justice, a willingness to self-improve and a desire to be a mover and shaker – someone at the hub of important things in life.

Meghan has an energy, generosity and openness that attracts others, but she can be impatient if people try to assert themselves. Sun Leo people are proud and naturally regal, often confident of success. When they achieve, they will unhesitatingly invite courtiers into their orbit, reject the ordinary and possibly concede ground to those of stature and nobility.

Saturn, planet of material security, rules the partnership area of Meghan's chart, suggesting the pragmatism that has helped Meghan become successful. Meghan will have been careful to choose a partner who will be worth her while. Equally, she will have been attracted to someone who can carry authority. Meghan will seek absolute commitment in marriage but will also give every bit as much as she gets, providing enormous support for her partner. Saturn is well placed, exalted in Libra, suggesting the strengths and benefits of her match. Again, focus is drawn to the importance of Libra, sign of the Scales, in Meghan's chart. Influencing the area associated with roots and home, there is a clear message that, in circumstances not dissimilar to that of her parents, she will need to find a balance between two cultures – to work at harmonising differences.

Will she be successful in this? There are a number of encouraging signs. Truthful Uranus, exalted in Scorpio, links supportively to Meghan's Ascendant and Descendent – chart points that influence relationships. Meghan was born to be a circuit breaker and introduce a fresh approach to things. Perhaps success will come from her readiness to shake up convention, perhaps because she is forward-focused and has the gift of surviving in a fast-changing world.

The compatible links between the Sun and Moon in Meghan's chart suggest her parents provided a good-enough and generally conventional example of partnership. This would have been important for the older Meghan's equilibrium and sense of well-being. Meghan would experience her father as big-hearted, extroverted, enthusiastic and able to inspire confidence. Her father would have taken his family responsibilities seriously but may have tended, on a fairly regular basis, to put off planning for the future. He would want to make his mark on the world, would hate to be humiliated and might struggle somewhat with self-control. Both parents would be excellent communicators, skilful with words.

Within the parental relationship, Meghan's Moon in Libra suggests her mother made the most of the accommodation needed, giving ground to avoid conflict. However, there is a picture of a serious and strong maternal influence, someone who is philosophical, future-focused with high standards, encouraging perfection in her daughter. As the Moon, the symbol of mother, is in the chart area associated with siblings, her mother may have been more like a sister and is someone who very much wants to be at the centre of the life of her loved ones. Meghan's mother is creative and dramatic with a strong drive to set things right and a willingness to be of use to others. Meghan may have experienced a volatile side to her mother's character when young but her mother also has a profound respect for elegance, decorum and good manners – the importance of appearance will have been instilled in Meghan from the word go.

Importantly, in her early years Meghan may well have felt the need to be peacemaker and mitigate any conflict threatening the family. She would have developed empathy with different perspectives – a useful skill for adult life and one she will need for the balancing act reflected by her commitment to living in multiple locations. Affectionate Venus in the chart area associated with siblings hints that although there may be criticism from both sides, there is an innate fondness for blood relatives. Early years may well have been marked by competition for resources and disputes may come and go, but ultimately there will be hope of reconciliation.

Glancing back before looking forward, February 2020 saw the transit of ambitious Saturn, planet of tests, restrictions and authority figures, move opposite Meghan's Ascendant and into the chart area associated with all formal partnerships. Saturn delivers exactly what has been earned and if Meghan had planned and worked hard on projects to advance her own life and that of her partner, this would be the time when she would begin to get ahead. With her free-spirited Aries Midheaven, regal Leo Sun and wilful Uranus, Meghan needs to shine and have opportunities to shine in her own right, and this will be a moment of breakthrough. From a modern perspective, this might mean that within a relationship, her wishes and career will win out. At the end of the day, shining in someone else's court may not be enough for her.

However, this area of the chart is also known as the house of open enemies. Understandably, Meghan's evolving objectives and aspirations would have upset many people and she would have faced considerable opposition. Saturn is known for bringing reality checks and Meghan may have felt she had achieved less than she was entitled to. This would have been painful – such is Saturn.

In March 2020, Pluto, planet of breakdown and regeneration, reached exactly the same position in Meghan's chart, opposite her Ascendant. This is another very powerful portent of uncomfortable and irrevocable change and the immediate effect would have been to bring out into the open any hidden stresses within her marriage. Fortunately, the presence of protective Jupiter should have consolidated respect between Meghan and her partner.

The bigger issue is that Pluto is concerned with power struggles and Meghan seems to be fiercely fighting a number of adversaries. Things may become intense again in January, September and November 2021.

There will be obvious opponents – open enemies – during this period, but in May 2021 it will be useful for Meghan to think once more about hidden opponents. On this occasion, she may need to consider not simply how her own actions may be undermining her, but in fact whether someone close or some faction is using her to fight their battles for them.

There are many life-advancing, supportive transits occurring for Meghan during the next five years. In her natal chart, volcanic Pluto is in the area associated with roots and home, suggesting that periodically she may feel the need to wipe out what she has established and build something new. For this reason, it is important for Meghan to find or create links worldwide with like-minded others who will accept her ideas and support her initiatives. This can be hard work but Meghan's well-placed Uranus, planet of originality and innovation, will support her humanitarian plans. Meghan has taken the first steps now towards this objective with many indications of success. Presently, positive Jupiter, planet of new horizons, is working towards the highest point in her chart, the Midheaven, associated with reputation and vocation, reaching this position in early March 2023. This should enhance her public standing and provide clarity to her ambitions. By looking at her past, Meghan will gain greater spiritual understanding, too, and can improve family links. This might be the time she moves into a larger property or makes improvements to an existing home.

Shortly after, in April 2024, Jupiter will link with wounded healer, Chiron, planet of wholeness and creative solutions, which is placed in the chart area associated with networks, hopes, dreams and wishes. Meghan will find that old insecurities melt away. This is also roughly the period when she will experience her Uranus opposition. This occurs when transiting Uranus in the sky will be opposite her natal Uranus and it will provide a further prompt to be true to herself – to break free from any scripts she may feel have been imposed upon her. This should mark a turning point for Meghan, when the impetus to seek approval in the outside world lessens and greater self-awareness means she can focus, during the second half of her life, towards inner fulfilment.

Madeleine Moore
July 2020

LIFE AND TIMES

————

4 August 1981: Rachel Meghan Markle is born at the West Park Hospital in Canoga Park, a suburb just north of the family home in Woodland Hills, an upscale neighbourhood of Los Angeles. She has an elder half-sister, Yvonne, who is sixteen, and an elder half-brother, Tom Jr, aged fifteen. Her father Thomas Markle is a lighting director on *General Hospital* and met Doria Ragland at the studio where she worked as a trainee make-up artist. They have been married for nineteen months when Meghan is born.

Dec 1986: Sings 'Wheels on the Bus' at the end-of-year talent show at the Hollywood Schoolhouse, her first school. Her mum and dad had split up when she was two but did not divorce until she was seven. She is living with Doria in an apartment in South Cloverdale Avenue, three miles from the school.

Oct 1990: Travels with Doria to Oaxaca City in Southern Mexico for the annual Day of the Dead Festival. She witnesses poor street children selling sweets to earn a few pesos to buy food.

April 1992: Is sent home early from school when rioting engulfs the streets of LA after a predominantly white jury acquits the police officers who had savagely beaten a black motorist, Rodney King.

June 1993: Appears on *Nick News W5* with Linda Ellerbee explaining how she persuaded Proctor & Gamble to change a sexist ad for dishwasher liquid. Linda said, 'It didn't matter that she was eleven years old. She believed in women and in her own power.'

June 1995: Makes her first serious public speech, aged thirteen, at her middle school graduation at the Immaculate Heart High School. She singles out the religious lessons that had taught her and her classmates 'a deep compassion to those who suffer from the Aids virus'.

August 1995: Celebrates her fourteenth birthday at the summer drama camp organised by the Agape International Spiritual Center in Santa Monica. Has her first kiss with a boy, Joshua Silverstein, later a well-known stand-up on the LA circuit.

Nov 1995: Takes the role of Delilah in the Immaculate Heart production of *Back County Crimes*. Her boyfriend, Luis Segura, a pupil at St Francis High School in La Cañada Flintridge, is also in the cast.

March 1996: Plays Star-To-Be in the school production of *Annie* and writes in the programme that she 'loves singing, smiling and dancing, and hopes to shuffle off to Broadway some day.'

June 1996: Holidays in Europe with best friend Ninaki Priddy and her family. Is photographed as a happy tourist in front of Buckingham Palace.

March 1997: Meghan is cast as Little Red Riding Hood in Immaculate Heart's version of the Stephen Sondheim musical *Into the Woods*. She still wants to go to Broadway but has her eye on studying drama at Northwestern University first.

Nov 1998: Meghan is crowned Homecoming Queen by the St Francis High School. She stars as Jocasta in the all-boys school's production of *Oedipus Rex*. It's a sell-out.

March 1999: She is chosen to be team leader at the Kairos senior retreat in Encino during her last year of high school. Meghan is selected because teachers thought she could 'take conversations to a deeper level'. Models on a catwalk for the first time when she takes part in the annual mothers and daughters fashion show at Immaculate Heart.

Brings the house down singing 'Whatever Lola Wants' in *Damn Yankees*, the annual musical at another boys school, Loyola High School in LA. Her father is in the audience sat beside her drama coach, Gigi Perreau, who called her performance 'thrilling'.

June 1999: Graduates at the Hollywood Bowl. She collects many awards including a commendation from the National Achievement Scholarship Programme for outstanding black students.

Aug 1999: Appears fleetingly as an extra in the video for the Tori Amos melancholic ballad '1000 Oceans' shot in a parking lot in downtown LA. Meghan can be seen in a crowd at thirty-seven seconds and at fifty-seven seconds.

Sept 1999: Enrols at Northwestern University in Evanston, Illinois, just north of Chicago to study English. Joins the Kappa Kappa Gamma Upsilon sorority chapter and supports the Glass Slipper Project, providing new and nearly new prom dresses for girls that could not afford their own. At uni, meets lifelong friends Lindsay Jill Roth and Genevieve Hillis.

March 2000: Takes part in the famous annual dance marathon at Northwestern, one of the biggest student-led philanthropic ventures in the US. Meghan has to stay on her feet for forty-five minutes out of every hour for thirty hours. More than half a million dollars is raised for a cancer support group.

Aug 2002: Travels in the US Treasury Secretary Paul O'Neill's motorcade in Buenos Aires, where she has a summer internship at the American Embassy. Describes being caught up in street protests as one of the scariest moments of her life. Fails the Foreign Service Officer Test, which halts her diplomatic ambitions.

Nov 2002: Speaks her first lines on television as Nurse Jill in *General Hospital*. They are 'Wait a second'. She has left Northwestern with a dual major in theatre and international relations.

April 2005: Her first film, a rom-com starring Ashton Kutcher called, *A Lot Like Love*, is released. She secured the role of Hot Girl #1 by convincingly saying the word 'Hi' at an audition.

June 2005: Writes the invitations for the wedding of singer Robin Thicke and Paula Patton, demonstrating her skill as a calligrapher, her go-to job between acting roles.

April 2006: Appears for the first time as a 'briefcase model' on the popular game show *Deal or No Deal*. She would appear in thirty-four episodes spanning the next ten months, mainly carrying Briefcase Number 24 and earning $800 per show.

Oct 2009: A role in sci-fi series *Fringe* seems promising but only lasts for two episodes. More significantly, at the audition, renowned casting agent April Webster tells her, 'You need to know that you're enough.'

Nov 2009: Accompanies film producer boyfriend Trevor Engelson to the awards party at the MyHouse lounge after he is named by the *Hollywood Reporter* one of the Top 35 under 35. They are living together in a small yellow villa in a street off Sunset Boulevard, close to the Viper Room.

Jan 2010: Begins writing an anonymous blog called 'Working Actress' that sharply chronicles the trials of being a jobbing actor.

March 2010: Finally secures a minor part in one of Trevor's movies: *Remember Me* is a romantic drama set in New York, starring Robert Pattinson. Meghan thought him 'gracious, humble and cool'.

July 2010: Meets one of her film idols, Donald Sutherland, on the LA set of *Horrible Bosses*. She has a thirty-second role as a FedEx girl.

Aug 2010: Travels to New York to shoot the pilot for a series called *A Legal Mind*. She plays a character called Rachel Lane but by the time the show is broadcast it has been renamed *Suits* and she is now Rachel Zane, a paralegal with the firm Pearson Hardman.

Jan 2011: Time to celebrate when *Suits* is commissioned for a whole series, which for economic reasons was set to film in Toronto. It would be her home city for seven years.

Sept 2011: Meghan and Trevor get married in an idyllic beach location in Jamaica where the bride and groom book all fifty-five rooms at the exclusive Jamaica Inn in Ocho Rios. It's a very relaxed affair with guests playing games on the beach before the ceremony.

Oct 2011: Chosen as a host for the first time, co-presenting the Anti Defamation League Entertainment Industry Awards at the Beverly Hilton Hotel, LA. The international Jewish organisation opposes anti-semitism and denounces racism.

Feb 2012: Puts on a crisp white t-shirt bearing the slogan 'I Won't Stand for Racism' to film a video in support of Erase the Hate campaign. Reveals the time her mother was called the 'N word'.

April 2013: For the first time, Meghan has to contend with racist tweets when her fictional father is revealed as black actor Wendell Pierce in *Suits* Season 2.

Aug 2013: Her divorce becomes finalised, citing irreconcilable differences. Details of any settlement are kept private and neither Trevor nor Meghan has spoken of it. She is living in a cottage in the Seaton Village area of Toronto with her rescue dog, Bogart, known as Bogs.

Nov 2013: Makes movie *Anti-Social* in Europe. Appears on the red carpet for the premiere of *The Hunger Games: Catching Fire* at the Odeon, Leicester Square, and receives first mention in tabloid newspaper; the *Sunday People* describes her as a 'Californian beauty'. Co-presents at the Global Gift Gala backed by the Eva Longoria Foundation at the ME London Hotel.

Feb 2014: Becomes instant best friends with Serena Williams when they play on the same team for a charity game of celebrity flag football in Manhattan. Films Hallmark movie *When Sparks Fly* in Vancouver, the first time she has had the starring role. Returns to Northwestern University for a Q and A as part of the pre-season *Suits* publicity tour.

May 2014: Launches new web site The Tig, named after Tignanello, a favourite Tuscan red wine. She describes it as a hub for the discerning palate or a conversation between girlfriends. Starts dating Canadian celebrity chef Cory Vitiello.

Oct 2014: Attends the One Young World conference in Dublin as a counsellor. Meghan tells the audience during a debate entitled 'Bridging the Gender Gap' that she would no longer be wearing just a towel for scenes in *Suits*. Meets designer Misha Nonoo when she and Cory fly to Miami for the Art Basel festival.

Dec 2014: Joins other celebrities on the USO Holiday Tour cheering up service personnel who would not be home for Christmas; visits Spain, Italy, Turkey, Afghanistan and the UK. Meghan and Cory spend Christmas at his parents' home: takes her two rescue dogs along – Bogart and the latest addition, Guy the Beagle.

Feb 2015: Visits Rwanda in East Africa for the first time as an advocate for UN Women. Meets with female parliamentarians in the capital, Kigali, celebrating that the country is the first in the world where women hold a majority. Sees for herself the hardship endured at the Gihembe Refugee Camp.

March 2015: Meghan receives a standing ovation when she addresses the UN Women's conference marking International Women's Day. She tells the audience which includes Ban Ki-moon, the UN Secretary-General: 'I am proud to be a woman and a feminist.' She stresses the need for greater female representation in politics worldwide.

July 2015: Writes her famous essay for *Elle* magazine entitled 'I'm More than an Other' about finding her voice as a biracial woman. Five years before the killing of George Floyd, she concludes that America has 'perhaps only placed bandages over the problems that have never healed at the root.'

Aug 2015: Appears in a PSA video for UN Women that proclaims, 'We see potential leaders everywhere.' Meghan is seen scribbling notes and walking to make a speech under the rallying call: 'Nominate a Woman in your Life.' Signs up to be the face of an affordable fashion campaign by Canadian store, Reitmans.

Oct 2015: As guest speaker at a Toronto workshop sponsored by Dove Self-Esteem Project, Meghan warns against believing too much in the smoke and mirrors of celebrity. Her character, Rachel Zane, was not real, she stressed.

March 2016: Meghan is named as a global ambassador for the charity World Vision Canada and returns to Rwanda, this time as part of a learning mission gathering insight and publicity for its Clean Water Campaign. On return to Toronto, she hosts The Watercolour Project painting exhibition that raises funds to build a new water source in Rwanda.

May 2016: Describes Donald Trump as 'misogynistic' and 'divisive' on an American TV show. Encourages a vote for Hillary Clinton in the upcoming presidential election. Her relationship with Cory has run its course.

July 2016: Meghan meets Prince Harry for the first time on a blind date set up for them by a female friend at the Dean Street Townhouse in Soho. There is a strong mutual attraction and they have two more dates before she has to return to Canada to film *Suits*. By now she is a millionaire earning a reported $50,000 an episode.

Aug 2016: She is maid of honour when her friend Lindsay Roth marries at the St Regis New York hotel. Spends five days in Botswana with Harry, who says, 'We camped out with each other under the stars.' They are in love.

Oct 2016: Tells her audience at the Create and Cultivate conference in Atlanta that, 'You can be a woman who wants to look good and still stand up for the equality of women.' Harry is staying with Meghan in Toronto when the *Sunday Express* reveals they are dating.

Nov 2016: *The Sun* declares, 'Harry's Girl on Pornhub'. The *Daily Mail* says, 'Harry's girl is (almost) straight outta Compton'. The paper's columnist refers to Meghan's 'rich and exotic DNA'. Harry asks the press to 'pause and reflect before any further damage is done'.

Jan 2017: Meghan is in India to spend time with the Myna Mahila Foundation and to see for herself the plight of teenage girls whose education was sorely affected by the stigma surrounding menstrual health and the lack of proper sanitation. Writes an article for *Time* magazine entitled 'How Periods Affect Potential.'

April 2017: Closes The Tig, one of many things she gives up to be with Harry including Reitmans, her agent, *Suits* and her home in Toronto.

July 2017: Appears on the front cover of *Pride* magazine under the banner 'Princess in Waiting' and the headline 'Most people could not tell I was half black'.

Oct 2017: Wears the famous 'Husband Shirt' when she is photographed with Harry at the Invictus Games in Toronto. Her mother Doria is also seen with them. Meets the Queen for the first time when Harry drives Meghan around to Buckingham Palace for tea.

Nov 2017: The engagement is announced on Twitter. Their engagement interview, conducted by broadcaster Mishal Husain, reveals that Harry has yet to meet Meghan's father. Harry's spokesman announces that she is stepping away from her charitable roles and would no longer work for World Vision Canada or as a UN Women's advocate.

Dec 2017: Makes first venture with Harry as a royal couple. They are in Nottingham to visit the Terence Higgins Trust World Aids Day Fair and meet counsellors working with Full Effect, an organisation that helps children vulnerable to gang influences. Meghan introduces herself to well-wishers: 'Hi, I'm Meghan.' Spends Christmas with the Royal Family at Sandringham.

Jan 2018: Pays a secret visit to the Hubb Community Kitchen, a group of women who had gathered in West London the day after the Grenfell Fire to cook food for their families and others displaced by the tragedy.

May 2018: Meghan and Harry marry at St George's Chapel, Windsor. Doria is the only member of her family who attends. Tom is recovering from heart problems at home in Mexico. Elton John plays three numbers at the afternoon reception in Windsor Castle. At the evening party in Frogmore House, Idris Elba does some DJing and Meghan makes a speech. The newlyweds first dance is the classic 'I'm in Love' by Wilson Pickett.

Sept 2018: Accompanied by Doria, hosts the launch in the gardens of Kensington Palace of *Together*, the Hubb Community cookbook for which she has written the foreword. Within six months the book sells more than 130,000 copies worldwide and raises more than half a million pounds for the kitchen and other Grenfell Tower support projects.

Oct 2018: An official announcement confirms Meghan is pregnant. She gives a speech on female empowerment at the University of the South Pacific in Fiji and another on women's suffrage at a reception in Wellington, New Zealand, where she sits beside Jacinda Ardern, the country's premier.

Jan 2019: The tabloid press criticise Meghan for cradling her baby bump. The *Daily Mail* lambasts her for eating avocado on toast, asking 'Is Meghan's favourite snack fuelling drought and murder?' Becomes patron of the National Theatre and of @themayhew, a London-based charity that rescues abandoned cats and dogs.

March 2019: Meghan and Harry move into Frogmore Cottage, Windsor. The cost of renovating the rundown property is £2.4 million, paid out of the Sovereign Grant. They leave the Royal Foundation, marking the official split from the household of William and Kate.

May 2019: Archie Harrison Mountbatten-Windsor is born at the Portland Hospital in London. His name is announced on Instagram two days later. There are no pictures of Meghan leaving hospital and the couple do not reveal the names of the godparents.

Sept 2019: The tabloid press criticise Meghan's guest editorship of *Vogue*. It features fifteen women who are 'Forces for Change'. The issue is the fastest selling in the magazine's history. Launches a new capsule collection as patron of Smart Works, a charity that provides good-quality interview clothes and coaching to boost the confidence of women struggling to find a job. Introduces Archie to Archbishop Desmond Tutu in Cape Town.

Oct 2019: Meghan announces she is suing the *Mail on Sunday* after the newspaper published part of a handwritten note she had written to her father. Harry says, 'I lost my mother and now I watch my wife falling victim to the same powerful forces.' He issues legal proceedings against *The Sun* and the *Daily Mirror* over alleged phone hacking. Seventy-two women MPs sign a letter expressing solidarity with Meghan against national newspaper coverage, calling out the 'outdated colonial undertones' of some of the stories. *Meghan and Harry: An African Journey* is broadcast in which, filled with emotion, she says, 'You've got to thrive. You've got to feel happy.'

Jan 2020: Harry and Meghan announce they will be dividing their time between North America and the UK and stepping back as senior members of the Royal Family. *The New York Times* describes their act of leaving as 'two fingers up at the racism of the British establishment.' They are living with Archie in a mansion on Vancouver Island.

March 2020: Meghan fulfils her last official engagements in the UK, including a visit to the Robert Clack Upper School in Dagenham, urging the boys to value and appreciate the women in their lives. She joins Harry at the Commonwealth Day service at Westminster Abbey. Relations with William and Kate appear decidedly frosty. Meghan flies out the same day to return to Vancouver and Archie.

April 2020: Meghan and Harry spend three days delivering food packages to the sick and vulnerable in West Hollywood on behalf of Project Angel Food. They have moved from Canada to LA before the lockdown prevents travel. They donate more than £90,000 of profits from their wedding broadcast to Feeding Britain, a UK charity distributing meals to families in need. Provides the voice-over for the Disney film *Elephant*.

June 2020: Meghan talks about the killing of George Floyd in a powerful graduation address to students of her old school, Immaculate Heart: 'I realised that the only wrong thing to say is to say nothing.'

July 2020: Meghan's issue of *Vogue* wins the Diversity Initiative of the Year at the PPA (Professional Publishers Association) Awards. Meghan and her family have moved to Montecito, Santa Barbara, described by the locals as 'Eden by the Sea'.

Aug 2020: Takes part in an online discussion with Emily Ramshaw, founder of The 19th, a news outlet named after the Nineteenth Amendment that gave women the right to vote in the US. Meghan says she is looking forward to using her own voice in the future, something she hadn't been able to do of late. She adds, 'It's good to be home.'

ACKNOWLEDGEMENTS

_____

Sometimes I feel that my books are on an ongoing soap opera set in the Rovers Return with a friendly and familiar set of faces popping in to share a Guinness with me before getting on with the other important things in their life. I've not exactly been going as long as _Coronation Street_ but it's reassuring to know that I can count on so many talented and trusted people to help me across the line once more.

I had a look and I think my longest-running collaboration is with the astrologer Madeleine Moore. She produced the Robbie Williams Birth Chart for me back in 2003 and has done a superb job on every book since then. Her thoughts on Meghan were as astute as ever. We don't discuss the subject at all before she prepares her thoughts so I was fascinated to read of Meghan: 'She is likely to be an informed and stimulating communicator on the issues of identity.'

Many thanks to Gordon Wise, my agent at Curtis Brown, who has looked after me astutely and enthusiastically since my biography of Jennifer Aniston in 2007; his assistant, Niall Harman, has been an efficient support as always. I don't know how my chief researcher Emily Jane Swanson finds the time to help me while successfully studying for a master's in psychology. She has been an invaluable part of the team since working on my book about Alesha Dixon in 2012. EJ was meant to be getting married this year but coronavirus has temporarily postponed things, so I'm looking forward to next year's celebration!

I am grateful to Jo Westaway who has helped me with all things online and technical since my biography of Victoria Beckham in 2008. Good luck with your master's degree in singing at the Royal Welsh College of Music & Drama. Hope it won't be long before a live audience can hear you again. Thanks also to Jen Westaway for transcribing my interviews, a task she took on for the first time when I wrote *Cheryl* back in 2009. It's been a pleasure working again with Helena Caldon, a terrific copy editor.

Alison Jane Reid has been my fashion guru for countless books since she cast an eye over the outfits worn by Tulisa back in 2012. Meghan was an ideal subject for her. Alison Jane has just relaunched her website, Ethical Hedonist, so do check it out here: www.ethical-hedonist.com.

Many of my books have a California connection – from Justin Timberlake in 2004 to Meghan, of course. Again, my old friends Gill Pringle, Cliff Renfrew, Chrissy Iley and Richard Mineards have been a great help. By coincidence, Richard lives in Montecito, the new home of Harry, Meghan and Archie. Tell me how you get on when you pop by for a pot of tea, Richard!

While I was in LA, I was lucky enough to meet up with Louisa Spring, who really does seem to know everybody. I loved the conversations I had with Gigi Perreau, John Dlugolecki, Toby Guidry, Callie Webb and Maureen Diekmann from Immaculate Heart High School, and with the multi-talented Joshua Silverstein. He has been running the Process Out Loud Creative Writing Class! during the 2020 pandemic. Discover all about his other projects here: https://linktr.ee/TheJoshuaSilverstein.

I had been hoping to have lunch with Andrew Morton, the renowned royal biographer, while I was in California, but we were both isolating in the UK so that plan was abandoned. Andrew and I used to play in the same Sunday cricket team – I don't recall us being much good – and he has always been a great help to me over the years. Thanks also to Phil Dampier for his assistance sorting out the chronology of events with Harry.

Another old friend, Christopher Wilson, is a very experienced writer on all things royal but, wearing another hat, he is the novelist TP Fielden, whose latest mystery, *Stealing the Crown*, is another superb read. It's set in Buckingham Palace in 1941, a few years before Meghan's time.

This is my seventh book for HarperCollins and, once more, everyone has been super helpful, in particular commissioning editor Zoe Berville who has been so enthusiastic about the project since I first mentioned it to her more than a year ago. Thanks also to Georgina Atsiaris, Senior Project Editor; Sarah Burke, Senior Production Controller; Fiona Greenway, Picture Research; Mark Rowland, Designer; Claire Ward, Creative Director; Hattie Evans, Marketing Executive; Josie Turner, Publicity Manager; Tom Dunstan, Sales Director; Alice Gomer, Key Account Manager; Zoe Shine, Head of UK Rights; and Charlotte Brown, Audio Assistant.

Finally I would like to thank the newest member of Team Sean, Talia Beresford, for reading the manuscript and sharing her insight.

You can read more about my books at seansmithceleb.com or follow me on Twitter and Facebook @seansmithceleb, although to be honest I've been neglecting them a bit lately in favour of my photogenic cat's Instagram page: the_queen_of_boop.

SELECT BIBLIOGRAPHY

————

Brett, Samantha & Adams, Steph, *The Game Changers*, Viking, 2017

Jones, Caroline, *Meghan: The Life and Style of a Modern Royal*, Carlton Books, 2019

Morton, Andrew, *Meghan: A Hollywood Princess*, Michael O'Mara Books, 2018

Scobie, Omid and Durand, Carolyn, *Finding Freedom: Harry and Meghan and the Making of a Modern Royal Family*, HQ, 2020

The Hubb Community Kitchen, *Together: Our Community Cookbook*, Ebury Press 2018

PICTURE CREDITS

—————

INDEX